First World War
and Army of Occupation
War Diary
France, Belgium and Germany

74 (YEOMANRY) DIVISION
Headquarters, Branches and Services
Adjutant and Quarter-Master General
1 May 1918 - 30 June 1919

WO95/3148/2

The Naval & Military Press Ltd
www.nmarchive.com
Published in association with The National Archives

Published by

The Naval & Military Press Ltd

Unit 10 Ridgewood Industrial Park,

Uckfield, East Sussex,

TN22 5QE England

Tel: +44 (0) 1825 749494

www.naval-military-press.com

www.nmarchive.com

This diary has been reprinted in facsimile from the original. Any imperfections are inevitably reproduced and the quality may fall short of modern type and cartographic standards.

© **Crown Copyright**
Images reproduced by permission of The National Archives, London, England, 2015.

Contents

Document type	Place/Title	Date From	Date To
Heading	74th Division 'A' & 'Q' Branch 1918 May-Jly 1919		
Heading	HQ A&Q 74 D Vol 2		
Miscellaneous	On His Majesty's Service.		
Heading	War Diary A & Q Branch HQ. Qr 74th (Yeo) Division From 1st To 31st May 18 Volume XV		
War Diary	Noyelles	01/05/1918	07/05/1918
War Diary	Rue	09/05/1918	20/05/1918
War Diary	Roellecourt	21/05/1918	24/05/1918
War Diary	Le Cauroy	25/05/1918	31/05/1918
Miscellaneous	Circular Memorandum	07/05/1918	07/05/1918
Miscellaneous	Table "A" Issued With Secret Memorandum No.B.A. 305 Of 7/4/1918.	07/04/1918	07/04/1918
Miscellaneous	Instructions Re Billeting Appendix II	09/05/1918	09/05/1918
Miscellaneous	Instructions Re Opening of An Imprest Account and Obtaining Officers Advance Books	07/05/1918	07/05/1918
Miscellaneous	Application for A.F.W.3100 Requisition for Cash Book		
Miscellaneous	Field Cashier Abbeville		
Miscellaneous			
Miscellaneous	Receipt For Officers Advance Forms "D"		
Miscellaneous	Imprest Account		
Miscellaneous	Circular Memorandum Kits Off Other Ranks	14/05/1918	14/05/1918
Miscellaneous	Billeting	15/05/1918	15/05/1918
Miscellaneous	Instructions re Reporting Absentees etc		
Miscellaneous	Instructions for Advanced Billeting Parties.74th (Yeomanry) Division	19/05/1918	19/05/1918
Miscellaneous	Administrative Instructions With Reference To 74th Divnl. Order No.59	10/05/1918	10/05/1918
Miscellaneous	Move Of 74th (Yeomanry) Division	20/05/1918	20/05/1918
Miscellaneous	When the Sentence "Part of Divnl Train" occurs in this State it means the barrage and Supply wagons attached from the Divnl Train to the Unit or units proceeding by that train.		
Miscellaneous	Location Return 74th (Yeomanry) Division		
Miscellaneous	Location Of 74th (Yeomanry) Division. (Les-s R.A)		
War Diary	Le Cauroy	01/06/1918	25/06/1918
War Diary	Norrent Fontes	26/06/1918	30/06/1918
Miscellaneous	Instructions Regarding Supply etc of Ordnance Stores	31/05/1918	31/05/1918
Miscellaneous	Schedule "A" Bulked Stores		
Miscellaneous	Circular Memorandum Salvage	01/06/1918	01/06/1918
Miscellaneous	74th (Yeomanry) Division Instructions On Reporting Casualties List of Casualty wires and Returns required		
Miscellaneous	74th (Yeomanry Division) Instructions on Reporting Casualties	06/06/1918	06/06/1918
Miscellaneous	Appendix I		
Miscellaneous	Daily Casualty Return		
Miscellaneous	Details Of Casualties To Officers		
Miscellaneous	Appendix 3 Pre-Forma "B"		
Miscellaneous	Provisional Entraining Instructions	12/06/1918	12/06/1918
Miscellaneous	Entraining Station-Tinques		
Miscellaneous	Entraining Station-Savy		

Miscellaneous	Entraining Station-Aubighy		
Miscellaneous	Instructions Re Move of the Division by Tactical Trains	24/06/1918	24/06/1918
Miscellaneous	Administrative Instructions Relative To Operation Order No.65	24/06/1918	24/06/1918
Miscellaneous	Administrative Instructions Relative To Operation Order No.63	25/06/1918	25/06/1918
Miscellaneous	Reference This Office S.G.21/4 Of 28th Inst	28/06/1918	28/06/1918
Heading	HQ A & Q 74 D Vol 4		
Miscellaneous	D.A.G 3rd Echelon Base		
War Diary	Norrent Fontes	01/07/1918	13/07/1918
War Diary	Lillette N.23.d.8.8	14/07/1918	15/07/1918
War Diary	Lillette N.33.d.8.8	16/07/1918	31/07/1918
Miscellaneous	Drinking Water		
Miscellaneous	Water Carts		
Miscellaneous	Instructions Re "B" Teams Reference Sheet 36 A 1/40,000	09/07/1918	09/07/1918
Miscellaneous	Administrative Instructions Relative To 74th Divisional Order No.66	09/07/1918	09/07/1918
Miscellaneous	Table Shewing Dates Units Will Commence Drawing Supplies From Mazinghem		
Miscellaneous	Appendix IV	12/07/1918	12/07/1918
Miscellaneous	Amendment To Administrative Instructions Relative To 74th Divisional Order No.66	13/07/1918	13/07/1918
Miscellaneous	O.C. 74th Divisional Reception Camp	17/07/1918	17/07/1918
Miscellaneous	74th (Yeomanry) Division Administrative Arrangements		
Miscellaneous	Schedule 1-Agriculture		
Miscellaneous	Schedule 2-Ammunition		
Miscellaneous	Schedule No.3 Areas		
Miscellaneous	Schedule No.4 Basic And Laundry		
Miscellaneous	Schedule No.5 Burials		
Miscellaneous	Schedule No.6 Divisional Canteens		
Miscellaneous	Schedule No. 7 Field Cashier		
Miscellaneous	Medical Arrangements During Normal Warfare		
Miscellaneous	Medical Arrangements for Heavy Fighting		
Miscellaneous	Ordnance		
Miscellaneous	Police Arrangements		
Miscellaneous	Water Supply		
Miscellaneous	Schedule 14-Reserve Rations And Water		
Miscellaneous	Salvage		
Miscellaneous	Supply Arrangements		
Miscellaneous	Schedule No.17-Veterinary		
Miscellaneous	Divisional Reception Camp		
Miscellaneous	Administrative Instructions Relative To 74th Division Order No.69	21/07/1918	21/07/1918
Miscellaneous	Appendix IX		
Heading	War Diary A & Q Branch Headqrs 74th (Yeo) Divn From 1st To 31st August 18 Volume XVIII		
War Diary	Lillette Chateau N.33.d.88	03/08/1918	22/08/1918
War Diary	Busnes Chateau P.31.C Central	24/08/1918	28/08/1918
War Diary	Beaucourt Chateau Sheet 57 C	29/08/1918	31/08/1918
Miscellaneous	Administrative Instructions Relative To 74th Divisional Order No.70	01/08/1918	01/08/1918
Miscellaneous	Administrative Instructions Relative To 74th Division Order No.75	15/08/1918	15/08/1918
Miscellaneous	Police Arrangements	13/08/1918	13/08/1918

Miscellaneous	74th (Yeomanry) Division Instructions On Reporting Casualties		
Miscellaneous	G.R.O.3867 As Amended By G.R.O.4693		
Miscellaneous	XI Corps Administrative Instructions Reference XI Corps Order No.390 dated 25.8.18 (Relief of 74th Division by 59th Division)	25/08/1918	25/08/1918
Miscellaneous	List Of Special Stores To Be Handed Over By 74th Division		
Miscellaneous	Administrative Instructions Relative To 74th Division Order No.79	26/08/1918	26/08/1918
Miscellaneous	74th Divisional Reception Camp		
Miscellaneous	Move of 74th Division With Artillery	26/08/1918	26/08/1918
Miscellaneous	Administrative Instructions Relative To 74th Division Order No.79	27/08/1918	27/08/1918
Miscellaneous	Distribution Of Motor Lorries		
Miscellaneous	229th Infantry Brigade Group Entraining Station Berguette		
Miscellaneous	230th Infantry Brigade Group Entraining Station Lillers		
Miscellaneous	231st Infantry Brigade Group Entraining Station Aire		
Miscellaneous	Divisional Artillery Entraining Station-Lillers		
Miscellaneous	Distributions Of Motor Lorries		
Miscellaneous	74th (Yeomanry) Division August Summaries Of Returns	06/09/1918	06/09/1918
Heading	A & Q 74th Division September 1918		
Heading	War Diary A & Q Branch 74th (Yeomanry) Division From 1st To 30th September 1918 Volume XIX		
War Diary	Beaucourt	01/09/1918	01/09/1918
War Diary	H.3.b.6.1 (Hem)	01/09/1918	06/09/1918
War Diary	J.10. Central (Near Haut Allaines)	07/09/1918	09/09/1918
War Diary	D.H.Q J.11.C.3.5	10/09/1918	10/09/1918
War Diary	J.11.c.3.5	13/09/1918	26/09/1918
War Diary	Norrent Fontes	27/09/1918	30/09/1918
Miscellaneous	Administrative Instructions Relative To 74th Divion Order No.81	01/09/1918	01/09/1918
Miscellaneous	Reference Sheet 62c Map 1/40,000	01/09/1918	01/09/1918
Miscellaneous	Q.L.27	01/09/1918	01/09/1918
Miscellaneous	Q.L.31	02/09/1918	02/09/1918
Miscellaneous	Q.L.49.	06/09/1918	06/09/1918
Miscellaneous	O.Q.68/3	09/09/1918	09/09/1918
Miscellaneous	Administrative Instructions Relative To 74th Division Order No.90		
Miscellaneous	Table "A" Kit To He Carried On The Man.		
Miscellaneous	Table "C"		
Miscellaneous	Administrative Instructions Relative To 74th Divisional Order No.90	16/09/1918	16/09/1918
Miscellaneous	Instructions for Advanced Billeting Parties Reference 74th Div. Order No.93	23/09/1918	23/09/1918
Miscellaneous	Amendments to Instructions for Advanced Billeting Parties Reference 74th Div Order No.93		
Miscellaneous	Administrative Instructions Relative To C.A 473/3 Operation Order No.93	24/09/1918	24/09/1918
Miscellaneous	Administrative Instructions Relative To 74 Division Order No.94	26/09/1918	26/09/1918
Miscellaneous	Table "D" For Move Of 74th Division Less Artillery		
Miscellaneous	Entrainment Programme for Move of 74th Division Less Artillery September 27th And 28th 1918	28/09/1918	28/09/1918

Miscellaneous	Administrative Instructions Relative To 74th Division Order No.95	29/09/1918	29/09/1918
Miscellaneous	Fourth Army No.G.S.2/17	28/09/1918	28/09/1918
Miscellaneous	74th (Yeomanry) Division Consolidated List Of Casualties For Period 1st-30th Sept.		
Miscellaneous	R.H.K Butler K.C.M.G C.B. Commanding III Corps	26/09/1918	26/09/1918
War Diary	Norrent Fontes	03/10/1918	03/10/1918
War Diary	W.30.d.7.8	04/10/1918	05/10/1918
War Diary	S.12.d.7.8	05/10/1918	16/10/1918
War Diary	Fournes Chateau	17/10/1918	18/10/1918
War Diary	Wattignies Chateau W.I.C.8.3	19/10/1918	20/10/1918
War Diary	Pont A Tressin M.21.a.5.3 Sheet 37	21/10/1918	31/10/1918
Miscellaneous	Administrative Instructions Relative To 74th Division Order No.97	06/10/1918	06/10/1918
Miscellaneous	Appendix II	25/10/1918	25/10/1918
Miscellaneous	Administrative Instructions Relative To 74th Division Order No.97	08/10/1918	08/10/1918
Miscellaneous	Appendix II	25/10/1918	25/10/1918
Miscellaneous	Headquarters 229th Inf Bde A.I.245/M	27/10/1918	27/10/1918
Miscellaneous	74th (Yeomanry) Division Mounted Squadron B. Qrs & 3 Troops War Establishment		
Miscellaneous	Mounted Squadron Personnel To Be Found By Units		
Heading	War Diary A & Q Branch Hd Qrs 74th (Yeo) Division From 1st To 30th June 1918 Volume XVI		
Miscellaneous	74th (Yeomanry) Division Consolidated List Of Casualties For Period 1st-31st Oct	31/10/1918	31/10/1918
Heading	War Diary 74d (Yeomanry) Division A & Q Branch From 1st To 31st October 1918 Volume XX Vol 7		
Heading	War Diary A & Q Branch 74th (Yeomanry) Division For Month Of November 1918 Vol 8		
War Diary	Pont A Tressin M.21.a.3.3 Sheet 37	04/11/1918	10/11/1918
War Diary	O.18.c.27 Fauborg De Chateau	10/11/1918	11/11/1918
War Diary	O.18.c.27	11/11/1918	11/11/1918
War Diary	L.23.a.27 Frasnes Lez Buissenal	11/11/1918	30/11/1918
Miscellaneous	Supplementary New Year's Despatch 1919	22/11/1918	22/11/1918
Heading	War Diary A & Q Branch 74th (Yeomanry) Division For Month Of December 1918 Vol 9		
War Diary	Frasnes Lez Buissenal L.23.a.2.7	07/12/1918	14/12/1918
War Diary	Lessines	15/12/1918	19/12/1918
Miscellaneous	Form "D"	01/02/1918	01/02/1918
Miscellaneous	Fighting Strength Of 231st Infantry Brigade	25/01/1918	25/01/1918
Miscellaneous	Form "D"	04/01/1918	04/01/1918
Miscellaneous	Fighting Strength Of 231st Infantry Brigade	05/01/1918	05/01/1918
Miscellaneous	Form "D"	11/01/1918	11/01/1918
Miscellaneous	Fighting Strength Of 231st Infantry Brigade	11/01/1918	11/01/1918
Miscellaneous	Form "D"	18/01/1918	18/01/1918
Miscellaneous	Remarks N Form "D"	18/01/1918	18/01/1918
Miscellaneous	Form "D"	25/01/1918	25/01/1918
Miscellaneous	Fighting Strength Of 231st Infantry Brigade	18/01/1918	18/01/1918
Miscellaneous	Form "D"	08/02/1918	08/02/1918
Miscellaneous	Fighting Strength Of 231st Infantry Brigade	08/02/1918	08/02/1918
Miscellaneous	Fighting Strength Of 231st Infantry Brigade	01/02/1918	01/02/1918
Miscellaneous	Form "D"	15/02/1918	15/02/1918
Miscellaneous	Fighting Strength Of 231st Infantry Brigade	15/02/1918	15/02/1918
Miscellaneous	Form "D"	22/02/1918	22/02/1918
Miscellaneous	Fighting Strength Of 231st Infantry Brigade	22/02/1918	22/02/1918

Miscellaneous	Form "D"	01/03/1918	01/03/1918
Miscellaneous	Fighting Strength Of 231st Infantry Brigade	01/03/1918	01/03/1918
Miscellaneous	Form "D"	08/03/1918	08/03/1918
Miscellaneous	Fighting Strength Of 231st Infantry Brigade	08/03/1918	08/03/1918
Miscellaneous	Form "D"	15/03/1918	15/03/1918
Miscellaneous	Fighting Strength 231st Infantry Brigade	15/03/1918	15/03/1918
Miscellaneous	Form "D"	30/03/1918	30/03/1918
Miscellaneous	Fighting Strength	30/03/1918	30/03/1918
Miscellaneous	Form "D"	23/03/1918	23/03/1918
Miscellaneous	Fighting Strength 231st Infantry Brigade	22/03/1918	22/03/1918
Miscellaneous	Form "Z"	30/03/1918	30/03/1918
Miscellaneous	Form "Z"	22/03/1918	22/03/1918
Miscellaneous	24th (Denbigh Fus) Bn R.W.F		
Miscellaneous	Form "Z"	15/03/1918	15/03/1918
Miscellaneous	Nominal Roll of Casualties Officer		
Miscellaneous	Form "Z"	08/03/1918	08/03/1918
Miscellaneous	Nominal Roll		
Miscellaneous	Form "Z"	01/03/1918	01/03/1918
Miscellaneous	Form "Z"	22/02/1918	22/02/1918
Miscellaneous	Nominal Roll of Officers Admitted Sick		
Miscellaneous	Form "Z"	15/02/1918	15/02/1918
Miscellaneous	Form "Z"	08/02/1918	08/02/1918
Miscellaneous	Nominal Roll of Officers Admitted Sick		
Miscellaneous	Form "Z"	01/02/1918	01/02/1918
Miscellaneous	Nominal Roll of Officers Admitted Sick	29/01/1918	29/01/1918
Miscellaneous	Form "Z"	25/01/1918	25/01/1918
Miscellaneous	Nominal Roll of Officers Admitted Sick		
Miscellaneous	Form "Z"	13/01/1918	13/01/1918
Miscellaneous	Form "Z"	11/01/1918	11/01/1918
Miscellaneous	Nominal Roll of Officers Admitted Sick	11/01/1918	11/01/1918
Miscellaneous	Form "Z"	04/01/1918	04/01/1918
Miscellaneous	Nominal Roll of Officers Admitted Sick	29/12/1917	29/12/1917
Miscellaneous	Form "Z"	12/03/1918	12/03/1918
Miscellaneous	Nominal Roll	12/03/1918	12/03/1918
Miscellaneous	Form "Z"	12/03/1918	12/03/1918
Miscellaneous	A Form Messages And Signals		
Miscellaneous	C Form Messages And Signals	15/03/1918	15/03/1918
Miscellaneous	A Form Messages And Signals		
Miscellaneous	C Form Messages And Signals	14/11/1918	14/11/1918
Miscellaneous	Form "Z"	12/03/1918	12/03/1918
Miscellaneous	Nominal Roll	11/03/1918	11/03/1918
Miscellaneous	C Form Messages And Signals		
Miscellaneous	A Form Messages And Signals		
Miscellaneous	Form "Z"	12/03/1918	12/03/1918
Miscellaneous	Nominal Roll	10/03/1918	10/03/1918
Miscellaneous	C Form Messages And Signals		
Miscellaneous	A Form Messages And Signals		
Miscellaneous	C Form Messages And Signals		
Miscellaneous	A Form Messages And Signals		
Miscellaneous	C Form Messages And Signals		
Miscellaneous	A Form Messages And Signals		
Miscellaneous	Form "Z"	10/03/1918	10/03/1918
Miscellaneous	Nominal Roll	09/03/1918	09/03/1918
Miscellaneous	Form "Z"		
War Diary	Lessines	07/01/1919	31/01/1919

Miscellaneous	Administrative Instructions Relative To 74th Divisional Order No.119	21/01/1919	21/01/1919
Heading	War Diary A & Q Branch 74th (Yeo) Division For Month Of February 1919 Vol 11		
War Diary	Lessines	05/02/1919	27/02/1919
Miscellaneous	Administrative Instructions Relative To Move Of 1/12th L.H Lancs To 2nd Army	20/02/1919	20/02/1919
Miscellaneous	Messages And Signals		
Heading	War Diary Hd Qrs 74th (Yeo) Division For Month Of March 1919 Vol 12		
War Diary	Lessines	03/03/1919	31/03/1919
Heading	War Diary Hd Qrs 74th (Yeo) Division For Month Of April 1919 Vol 13		
War Diary	Lessines	01/04/1919	30/04/1919
Heading	War Diary Hd Qrs 74th (Yeo) Div Period 1st To 31st May 19 Vol 14		
War Diary	Lessines	08/05/1919	31/05/1919
Miscellaneous	Appendix I	27/05/1919	27/05/1919
Miscellaneous	Copies of Telegrams.		
Operation(al) Order(s)	74th Divisional Order No.120	30/05/1919	30/05/1919
Heading	War Diary H.Q.74th (Yeo) Divn June 1919 Vol 15		
War Diary	Lessines	02/06/1919	30/06/1919
Miscellaneous	3rd Corps	04/06/1919	04/06/1919
Miscellaneous	A.Z.B.2/41/4.	09/06/1919	09/06/1919
Miscellaneous	A.Z.B.2/41/4	12/06/1919	12/06/1919
Miscellaneous	A.Z.B.2/41/4	14/06/1919	14/06/1919
Miscellaneous	D.H.1/75	02/06/1919	02/06/1919
Miscellaneous	Q.D.1961	29/05/1919	29/05/1919
Miscellaneous	Extract from Schedule Showing Strength of Personnel for "Equipment Guards" of Units		
Miscellaneous	A.Z.B.2/41/2	19/06/1919	19/06/1919
Miscellaneous	Schedule Issued With A.Z.B.2/41/2	19/06/1919	19/06/1919
Miscellaneous	A.Z.B.2/41/2	19/06/1919	19/06/1919
Miscellaneous	Schedule Issued With Addendum To A.Z.B.2/41/2	21/06/1919	21/06/1919
Operation(al) Order(s)	74th Divisional Order No.121	20/06/1919	20/06/1919
Miscellaneous	Schedule		
Operation(al) Order(s)	74th Divisional Order No.122	26/06/1919	26/06/1919
Miscellaneous	Schedule "A" Issued With Divisional Order No.122		
Miscellaneous	Addendum To Divisional Order No.122	25/06/1919	25/06/1919
Operation(al) Order(s)	74th Divisional Order No.125	26/06/1919	26/06/1919
Miscellaneous	Schedule Issued With Divisional Order No.123		
Miscellaneous	Amendment To Divisional Order No.123	30/06/1919	30/06/1919
Miscellaneous	Equipment and Stores Handed in to I.C.S Ath		
Operation(al) Order(s)	74th Divisional Order No.124	27/06/1919	27/06/1919
Miscellaneous	Schedule "A" Issued With Divisional Order No.124		
Miscellaneous	Amendment To Divisional Order No.124	30/06/1919	30/06/1919

74TH DIVISION

'A' & 'Q' BRANCH
1918 MAY - ~~DEC 1918~~.
~~JAN~~ - JLY 1919.

HO 09 Q 74 P
Vol 2

On His Majesty's Service.

SECRET.

D.A.G.

G.H.Q.

3rd Echelon.

War Diary
A. & Q. Branch
Hd Qrs 24th (Vic) Division
from 1st to 31st May/18

VOLUME XV.

Army Form C. 2118

WAR DIARY
or
INTELLIGENCE SUMMARY
(Erase heading not required.)

Ammunition Branch
Headquarters 74 (Yeo) Division
May 1918

Place	Date	Hour	Summary of Events and Information	Remarks and references to Appendices
NOYELLES	1	22.00	1st Horse train arrived at 22.00	
	2		2nd, 3rd & 4th Trains arrived at 0300, 0730 & 1730 respectively. The advance parties of the Division went into Billets in the RUE FAVIERS, FOREST MONTIERS except Advance Party of M.C.B. & 231st Inf Bde which went into NUVION Camp	
	3		Advance parties of 23rd Inf Bde moved into CANCHY Area	Appendix I
	5.		Billets, rendezvous and advance parties put in accordance with distribution given in Appendix 'A' attached to Circular Memorandum BA 205 dated 5th May 1918	Appendix I Appendix II Appendix III Appendix IV
	7.		Administrative Instructions prepared in form of a Circular Memorandum to be issued to Units and formations on arrival. Separate instructions were issued re Billets and Imprest accounts	
RUE	9.		The G.O.C., G.S.I., A.A. & Q.M.G., A.D.C. & A.D.M.S. arrived at NOYELLES and Divisional H.Q. were opened at RUE	
	10.		D.A.D.S. remained at RUE until all trains except those of R.A. had arrived. Major A.D.V.S., A.P.M., Camp Cmdt & S.C.F. arrived. The Establishment of Lewis Guns exclusive of those for A.A. purposes increased from 16 to 24 Per Inf Bn. Auth. G.H.Q. O.B., 1215 of 9/4/18. Auth that of Pioneer Bn increased to 12	
	14.		Railway points fixed as follows. 229 Infty Bde Group & D.H.Q. at RUE. 230 Inf Bde Group at LE TITRE. 231st Inf Bde at CANCHY. Instructions re disposal of Tickets issued to all concerned. Divisional Am. R.A. & Employment Coy completed detrainment at NOYELLES	Appendix V
	15.		Further instruction re Billeting issued. Instruction re Specially absentees issued. The Division less Divnl Ammn completed to establishment in horses and vehicles	Appendix VI

A.G. Anderson-Major
D.A.Q.M.G. 74 (Yeo) Divn

WAR DIARY or INTELLIGENCE SUMMARY.

(Erase heading not required.)

Army Form C. 2118.

Commanding Branch
Headquarters 74 (Yeo) Division

May 1918.

Place	Date	Hour	Summary of Events and Information	Remarks and references to Appendices
RUE	16		Divl R.A. commenced to detrain at NOYELLES	
	17.		Divl R.A. & Divl Employment Coy completed detrainment	
	18.		Orders received for Division to move to ROELLECOURT MAIZIERES and SUS ST LEGER Areas.	
			Representative of 4 Bde R.F.A in accordance with instruction from Corps Army drew 6, 4.5" Howitzers, 12 Wagons Ammn How 4.5, and 36, 18 pdr Wagons Ammn at Ordnance Calais.	appendix VII
	19.		Representative of 117 Bde R.F.A drew at Calais similar stores & & as 4 Bde. Instruction for Ordnance Billeting Parties issued at 0100 DAQMG, APM & Interpreter proceeded to new area by Motor Car	Appendix VIII
	20.		Accumulating Instructions issued. Divl Ammn Column drew 12 Wagons Ammn 4.5 How and 36 Wagons Ammn 18 pdr. Division commenced entraining at RUE for LIGNY ST FLOCHEL. A few men (about 6 officers & 60 O.R.) billeted at train was detailed from first Duty Bn. which arrived this party remained at the station until detrainment was completed. It was found that this party effected a great saving of time.	
			Divl H.Q. closed at RUE at 16.00 and opened at ROELLECOURT at unknown hour. Guns from 4.A work on rail 4.B. 26 Bally R.4A 17 Sedan D.A.C. and 1.	
ROELLECOURT	21		B. Buttery R.E. Auth GHQ 0/3.1939 dates 3/9/18. Detrainment of Division less R.A. at LIGNY ST FLOCHEL completed & billets recorded to Roellecourt Rest	Appendix IX
	23.			
	24.		Division moved into new Billeting areas as per locations list AD Div H.Q. opened at 1300 at LE CAUROY	Appendix X
LE CAUROY	25			Appendix
	30		Divl Artillery arrived in new area by road & were billeted as per locations list Refilling Point 820 & Div train at LIENCOURT 230 of Brd Train VILLERS SUR SIMON 231. Divl Bn Supply at LE HAMEAU R.A. & MAGNICOURT	
	31.		On the whole during the month the weather was exceptionally fine & condusive to the end of the training. Per Gen. Employment Cy issued Aas with HQ Butchart Hy.Div.	

Beasy Lt Col GSO.

appendix I diary May
War Diary
CA/157

SECRET

B.A. 305.

CIRCULAR MEMORANDUM.

With reference to the present move of the Division, the following instructions and information are issued :-

1. **DETRAINMENT.**
On arrival troops will be provided with a hot meal at the Staging Camp, NOYELLES. Troops arriving too late to get into billets before dark will use the Staging Camp for the night.

2. **BLANKETS.**
One blanket per man will be drawn at NOYELLES Staging Camp on arrival.

3. **ACCOMMODATION.**
(a). The Division will be accommodated in Camps and Billets in the under-noted sub-areas. The name and address of each Sub-area Commandant is given :-

Sub-Area.	Sub-Area Comdt.	Address.
RUE	Captain KNIGHT,	Rue de la Porte de BOCQUY, RUE.
FAVIERS	Lieut.-Colonel REITH,	NEUVILLE-les-FOREST MONTIERS.
NOUVION	Lieut.-Colonel GRAHAM,	NOUVION.
BUIGNY	Captain BUNT,	BUIGNY ST.MACLOU.
PORT LE GRAND	Major WILLIAMS,	Villa mon Plaisir, PORT LE GRAND
BRAILLY	Major HARRISON,	CRECY.

NOTE :- SAILLY-le-SEC is administered by the Reserve Army Artillery School, SAILLY-le-SEC.

(b). Sub-Area Commandants have full particulars of all billets in their respective areas, and the purposes for which these billets are to be used. All questions between the troops and the French should be referred to the Sub-Area Commandants.
(c). The distribution of units is shown in Table "A" attached.
(d). Detailed instructions as to billeting are being issued separately.

4. **SUPPLIES.**
Until the necessary H.T. has been drawn, the O.C. 74th Divisional M.T. Company will arrange for Rations and Forage to be delivered to units by motor lorry.

5. **E.F. CANTEENS.**
(a). There are Canteens at WAILLY, MONTREUIL and ABBEVILLE.
(b). Spirits will be sold only for comsumption by officers, and all orders for such will be in the form of bulk orders. Spirits will be issued to Messes only on the production of a PRINTED liquor voucher signed by a Staff Officer of the formation concerned. The quantity of liquor required must be entered in words on the vouchers and NOT in figures. Printed liquor vouchers will be provided by the E.F.C. at their various branches.
(c). No spirits will be allowed to be sold by the E.F.C. to Sergeants' Messes.

6. **Y.M.C.A.**
Y.M.C.A. Canteens have been established at RUE, NOUVION, HAUTVILLERS and FOREST MONTIERS.

7. **FIELD CASHIER.**
There is a Field Cashier at ABBEVILLE. His office is open daily from 0900 to 1230 and from 1430 to 1830. No imprest money can be obtained without an A.F.W.3100. Requisition for cash book. Detailed instructions as to obtaining these and officers' Advance Books are being issued separately.

P.T.O.

- 2 -

8. **CENSOR STAMPS.** Censor stamps have been issued to all units whose horses were sent on in advance. Units not having advance parties will be issued with censor stamps on arrival.

9. **IRON RATIONS AND FIELD DRESSINGS.** Iron Rations and Field Dressings will be inspected on arrival and any deficiencies made good forthwith.

10. **OFFICERS' CLOTHING DEPOT.** There is an Officers' Clothing Depot at ABBEVILLE (Boulevard de la Republique). Officers must produce their Advance Books when purchasing.

11. **AMMUNITION.** Requirements in ammunition to complete R.A. and Infantry Echelons to Establishment will be wired to this office without delay.

12. **CAMERAS.** All cameras will be withdrawn under arrangements to be made by C.Os. and despatched by parcel post. A slip will be enclosed before despatch, stating that the unit has recently arrived from abroad and that the camera is now sent home under Reserve Army Authority. In addition to the address, the label will have endorsed on it the following certificate which will be signed by the officer concerned :-
"Contents - Camera, sent home in the Public Service, on Army Authority"

13. **OFFICERS' KITS.**
    (a). The total weight (excluding articles in Camp Kettles) of 70 lbs. for a Commanding Officer and 55 lbs. for other officers must not be exceeded. As soon as possible after detrainment all surplus officers' kits will be sent to the Base for despatch to ENGLAND.
    (b). Immediately kits are ready for despatch notice will be sent to this office through the usual channels, stating by units :-
        (1) The total number of packages, and (2). The approximate weight.
    (c). No Government property must be included in these kits, and Os.C. will censor all kits prior to despatch. Each package must bear the censor stamp of the unit concerned.
    (d). Labels must state, in addition to the address, the name of the sender, and in general terms the contents of the package.

14. **SANITATION.**
    (a). All units will immediately on arrival construct permanent deep pit latrines in their areas. These latrines will be at least 10 feet deep. Pits will be boxed in and be fitted with self-closing lids. Every care must be taken to ensure that the covers are fly proof. The necessary material for this work has been dumped with Area Commandants.
    (b). All camp refuse & tins which have contained food will be incinerated.

15. **MAPS.** A full issue of maps covering this area has been made to all units which sent forward advance parties. Maps will be issued to other units on arrival.

16. ACKNOWLEDGE.

7th May, 1918.

Lieut.-Colonel,
A.A.& Q.M.G. 74th (Yeo.) Division.

Copies to :-
H.Q. Reserve Army.
"G".
229th Brigade.
230th Brigade.
231st Brigade.
C.R.A.
C.R.E.
A.D.M.S.
A.D.V.S.
Divl.Sig.Coy.
Div.M.G.Bn.
Div. Train.
74th Div.M.T.Coy.

Camp Commandant.
A.P.M.
Chemical Adviser, Reserve Army.
Gas Officer, 74th Division.
Sub-Area Commandants at :-
 RUE.
 NEUVILLE-les-FORET MONTIERS.
 NOUVION.
 BUIGNY ST.MACLOU.
 PORT LE GRAND.
 CRECY.
D.A.D.O.S.
Diary.

TABLE "A".

ISSUED WITH SECRET MEMORANDUM No. B.A. 305 OF 7/4/1918.

Unit.	Place.	Sub-Area.	Water Supply. Men.	Water Supply. Animals.
Div. H.Q.	RUE.	RUE.	Wells & Pumps	River.
Div. Sig. Coy.	RUE.	RUE.	do.	do.
H.Q. Div. R.E.	RUE.	RUE.	do.	do.
Sanitary Sect.	RUE.	RUE.	do.	do.
229th Inf. Bde. H.Q.	St. FIRMIN.	RUE.	do.	Stream & River.
14th R. Highrs.	St. FIRMIN.	RUE.	do.	do.
229 L.T.M. Bty.	St. FIRMIN.	RUE.	do.	do.
12th R. Scots Fus.	RUE Camp.	RUE.	do.	do.
16th Devons.	FAVIERC & BECQUERELLE.	FAVIERS.	do.	Stream.
12th Som. L.I.	FOREST MONTIERS.	FAVIERS.	do	do
229th F. Ambul.	RUE.	FAVIERS.	do	do
448 Coy. D. Train.	BERNAY.	FAVIERS.	do	Stream & River.
5th R.A.R.E. Fld. Coy.	BERNAY.	FAVIERS.	do	do
230th Inf. Bde. H.Q.	PONTHOILE.	FAVIERS.	do	Stream.
230 L.T.M.B.	PONTHOILE.	FAVIERS.	do	do
16th Sussex.	PONTHOILE., MORLAY & HAMEL.	FAVIERS.	do	do
12th Norfolks.	NOUVION CAMP.	NOUVION.	do	do
15th Suffolks.	LAMOTTE BULEUX.	BRAILLY.	Wells.	Ponds.
10th E. Kents.	FOREST L'ABBAYE.	BRAILLY.	do	do
5th R.M.R.E. Fld. Coy.	SAILLY BRAY.	FAVIERS.	do	River.
449th Coy. D. Train.	LE TITRE.	BRAILLY.	do	Ponds.
230 Fld. Ambul.	LE TITRE.	BRAILLY.	do	do
231st Inf. Bde. H.Q.	CANCHY.	BRAILLY.	Wells	Large Pond.
231 L.T.M.B.	CANCHY.	BRAILLY.	do	do
10th K.S.L.I.	CANCHY.	BRAILLY.	do	do
24th Welsh Rgt.	CANCHY.	BRAILLY.	do	do
24th R.W. Fus.	DOMVAST.	BRAILLY.	do	do
25th R.W. Fus.	DOMVAST.	BRAILLY.	Wells & Pumps	Ponds.
439th Fld. Coy.	MARCHEVILLE.	BRAILLY.	do	do
231st Field Ambul.	MARCHEVILLE.	BRAILLY.	do	do
450th Coy. D. Train.	CANCHY.	BRAILLY.	Wells.	Large Pond.
Divl. M.G. Bn.	NOUVION CAMP.	NOUVION.	Wells & Pumps	Stream.
12th L. North Lancs.	HAUTVILLERS.	BUIGNY.	Wells.	Stream & Troughs.
H.Q. & 447th Coy. D. Train	SAILLY BRAY.	FAVIERS.	Wells.	River.
H.Q. Div. R.A.	PORT LE GRAND.	PORT LE GRAND.	Wells.	Springs & Canal.
74th D.A.C.	PORT LE GRAND.	PORT LE GRAND.	Wells.	do
2 Medium T.M.B.	PORT LE GRAND.	PORT LE GRAND.	do	do
117 Bde. R.F.A.	GRAND LAVIERS.	PORT LE GRAND.	do	do
Mob. Vet. Sect.	GRAND LAVIERS.	PORT LE GRAND.	do	do
44th Bde. R.F.A.	SAILLY-le-SEC.	Res. Army. Art. School.	do	do
74th Divl. M.T. Coy.	FOREST MONTIERS.	FAVIERS.	Wells & Pumps	-

Diary / Appendix II Diary May

B.A.311.

INSTRUCTIONS re BILLETING.

1. Detailed Instructions regarding Billeting are given in Army Book 397 - Billeting Instructions. Every Officer will make himself thoroughly acquainted with these instructions. Particular attention is directed to paras. 4. 5.(c). 8. 9 13.

2. Billets will invariably be arranged with the Area or Sub-Area Commandant, or where there is no Area or Sub-Area Commandant, with the Mayor or his representative.

3. Billeting Certificates for each commune will be made out Weekly or PRIOR to departure in the case of a shorter stay. The duplicate certificate will be forwarded each Week so as to arrive on MONDAYS at the Branch Requisition Office, Army H.Q.- while in the present Area to Branch Requisition Office, Reserve Army H.Q.

4. On every occasion on which Billets are vacated, a certificate will be rendered to this office through the usual channels to the effect that Billeting Certificates for all Billets vacated have been issued and forwarded to the proper authorities.

5. Offices. Workhouses. Storerooms.
   The Weekly return of Offices etc., hired at the rate not exceeding 25 francs per week will be sent to the Branch Requisitioning Services Officer of the Army, and NOT to Director of Requisition Services, G.H.Q. as stated in para.8.a.(iii)., of General Instructions in A.B.397.
   Particular care must be taken to ensure that the Certificate required under para 8.a. IV. is endorsed on A.F.W. 3401 in the case of hirings under para 8. (b).

6. MESSES.
   No expense either direct or indirect can be allowed to fall on the Public for Officers', N.C.O's, and Mens' Messes, whether furnished or unfurnished, the SUMS DUE FOR THEM must NOT be included on Billeting CERTIFICATES.

7. ACKNOWLEDGE.

sd. H.J.Butchart. Major for,
Lieut-Colonel.,
9/5/18.   A.A.& Q.M.G., 74th (Yeomanry) Division.

Copies to :-
(1)	"G".	(1)	Div.Signal.Coy.
(6)	229th Inf.Bde.	(1)	Div.M.G.Battn.
(6)	230th Inf.Bde.	(1)	Div.Train.
(6)	231st Inf.Bde.	(1)	74th Div.M.T.Coy.
(6)	C.R.A.	(1)	Camp Commdt.
(5)	C.R.E.	(1)	A.P.M.
(5)	A.D.M.S.	(1)	Gas Officer.
(2)	A.D.V.S.	(1)	DIARY.
(1)	D.A.D.O.S.		

Appendix III Diary May.

E.A. 307.

INSTRUCTIONS

re

OPENING OF AN IMPREST ACCOUNT

and

OBTAINING OFFICERS' ADVANCE BOOKS.

OPENING AN IMPREST ACCOUNT.

1. All units with the exception of Infantry, must first apply to :-

    Staff Paymaster i/c Clearing House,

    A.P.O. S.38,

    B.E.F.

    who will allot a number to the Imprest Holder.

2. The Authority mentioned in 1 having been obtained (where necessary) an application (proforma "A" attached) will be signed by the Imprest Holder and counter-signed by the D.A.A.G. of the Division. The Imprest Holder will attend personally at the Field Cashier's and present the authority and application form.

3. Where the Imprest Holder does not attend personnaly to draw the Book he will sign an Authorisation (proforma "B" attached) for another officer to draw the A.F. W.3,100, in which case the signature of the officer sent to draw the Book must be embodied in the Authorisation.

4. Only <u>one</u> Requisition Book can be issued for each unit.

5. Particular attention is directed to the attached "Notes for the Guidance of Holders of Imprest Accounts".

OBTAINING OFFICERS' ADVANCE BOOKS.

1. Every Officer requiring an Advance Book will fill up an application form (proforma "C" attached) and sign it in the presence of the O.C. or Adjutant of his unit who will counter-sign the application.

2. The Officers of one unit may sign the same application form provided they draw from the same Agents, the O.C. or Adjutant countersigning after the last signature.

3. One Officer may draw the officers Advance Books for his unit provided he is given a mandate authorising him to do so and takes with him the application forms and Receipt forms duly completed.

4. Each officer must fill up the buff receipt form "D" (attached) and sign the certificate in the last column of the form. In filling in the 3rd column (Rank and Name) officers names must be entered in BLOCK-CAPITALS.

P.T.O.

5. One Buff Receipt Form will be used for all the officers of a unit drawing from the same Agents.

H. J. O. Butchant

Major,
D.A.A.G,
74th (Yeomanry) Division.

7th May, 1918.

Copies to :-

H.Q. Reserve Army.
Field Cashier, ABBEVILLE.
"G".
H.Q. 229th Infantry Bde.
" 230th " "
" 231st " "
C.R.A.
C.R.E.
A.D.M.S.
A.D.V.S.
D.A.D.O.S.

Div. Signal Coy.
Div. M.G. Battn.
Div. Train.
74th Div. M.T. Coy.
Camp Commandant.
A.P.M.
Div. Chemical Adviser.
Diary.

APPLICATION FOR A.F. W.3100,
REQUISITION FOR CASH BOOK.

"A"

Field Cashier.

    I request that you will supply me with an A.F. W.3100, Requisition for Cash Book.

(Date)............ (Signature of Imprest Holder)...........................

                                     (Unit).........................

                         Countersigned
(Date)............   ....

                                   D.A.A.G. 74 (Yeomanry) Division.

==

"B".

Authorisation for an officer other than the Imprest Holder to draw A.F. W.3100, Requisition for Cash Book

(Signature of officer drawing A.F. W.3100) ....

    The foregoing is the signature of

    ....

whom I hereby authorise to draw A.F. W.3100 on my behalf.

(Date).............. (Signature of Imprest
                          Holder)   ....

                          (Unit)........................

Field Cashier,
   ABBEVILLE.   "C".

      Will you please supply me with an Officer's Advance Book, A.F. W.3241 on my Agents, Messrs. ....

      I certify that this is the only application that has been, or will be, made by me for a first issue of A.F. W.3241, that I have not received a book direct from my Agents, and that if I do, same will be returned to them by me.

                                      Signed ....

The above was signed in my presence.

                                    Countersigned...................................

                                      O/C..

.....................1918.

Field Cashier,   "C".
   ABBEVILLE.

      Will you please supply me with an Officer's Advance Book, A.F. W.3241, on my Agents, Messrs...

      I certify that this is the only application that has been, or will be, made by me for a first issue of A.F. W.3241, that I have not received a book direct from my Agents, and that if I do, same will be returned to them by me.

                                    Signed......................................

The above was signed in my presence.

                                  Countersigned..................................

.....................1918.

No. of Book.	Name of Agent.	Rank and Name.	Unit.	SIGNATURE FOR RECEIPT:— "I certify that I am acquainted with the instructions printed on the inside of the cover of the book, and am aware that I am bound by them."

CERTIFIED that the name of each Officer who obtained a Book has been entered on this List, and that the name of the Officer has been inserted on Cover of Book. ....Signature of Officer issuing Book.

PRINTED IN FRANCE BY ARMY PRINTING AND STATIONERY SERVICES.

PRESS A—4/12—5986B—15,000.

"D"

Receipt for Officers' Advance Forms

No. of Book.	Name of Agent.	Rank and Name.	Unit.	SIGNATURE FOR RECEIPT:— "I certify that I am acquainted with the instructions printed on the inside of the cover of the book, and am aware that I am bound by them."

[P.T.O.

IMPREST ACCOUNT.

Notes for the Guidance of Holders of Imprest Accounts serving with the B.E.F., France.

1.—TO OPEN AN IMPREST ACCOUNT.

Application for authority to open an Imprest account (except in the case of Cavalry and Infantry Units) should first be made to the :—

>STAFF PAYMASTER i/c
>Clearing House,
>A.P.O. S.38. B.E.F.

who will allot a number to the Imprest Holder.

This authority will be presented to the FIELD or BASE CASHIER who will supply A.F. W.3100 without which no Imprest Money can be issued.

2.—COMPLETION OF THE A.F. W. 3100.

The name and allotted number of the account should be filled in the space provided.

An Officer delegated by an Imprest Holder to draw money on his behalf, should sign the front of the form in the Imprest Holder's presence, the latter signing as a witness to his signature. The Cashier is thus enabled to compare the signature of the Officer authorised to draw, with that of the Recipient of the money.

>N.B.—Under no circumstances should the Imprest Holder sign the form before the other signature is inserted, as to do so amounts to drawing a cheque payable to bearer, which in the event of its being mislaid can be cashed by anybody.

In Units where the C.O. is not also the Imprest Holder, the C.O. should sign the otherwise completed form as "seen" in the space provided for the purpose.

3.—CHANGE OF IMPREST HOLDER.

In the event of a change of Imprest Holder, notification of such change should be made by the C.O. or late Imprest Holder to the Field Cashier, and the name, rank, etc., of the new Imprest Holder must be stated and a specimen signature attached.

Notification must also be sent to the Paymaster i/c Clearing House in accordance with G.R.O., 1912, of 2-11-16.

4.—TEMPORARY ABSENCE OF IMPREST HOLDER.

If an Imprest Holder is temporarily absent on leave or duty elsewhere, he (or in the case of Cavalry and Infantry Units, the C.O.) must give written authority to the Field Cashier as follows :—

A.

Imprest Account of..

Authority is given for ....to hold the

Imprest Account during the absence of ....

the present Imprest Holder from..

....
(old) Imprest Holder,
or C.O. (Cavalry or Infantry).

Cash taken over, Francs ....

....
Signature of New Imprest Holder.

(To be attached to A.F. 01817, by Field Cashier.)

Failure to comply with this will entail the refusal of money.

5.—EMERGENCIES.

In cases of emergency which may not be covered by these Instructions, Officers should produce written application countersigned by their Divisional H.Q., C.R.As., C.R.Es., etc., as the case may be.

It is advisable where possible for Imprest Forms to bear the official stamp of the Unit concerned.

6.—NOTE.

Officers should bear in mind that the Field Cashier is personally responsible for the money entrusted to him and liable to make it good in the event of loss. He cannot in consequence be expected to issue money unless the above rules are strictly observed.

Appendix IV

Diary.

CIRCULAR MEMORANDUM.
KITS OF OTHER RANKS.

AV.5.

1. On moving from the present area other Ranks will not be permitted to take kit bags with them. O.s C. Units will therefore have all kit-bags inspected and dealt with as follows:-

   (a) All Government Property will be returned to Ordnance.
   (b) Any Private articles which cannot be carried in the Pack or Haversack will be sent Home.
      (I) If the articles are under 11 lbs they will be sent by Parcel Post.
      (II) If the articles are over 11 lbs they will be sent through the M.F.O. In which case Packages must conform with the Instructions contained in Para: 13 b,c,& d. of this Office B.A.305 of 7th inst. These Packages will be sent to their destination carriage forward from the Port at which they are landed in England.

2. A Report will be rendered by O's C. Formations and Units so as to reach this Office by 12 noon on the 17th inst. certifying that all Other Ranks Kits have been inspected and giving by Units the number of Packages belonging to Other Ranks to be sent Home through the M.F.O. and the approximate weight of same.

H.J. Butchart
Major D.A.A.G.
7th (Yeomanry) Division.

14/5/18.

Copies to: 229th Bde.   O.C. Div. Train
           230th Bde.   O.C. Div. Signals
           231st Bde.   O.C. M.G.Bn.
           A.D.M.S.   C.R.E.
           D.A.D.V.S   D.A.D.O.B
           C.Commdt.   A.P.M.
           Diary.   File.

Appendix IV May

B.A. 311.

BILLETING.

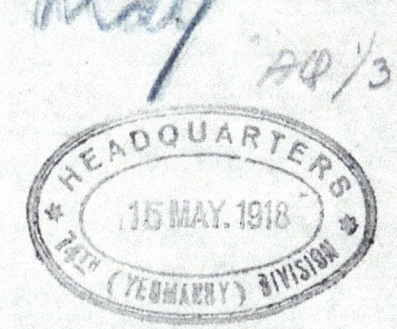

The normal procedure in billeting and allotting Areas is as follows :-

Prior to the move of the Division, Brigade Groups will be constituted. Each Brigade Group will move as a Group under the orders of their Commander.

The future Areas of these Groups will be specified in Divisional Operation Orders and the Staff Captains of Brigades will be responsible for the billeting of all Units allotted to their Groups. Groups are formed for administrative purposes only (unless otherwise ordered) and may be changed from time to time according to orders issued by Divisional Headquarters.

Lieut. Colonel,
15/5/18. A.A.& Q.M.G. 74th (Yeomanry) Division.,

Copies to :- "B"
"A"   229th Bde.   C.R.E.   A.D.V.S.   Div.Sig.Coy.
Diary.   230th Bde.   C.R.A.   A.D.M.S.   Div.M.G.Bn.
         231st Bde.   A.P.M.   D.A.D.O.S. Div.Train.
         C.Comdt.   Div.M.T.Coy.   Gas Officer

Appendix VI  AD/2
War Diary

Instructions re Reporting Absentees etc.

When notifying the A.P.M. of Deserters, Absentees, Escapes from Custody, etc. Units will give the following particulars ; and in the order stated:-

(1). Number, rank, name, initials and unit.
(2). Age, height and build.
(3). Complexion, colour of hair, eyes, growth of hair on face, shape of face.
(4). Peculiarities and distinctive marks.
(5). Description of dress when last seen.
(6). Where last seen and circumstances.
(7). Point to which might be making.
(8). Any other information available.

A specimen report is appended :-

"The following prisoner has escaped:-

(1). No. 16772 Pte. Smith J. 13th Battn. Blankshire Regt.
(2). Age 45 years, height 5'3", build - thick set.
(3). Complexion florid, hair light, eyes hazel, clean shaven, face round, erect carriage. Cut on left side of forehead.
(4). Dressed in F.S. tunic, trousers, puttees and cap.
(5). Last seen at "PERONNE"
(6). Probably making for HAVRE.
(7). Frequents Y.M.C.A. Canteens and is suspected of stealing sums of money"

H.L. Burchart Major
for Lieut. Colonel.

A.A. & Q.M.G. 74th (Yeomanry) Division.

Copies to :-
"G"   229th Bde.   C.R.E.   A.D.M.S.   Div.M.G.Bn.
War Diary.   230th Bde.   C.R.A.   A.D.V.S.   Div.M.T.Coy.
              231st Bde.   A.P.M.   D.A.D.O.S. Div.Sigs.
              C.Comdt.   Div.Gas Officer.   Div.Train.

Diary Appendix VII

SECRET.

INSTRUCTIONS FOR ADVANCED BILLETING PARTIES.
74th (Yeomanry) Division.

AQ.7.

1. Advanced Billeting parties will move to LE CAUROY on 19th inst. by Motor Lorries as follows:-
2. Composition of Party:-
   D.H.Q. D.A.D.M.S., Camp Commdt., and 4 Police.
   Each Infy. Bde.H.Q.:- Staff Captain.
   Each Infantry, M.G., & Pioneer Battn.: One Officer 4 C.Q.M.S., and one representative of Bn. H.Q.
   Each Field Coy. R.E. Field Amb. & Div. Signals.:- 1 Officer & 1 Sergeant.
   74th Div. Train.:- 3 Supply Officers and 4 N.C.Os.

3. Lorries will report at 0800 as under:- and advanced Billeting Parties will join Lorries at Places stated:-

No. of Lorry.	Place at which Lorry Reports.	Units.
1.	229 Bde. H.Q. ST.FIRMIN	229th Inf. Bde.H.Q., 14 Bn.R.H., 13 Devons.
	5th R.A.R.E. BERNAY	5th R.A.R.E., 448th Coy. A.S.C.
2.	D.H.Q. RUE 12th S.L.I.HQ. FOREST MONTIERS	D.H.Q. 229th Field Amb. 12th R.S.F. Div. Signals 12th S.L.I.
3.	230th Inf. Bde. H.Q. POINTHOILE	H.Q. 230th Inf. Bde. 13th Sussex.
	5th R.M.R.E. SAILLY BRAY.	5th R.M.R.E., 447th Coy. ASC.
4.	NOUVION CAMP 15th Suffolks LAMOTTE BOLEUX	12th Norfolks & 74th M.Gun Bn. 15th Suffolks & 10th E.Kents.
5.	230 Field Amb. LE TITRE.	449th Coy. ASC, 230th F.Amb. 1/12th L.N.Lancs.
6.	231st Inf. Bde H.Q. CANCHY	231st Inf. Bde. H.Q., 10th K.S.L.I. 24th Welsh Rgt., 231st F.Amb. 450th Coy. A.S.C.
7.	- do -	24th R.W.F., 25th R.W.F., 439th Fld.Coy. R.E.

4. All Lorries will rendezvous at 231st Infy. Bde H.Q.CANCHY by 10.am. and proceed via., AUX le CHATEAU to LE CAUROY where Parties will report to the Area Commandant.
5. Each Officer and Man will take with him 1 day's ration in addition to that for the day on which they proceed.
6. Each Infy. Bde will take 1 Bicycle to be carried on the Lorries.

H.J. Butcher
Major D.A.A.G.
For Lieut. Colonel A.A.& Q.M.G.
74th (Yeomanry)Division.

19/5/18.
Copies to:-
229 Bde. who will notify 5th RARE & 229 F.Amb.
230 Bde. "   "   "   5th RMRE ,230 F.Amb & M.G.Bn.
231st Inf.Bde. "   "   439 F.Co.RE.,1/12 L.N.Lancs & 231 F.Amb.
Camp Commandant C.R.E.
A.D.M.S.   Div. Train.
A.P.M.

War Diary Appendix VIII

SECRET.   ADMINISTRATIVE INSTRUCTIONS   O.A./174

With reference to 74th Divnl. Order No. 59 -

1. Orders with regard to the move of the 74th M.T. Company will be issued separately to the Officer Commanding that Unit.
2. Lieutenant A.M. Montgomery, Ayrshire Yeo. will superintend the entrainment of the Division which will take place at RUE. The Units will entrain according to attached schedule. Lieutenant H.P. Woods, Suffolk Yeo. will superintend the detrainment at LIGNY St. FLOCHEL.
3. Each Brigade Group Commander will detail 3 Officers for entraining and detraining, one of these always to be on duty until the entrainment or detrainment of the Group is completed.
4. Special loading parties should be told off by Units and will accompany vehicles to the station.
5. Rations for day following the day of entrainment will be taken by Troops.
6. Supply and Baggage Wagons of Divisional Train will be entrained with the Units to which they are affiliated, all wagons and water carts will travel full.
7. All Transport including Baggage and Supply wagons with loading parties will be at the entraining station 3 hours and personnel 1 hour before the time of departure of train.
8. Breast ropes and headcollars will be provided by Units for all Horses entraining.
9. Entraining States will be prepared by all Units and handed to the R.T.O. at the entraining Station.
10. All Divisional Train wagons will be returned to affiliated Train Company as soon as possible after detrainment.
11. Baggage and filled Supply wagons will be drawn from the Refilling Points at 5 p.m. on the day prior to the commencement of the entrainment of Groups by each Unit within the Group.
12. Units or parts of Units entraining on a day subsequent to the commencement of entraining of their Group will consume their portion of the rations drawn the previous evening and will again draw rations for the following day.
13. All horses will be watered immediately prior to entrainment.
14. Detonated Bombs are not to be carried.
15. No lights are allowed when travelling in trains.
16. One Motor Ambulance will be present at both entraining and detraining stations.
17. Motor Lorries will be provided by 1st Army for the carriage of Packs of Troops proceeding to SUS St LEGER, HUMBERCOURT and COULLEMONT.
18. ACKNOWLEDGE.

Headquarters,
10th May 1918.

Cowans Lieut-Colonel
A.A. & Q.M.G.
74th (Yeo) Division.

Copies to :-
229th Inf. Bde.   C.R.A.   74th Div. Train.
230th Inf. Bde.   C.R.E.   74th M.G. Bn.
231st Inf. Bde.   A.D.M.S.   74th M.T. Company.
H.Q. Reserve Army.   A.D.V.S.   935th Div. Emplot. Coy.
1st Army.   D.A.D.O.S.   War Diary.
Canadian Corps.   A.P.M.   Sub. Area Comdt. RUE.
"G"   File.   Camp Comdt,

SECRET.   MOVE OF 74TH (YEOMANRY) DIVISION, MAY 20TH. 1918.

Entrain at RUE..........................Consign to LIGNY ST. FLOCHEL.

Train No.	Marche.	Depart.	Date.	Contents.
1	T. 2	9.34	20/5/18.	H.Q.Divl.Train. - H.Q.Divl.R.E. 985th D.E.Coy. - 448th Coy.A.S.C.
2	T. 6	13.44	..	229th Bge.H.Q. - Part of Divl.Train. No.2 Section Divl. Signals. 5th R.A.R.E.
3	T.10	17.44	..	16th Devons(less 1 Coy.Cooker & team). Part of Divl.Train. - 229th T.M.B.
4	T.14	21.34	..	12th Somersets(less 1 Coy.Cooker & team). - Part of Divl.Train.
5	T.18	1.34	21/5/18.	12th R.S.F.(less 1 Coy.Cooker & team). Part of Divl. Train.
6	T.22	5.34	..	14th R.H.(less 1 Coy.Cooker & team). Part of Divl.Train.
7	T. 2	9.34	..	1 Coy.Cooker & team of 12th Somersets. do. do. 12th R.S.F. do. do. 16th Devons. Part of Divl.Train.
8	T. 6	13.44	..	Divl.H.Q. - Part of Divl.Train. H.Q., Divl.Signals.
9	T.10	17.44	..	229th Field Amb. - Part of Divl.Train. 59th Mobile Vet.Section. 1 Coy.Cooker & team of 14th R.H.
10	T.14	21.34	..	230th Bge.H.Q. - No.3 Sect.Signal Coy. 1 Coy.Cooker & team of 10th E.Kents. do. do. 12th Norfolks. do. do. 15th Suffolks. Part of Divl. Train.
11	T. 18	1.34	22/5/18.	15th Suffolks(less 1 Coy.Cooker & team) 449th Coy.Divl.Train. Part of Divl. Train.
12	T.22	5.34	..	12th Norfolks(less 1 Coy.Cooker & team). 230th L.T.M.Bty. - Part of Divl.Train.
13	T. 2	9.34	..	10th E.Kents(less 1 Coy.Cooker & team). Part of Divl.Train.
14	T. 6	13.44	..	16th Sussex(less 1 Coy.Cooker & team). Part of Divl.Train.
15	T.10	17.44	..	5th R.M.R.E. - Part of Divl.Train. 1 Coy.Cooker & team of 16th Sussex.
16	T.14	21.34	..	½ 74th M.G.Btn. & transport. 5th Signal Section.- Part of Divl.Train.
17	T.18	1.34	23/5/18.	½ 74th M.G.Btn., horses & transport.

- 2 -

Train No.	Marche.	Depart.	Date.	Contents.
18	T. 22	5.34	23/5/18.	231st Bge.H.Q. - 230th Field Amb. Part of Divl.Train. 4th Signal Section. 231st L.T.M.Bty. 1 Coy.Cooker & team of 24th R.W.F.
19	T. 2	9.34	..	24th R.W.F.(less 1 Coy.Cooker & team). - Part of Divl.Train.
20	T. 6	13.44	..	1 Coy.Cooker & team of 25th R.W.F. do. do. 24th Welsh do. do. 10th K.S.L.I. Part of Divl. Train.
21	T. 10	17.44	..	25th R.W.F.(less 1 Coy.Cooker & team). - Half 231st Field Amb. Part of Divl.Train.
22	T. 14	21.34	..	24th Welsh Rgt(less 1 Coy.Cooker & team). - Part of Divl.Train. ½ 231st Field Amb.
23	T. 18	1.34	24/5/18.	10th K.S.L.I.(less 1 Coy.Cooker & team). - Part of Divl. Train.
24	T. 22	5.34	..	439th Field Coy.R.E. 1 Coy.Cooker & team of 1/12th L.N.Lancs. - Part of Divl.Train. 1/12th L.N.Lancs.(part horses & transport.
25	T. 2	9.34	..	1/12th L.N.Lancs.(less 1 Coy. Cooker & team) and part horses & transport. - Part of Divl.Train.

T.A. 1864 S.

I enclose herewith _____ copies of entrainment programme for move of 74th (Yeomanry) Division less Artillery.

H.Q., L. of C. Area.
May 19th., 1918.

Douglas Wilson
Lieut-Colonel,
A.D.R.T. (S).

Addressed:- D.D.R.T.(S). - D.D.R.T. (E). - "Q" 4th Army.
A.D.G.T., 4th Army. - 74th Division H.Q. - C.R.N.
C.R., ABBEVILLE. - Traffic, PERNES. - Captain Hartopp.
Major Christie. - R.T.O.,RUE.

P.T.O.

When the Sentence "Part of Divnl Train" occurs in this Stab it means the baggage and Supply wagons attached from the Divnl Train to the Unit or units proceeding by that train.

Appendix IX

LOCATION RETURN 74th (YEOMANRY) DIVISION.

UNIT.	LOCATION.
74th Divnl. Head Quarters.	ROELLECOURT.
Head Quarters Divisional Signals.	"
Head Quarters Divisional Train.	"
No. 985 Employment Company.	"
Head Quarters Divisional Royal Engineers.	"
447 Company. A.S.C.	ROCOURT ST.AURENT.

229th Inf. Brigade Group.

Head Quarters 229th Inf. Bde.	SUS ST LEGER.
16th (R.N.Devon Hrs & 1/1 Devon Yeo)Battn. Devon Rgt.	"
12th (W.Somerset Yeo) Bn. S.L.Inf.	"
448 Company A.S.C.	"
229th Field Ambulance.	"
14th (Fife & Forfar Yeo) Bn. R.Highlanders.	HUMBERCOURT.
229th L.T.M.Battery.	"
439 (Cheshire) Fd. Coy. Royal Engineers.	"
12th (Lanark Yeo) Bn. R.S.Fusiliers.	COULLEMONT.

230th Inf. Brigade Group.

Head Quarters 230th Inf. Bde.	BUNEVILLE.
10th (R.East & West Kent Yeo) Bn. The Buffs.	"
12th (Norfolk Yeo) Bn. Norfolk Regt	(Maisnil St Pol.
	(NEUVILLE AU-CORNET.
15th (Suffolk Yeo) Bn. Suffolk Regt.	(HERLIN LE SEC
	(OCOCHE.
	(TACHINCOURT.
	(MAISNIL ST POL.
16th (Sussex Yeo) Bn. Sussex Regt.	FOUFFLIN-RICAMETZ
74th Machine Gun Battalion.	TERNAS.
230th L.T.M.Battery.	MONTS-EN-TERNOIS.
230th Field Ambulance.	"
5th Fd.Coy. Royal Monmouth Royal Engineers.	PT HOUVIN.
449 Coy. A.S.C.	FOUFFLIN-RICAMETZ.

231st Inf. Bde. Group.

Head Quarters 231st Inf. Bde.	AMBRINES.
10th (Shropshire & Ches Yeo) Bn. K.S.L.Inf.	"
5th Fd. Coy. Royal Anglesea. R.E.	"
450 Coy. A.S.C.	"
231st L.T.M.Battery.	"
24th (Welsh Horse) Welch Regt (Pem & Glam Yeo) Bn Welsh Regt	COUY EN TERNOIS.
24th (Pembroke & Glamorgan Yeo) Bn.R.W.Fusiliers (Denbigh Yeo)	MONCHEAUX.
25th (Denbigh Yeo) Bn. R.W.Fusiliers. (Mmo-Welsh H)	MAGNICOURT.
1/12 Bn. (Pioneers) Bn L.N.Lancs.	MEZIERES.
231st Field Ambulance.	SARS LEZ BOIS.

74th M.T. Company.	TINQUES.

Appendix X   May

LOCATION OF 74th (YEOMANRY) DIVISION. (Lee-s R.A.)

D.H.Q Group

D.H.Q.	LE CAUROY
H.Q. Signals.	do
59th M.V.S.	do
985th Div Emp. Coy.	do
H.Q. Div. Train.	do
447th Coy. A.S.C.	ETREE WAMIN.

229th INF. BDE GROUP.

229th Inf. Bde HQ.	LIGNEREUIL
12th S.L.I.	do
12th R.S.F.	GRAND RULLECOURT
14th R. Highldrs.	do
439th F. Coy. R.E.	do
16th Devons.	LEINCOURT
229th L.T.M.B	do
448th Coy. A.S.C.	do
229th F. Amb.	DENIER
74th M G. Bn.	BEAUFORT.

230th Inf. Bde. GROUP.

230th Inf. Bde H.Q.	IZELLEZ HAMEAU
10th Buffs.	do
12th Norfolks.	do
15th Suffolks	PENIN
16th Sussex.	MANIN
449th Coy. A.S.C.	DOFFINE
230th L.T.M.B.	VILLERS SUR SIMON
230th F. Amb.	do
5th R.M.R.E.	do

231st INF. BDE GROUP.

231st Inf. Bde HQ.	AVESNES LES COMTE
10th K.S.L.I.	LETTRE ST. QUINTIN
24th Welsh.	do
231st F. Amb.	do
24th R.W.F.	HAUTVILLE
25th R.W.F.	HABARCQ
231st L.T.M.B.	NOYELLETTE
1/12th L.N.Lancs.	FAUSSEUX
5th R.A.R.E.	do
450th Coy. A.S.C.	LE HAMEAU

74th Div M.T.Coy.	TINQUES.
H.Q. Div R.A.	HOUVIN HOUVIGNEUL
44 Bde R.F.A	ETRÉE WAMIN
117 Bde R.F.A	BERLENCOURT & SARS LE BOIS
74 Div D.A.C.	MAGNICOURT

WAR DIARY or INTELLIGENCE SUMMARY.

Army Form C. 2118.

A & Q Branch Headquarters 74 (Yeo) Division
June 1918.

Place	Date	Hour	Summary of Events and Information	Remarks and references to Appendices
LE CAUROY	1		Instructions issued regarding supply of Ordnance Stores	Appendix I
"	5		Instructions issued regarding Salvage	Appendix II
"	5		Warning order issued that the Division will probably relieve the 3rd Canadian Division about June 14th. 8 Lewis Gun P. Battalions (including Pioneers) issued thus bringing Battalions up to 32 Lewis Guns p. Infy Battalion	
"	6		Division ordered to be in readiness to move at 9 hours notice	
"	6		Instructions issued as to reporting of Casualties	
"	18		Provisional instructions re Entraining of Division issued	Appendix III
"	18		Division ordered to be in readiness to move at 24 hours notice from 24.00 today. Intimation received that Battalions would go into the line with the 3rd Canadian Division for 2 days, 2 Battalions to be in the line at a time commencing on 20th. Each Battalion would be split up so that a 74 Division Platoon would be attached to each Canadian Coy. All transport & "B" Teams to be left behind. Division to be sent from Divisional Railhead by Motor lorry to 2nd Canadian Refilling Point.	Appendix IV
"	24		Division ordered to move to NORRENT FONTES area by Tactical Trains & Road commencing June 25th.	Appendix V
"	25		Instructions issued as to move by Tactical Trains	Appendix VI
"	"		Administrative instructions for move issued	Appendix VII
"	"		Further Administrative instructions for move issued	
NORRENT FONTES	26		Divisional Headquarters closed at LE CAUROY at 1500 hours and opened at NORRENT FONTES at the same hour. A very large number of the Division was suffering from P.U.O. and over 800 "sick in billets" had to be moved to the new area by Motor lorry.	

H.J. Buckhan Mayor
A.A. & Q.M.G. 74 (Yeo) Division

Army Form C. 2118.

WAR DIARY
or
INTELLIGENCE SUMMARY.
(Erase heading not required)

A+Q Branch
Headquarters
74th (Yeomanry) Division
June 1918

Place	Date	Hour	Summary of Events and Information	Remarks and references to Appendices
NORRENT FONTES	26		The 229th Inf. Bde. Group was billeted in the Fontes, Lambres Witternesse, RELY area with their refilling point at RELY	
			The 230th Inf. Bde. Group was billeted in the Flechin, Enquin Les Mines, Estrée Blanche area with their refilling point at ESTRÉE BLANCHE	
			The 231st Inf. Bde. Group was billeted in ST HILAIRE FANCQUENHEIM & LIERES area with their refilling point at ST HILAIRE	
			Divisional Artillery were billeted in FONTAINES LES HERMAIN, AMES, NEDON NEDONCHELLE area with their refilling point of AUCHY AU BOIS.	
			Supply Railhead was at WITTERNESSE and supplies were taken from Railhead to Refilling points daily by Motor Lorry.	
	28		2 Battalion of 229 Inf. Bde ordered to move 1 Co. & L Coys to 119th d (Sheet 36 A 1/40,000) 1 Coy locale of ST VENNANT and BUSNES for work under 3rd & 61st Divisions & Administrative instructions for foregoing were issued.	Appendix VII
	29		1 Battalion 231st Inf Bde ordered to CHOCQUES for work under XIII Corps.	
			Intimation received that Colonel (Temp. Brig. Gen.) A.A. KENNEDY C.M.G. (then Cmdg 75th Inf. Bde) had been appointed to command the 230th Inf. Bde vice Major (Temp. Brig. Gen.) W.J. BOWKER. C.M.G., D.S.O. Somerset L.I. to England.	
	30		Divisional Reception Camp moved to WITTERNESSE.	

A.C. Chant Chaplin
AA&Q 74 (Yeo) Division

"A" War Diary June Appendix 1   QL-11.

INSTRUCTIONS REGARDING SUPPLY ETC. OF ORDNANCE STORES.

1. All Units will submit Indents for Ordnance Stores to D.A.D.O.S. as per attached schedules "A" and "B". Failure to comply with the dates shown will entail several days delay.
   Stores of a very important nature which have been lost or damaged during an action, however, should be demanded at once.

11. Except in the case of expendible stores, such as - Soap, Dubbin, Oil, Flannelette, Grease and materials for Repair of Boots, Saddlery etc, Indents to "replace" will not be approved of by D.A.D.O.S. unless a receipt from the Salvage Dump for the unserviceable article is produced.

111. To enable Units to comply with this Instruction, D.A.D.O.S. is arranging to issue a preliminary "Working Stock" on the following scale :-

	Puttees.	Boots(prs)	Jackets S.D.	Trousers S.D.	Pants S.D.
M.G., Pioneer, & Inf. Battns	50	50	40	40	2
Fld. Coy. R.E.	12	12	10	10	4
Inf. Bde. H.Q.	4	4	2	2	1
Div. Signal Coy.	12	12	10	-	10
No.1 Coy. A.S.C.	10	10	8	-	8
Nos. 2,3 & 4 Coys A.S.C.	4	4	2	-	2
Battery R.A.	12	12	10	-	10
D.A.C.	40	40	30	-	30
T.M.B.	4	4	2	2	-
Employ. Coy.	12	12	10	10	-
M.T. Company.	12	14	12	12	-
Fld. Ambulance.	12	12	10	10	-
Div. H.Q.	6	6	4	4	-
TOTAL=	190	192	140	90	67

A "Working Stock" is not considered necessary for items other than those mentioned above.

1V. Before submitting Indents to replace "Losses" Commanding Officers must fully investigate the circumstances under which the loss occurred and forward a statement of all these circumstances with the Indent. If the loss is due to neglect the individual responsible must bear the cost of the article and A.F.W. 3069 should be attached to the Indent.

V. All Indents for stores shown on Schedule "B" must show numbers in possession and strength of Men & Animals. Indents for Stores on Schedule "A" will only show strength of men and Horses.

Vl. Indents for Stores demanded as a "First Supply" must invariably quote the authority therefor, also the numbers in possession.

Vll. The following numbers of G.R.O's are quoted herewith for information. Commanding Officers are personally responsible that the instructions contained in these orders are strictly adhered to, viz,

    Clothing -   G.R.O. 3586 dated 9-3-18.
    Puttees -   G.R.O. 3426 dated 21-2-18.
    Mess Tins & Camp Kettles - G.R.O. 3279 dated 31-1-18.
    Binoculars -   G.R.O. 1956 dated 19-11-16.

P.T.O.

#2#

VIII. Commanding Officers will arrange for an Officer to visit D.A.D.
O.S. at least twice weekly. It is not considered advisable for
D.A.D.O.S. to send telegrams or D.R.L.S. messages to individual
Units notifying them that stores are awaiting removal. As far as
possible he will notify Staff Captains by phone, but Units' representatives when handing in Indents on days shown on attached Schedules
will ascertain from D.A.D.O.S. or his Warrant Officers what stores
are awaiting removal and will arrange to collect same next day
without fail.

(signed)

Major
D.A.Q.M.G.
74th (Yeo) Division.

Headquarters.

31st May 1918.

Copies to :-

229th Infantry Brigade.	C.R.A. 74th Division.
230th Infantry Brigade.	C.R.E. -do-
231st Infantry Brigade.	A.D.M.S. -do-
O.C. 74th Div. Train.	A.D.V.S. -do-
O.C. 74th Div. Signal Coy.	Camp Commandant.
O.C. 74th M.T. Company.	O.C. Div. Employ. Coy.
D.A.D.O.S.	O.C. 74th M.G. Battn.
A.P.M.	

SCHEDULE "A" BULKED STORES.

Indents for items shown below should reach D.A.D.O.S. by 10 a.m. on the days stated.

MONDAY.
Bags, ration.
Bottles Water.
Carriers Water.
Covers Mess tin.
Haversacks.
Tins Mess.
Axes Pick.
Shovels.
Spades.
Implements, entrenching.
Kettles Camp.
Pads surcingle.
All Picketting Gear.
Rugs Horse.
Sheets Ground.
Dubbin.
Grease.
Mineral Jelly.
Oil lubricating.
Paint Service Colour.
Soap.
Blankets.
Cotton Waste.
Flannelette.
Sponge Cloths.
Steel Helmets.
Bottles oil.

THURSDAY.
All Clothing, Necessaries & all articles of Grindery.

Saturday.
Bags, nose.
Blankets Saddle.
Brushes Horse.
Rubbers Horse.
Stable necessaries.
Horse & Mule Shoes.
Batteries torch.
Lamps electric torch.
Covers breech.
Pullthrough Cords.
Pullthrough gauzes.
Respirators, small box.
Anti Gas appliances.

SCHEDULE "B".
****

Indents for all Stores, not shown in Schedule "A" will be sent to D.A.D.O.S. on days allotted hereunder. Indents to be delivered by hand before 10 a.m.

MONDAY.
24th Bn. R.W.F.
25th Bn. R.W.F.
H.Q. & Signal 231st Bde.
12th Bn. R.S.F.
H.Q. & Signals 229th Bde.
74th Divisional Train.
74th Divl. Headquarters.
14th Bn. R.H.

TUESDAY.
24th Bn. Welsh Regt.
10th Bn. K.S.L.I.
231st L.T.M.B.
16th Bn. Devon Regt.
12th Bn. Somerset L.I.
229th L.T.M.B.
74th Div. Amm. Column.
74th Div. M.T. Coy.

WEDNESDAY.
74th M.G. Battn.
5th Fld. Coy. R.A.R.E.
H.Q. & Signals 230 Bde.
12th Bn Norfolk Regt.
X Battery M.T.M.B.
Y Battery M.T.M.B.
H.Q. Divl. Artillery.
985th Div. Employ. Coy.

THURSDAY.
1/12th Bn. Lancs.
231st Fld. Ambulance.
5th Fld. Coy. R.M.R.E.
229th Field Ambulance.
230th Field Ambulance.
44th Brigade R.F.A.
Headquarters R.E.
M.M.P.

P.T.O.

SCHEDULE "B" (continued)

FRIDAY.
15th Bn. Suffolk Regt.
16th Sussex.
230th L.T.M.B.
439th Fld. Coy. R.E.
117th Brigade R.F.A.
59th Mob. Vety. Section.

SATURDAY.
H.Q. & Nos. 1 & 5 Sections of
74th Div. Signal Coy.
10th Bn. E. Kent Regt.

A. War Diary June Appendix II

CIRCULAR MEMORANDUM.

SALVAGE.

Qs.2.

1. In order to reduce to a minimum the wastage in War material it is of great importance that a systematic system of Salvage should be in operation in the Division.

2. A Divisional Salvage party has been formed consisting of 50 O.R. under a Salvage Officer.

3. 2/Lt. A.C. UNWIN, 3rd Somerset Light Infantry is appointed Divisional Salvage Officer.

4. Salvage Receiving Stations have been formed in Brigade Areas as follows :-

    229th Brigade Area ... LIENCOURT.

    230th Brigade Area ...) IZEL LES HAMEAU.
) VILLERS SUR SIMON.

    231st Brigade Area.   LATTRE ST QUENTIN.

5. All Salved articles or wornout clothing and equipment will be sent in to these Receiving Stations by Units, where the N.C.O. in charge will check and give a receipt.

6. It is most important that Units should obtain receipts for the articles handed in to the Salvage N.C.O. i/c of the Receiving Station as when Indenting to replace wornout clothing or equipment, this receipt must be produced with the Indent to replace.

7. On no account will stores or equipment be re-issued direct to Units from the Salvage Dumps. Any articles classified as fit for Re-issue will be re-issued through D.A.D.O.S.

8. The various articles returned to the Dumps will be made up in separate lots or bundles, clearly marked with the <u>name of the Unit</u> and <u>number of articles</u> in each Bundle.

9. The Salvage Officer will apply to Staff Captains for Transport as required for removal of salvaged stores from Billets etc to the Dumps within the Brigade Areas.

10. ~~Enclosed is a copy of a pamphlet on Salvage (S.S./640).~~

                                              Major
Headquarters.   D.A.Q.M.G.
1st June 1918.   74th (Yeo) Division.

Copies to :-

229th Bde.	C.R.A.	O.C. 74th Div. Train.
230th Bde.	C.R.E.	O.C. 74th Div. Signals.
231st Bde.	A.D.M.S.	O.C. 74th M.T. Coy.
Camp Comdt.	D.A.D.V.S.	O.C. 74th M.G. Battn.
"A"	D.A.D.O.S.	O.C. Div. Employ. Coy.
	A.P.M.	Div. Salvage Officer.

Diary

War Diary June
Appendix VII

A 11

74th (YEOMANRY) DIVISION.
INSTRUCTIONS ON REPORTING CASUALTIES.
List of Casualty Wires and Returns required.

RETURN.	By whom Rendered.	For which period.	When due at D.H.Q.
I. APPROXIMATE CASUALTIES WHEN HEAVY FIGHTING IS IN PROGRESS.			
(a) Estimated Wire.	(a) Infantry, M.Gun & Pioneer Bns.	(a) 24 hours 6pm–6pm plus period from commencement of phase.	(a) 7 pm daily
(b) Supplementary Wire.	(b) –do–	(b) 12 hours 6pm–6am plus period from commencement of phase.	(b) 7a.m. if necessary.
II. ORDINARY CASUALTY REPORTS TO BE RENDERED BY ALL UNITS AND FORMATIONS.			
A. Casualties to General Offrs. Staff Offrs & Comndg. Offrs. (a) Wire. (b) Return.	All Units and Formations.	(a) As they occur. (b) As they occur.	(a) As they occur. (b) Within 12 hours of casualty.
B. Accurate daily wire. Incldg. names of Offrs.	All Units and Formations.	24 hours 12 noon–12 noon.	3 pm daily.
C. Accurate Daily Return. Incldg. Names of Offrs.	All Units and Formations.	24 hours 12 noon–12 noon.	8 pm daily.
D. Weekly return of Missing.	All Units and Formations.	Weekly 12 noon on Saturdays to 12 noon on Saturdays.	12 noon Sundays.
E. Weekly nominal rolls of O/R Casualties on A.F.B. 213.	All Units and Formations.	Weekly 12 noon on Saturday to 12 noon Saturday.	6 pm Sundays.

2.

SECRET.

74th (YEOMANRY DIVISION)

INSTRUCTIONS ON REPORTING CASUALTIES.

1. DESCRIPTION OF CASUALTIES. The attention of all concerned is particularly directed to the Instructions regarding the Reporting of Casualties issued under G.R.O. 3867 of 25th April, 1918 (see Appendix 1 attached)

2. MISSING OFFICERS. In all cases where an Officer is reported Missing a brief statement explaining the circumstances should be rendered without delay. A brief account being given in the Casualty Wire and full particulars given in the Daily Casualty Return.

3. Casualties exceeding 15 per Unit. During periods when no special operations are taking place, if casualties of any one Unit exceed 15 on any one day, a brief explanation will be added e.g., "Mine Explosion", "Heavy Shelling", "Hostile Raid" as the case may be.

---

1. APPROXIMATE CASUALTIES WHEN HEAVY FIGHTING IS IN PROGRESS.

To be rendered for Infantry (Including Pioneers) and Machine Gun Battalions only.

1. Brigades in which any Battalion has suffered 50 or more casualties will wire the number by Battalions to reach D.H.Q. not later than 7 p.m. daily made up for the 24 hours ending 6 p.m. If further heavy casualties occur during the night another wire will be sent to reach D.H.Q. by 7 a.m next morning, to include casualties up to 6 a.m. No wire is to be sent unless at least 50 more casualties in the case of Infantry Battalions and 25 in the case of M.G.Bn have occurred since the previous wire.

2. The casualties will be reported by "Phases", the date of commencing and closing each phase will be notified from this Office. The duration of each phase will vary according to the fighting and the casualties suffered, but will normally be about three weeks.

3. Each wire will include the number reported since the commencement of the phase, and will begin with the following words: "Total estimated casualties from ....(here insert date of commencement of phase). The word "Additional" will on no account be used in any wire.

4. When a Formation or Unit is resting it will take the opportunity of verifying the casualties it has reported for the current phase, and on going into action again for the second or third time will start reporting from the corrected figures and not from zero, unless in the meanwhile a new phase has been started.

5. Approximate Casualty Wires are to be sent only for Infantry Battalions, Machine Gun Battalions and Pioneer Battalions.

6. The following code will be used when reporting estimated casualties. Battalions will be represented by Alphabetical letters in order of succession as follows :

6. (Continued)

A. 16th Devons.	E. 10th E.Kents.	K. 24th R.W.F.
B. 12th Somerset LI	F. 12th Norfolks.	L. 25th R.W.F.
C. 12th R.Scots Fus.	G. 15th Suffolks.	M. 24th Welsh Regt.
D. 14th R.Highlanders.	H. 13th Sussex.	N. 10th K.S.L.I.
		P. 12th L.N.Lancs.
		X. M.Gun.Battn.

7. If a Battalions has not had more than 50 casualties (or 25 casualties in the case of the M.G.Bn.) since the previous wire, it will not be referred to in the previous wire.

8. The words "Officers" and "Other Ranks" will not be employed in these wires, numbers being used in each case separated by the word "and". If there are no Officer Casualties the word "NIL" must be used. "AAA" representing fullstop will not be used in those wires.

9. The following is an example of an Estimated Casualty wire:-

    "Total estimated casualties from 10th March A 2 and 58 C NIL and 75
    "D 8 and 86"

    It will be understood in this Office that the Units mentioned have suffered the following total casualties from 10th March to the date the wire was sent.

    <u>229th Inf. Bde.</u>

16th Devon Regt.	2 Officers and 58	Other Ranks.
12th R.Scots Fus.	Nil " 75	"
14th R.Highlanders.	8 " 86	"

10. This wire will give roughly approximate numbers of Officer and Other Rank Casualties. NO DISTINCTION WILL BE MADE BETWEEN KILLED, WOUNDED AND MISSING.

11. If Units over-estimate their casualties and subsequently recognize the fact, the error should be corrected by reporting the correct total figures in the next estimated casualty wire.

II. <u>ORDINARY CASUALTY REPORTS TO BE RENDERED BY ALL UNITS AND FORMATIONS.</u>

A. <u>Casualties to General Officers, Staff Officers and Commanding Officers</u>

   1. <u>WIRE.</u> Casualties to General Officers, Staff Officers and Commanding Officers will be wired to D.H.Q. immediately they occur, giving a brief statement showing how the Casualty occurred.

   2. <u>WRITTEN REPORT.</u> A written report will be rendered to reach this Office within 12 hours of the casualty, confirming same and giving full particulars.

   3. These Casualties will be included in the Daily Casualty Return and Wire in addition to being dealt with as above.

B. <u>ACCURATE DAILY WIRE.</u>

   1. All Units and Formations will render through the usual Channels an accurate Daily Casualty Wire.

   2. This wire will be made up to 12 noon for the preceding 24 hours and will be forwarded to reach D.H.Q. at 3.p.m. on the same day, thus casualties occuring between 12 noon 2nd May and 12 noon 3rd May must

P.T.O.

B. 2)(Continued)

must reach D.H.Q. by 3 p.m. 3rd May and will be termed casualties for the 3rd May. Nil wires will be rendered.

3. Casualties will be shown by Units (in clear as distinct from the estimated wire) showing the numbers Killed, Wounded, Missing, Died of Injuries, distinguishing Officers and Other Ranks. In the case of Officers the Unit, attached Unit, Rank, initials and name will be stated but in the case of other Ranks the numbers only will be given.

x Injured

4. In the case of Officers the actual date on which the casualty occurred will be added after the name of the Officer. (In the same way Officers Commanding Units when reporting Other Rank Casualties on A.Fs B.213 will endeavour to give the exact date on which the casualty occurred)

5. Specimen Wire.

74th Division.

"Casualties for 3rd May AAA 12th Norfolks Killed 2/Lt.A.B.Brown Norfolk Yeo 3rd O/R 3 Wounded O/R 8 Injured Capt F.P. White 3rd Bn.Norfolk Regt and at duty revolver AAA 15th Suffolks Killed O/R 2 Wounded 2/Lt. Green Lovat Scouts 3rd O/R 6 includes 4 at duty Missing O/R 2 on patrol AAA 16th Sussex Died of Injuries O/R 3 bomb explosion.

6. Before reporting names of Officers these must always be verified in the Army List to ensure that the correct Unit, initials and spelling are given. Carefully compiled Nominal Rolls of Officers should always be kept up-to-date by each Unit.

C. Accurate Daily Return.

1. All Units and Formations will render through the usual channels an accurate Daily Casualty Return on Pro-forma A (Appendix 2 attached)

2. This Return will be made up to 12 noon for the preceding 24 hours and will be rendered so as to reach this Office by 8 p.m. each day.

3. This Return will confirm the Daily Wire and will give any further particulars not included in the wire.

D. Weekly Return of Missing (On pro-forma "B" (appendix 3 attached).)

1. It will be made up to 12 noon on Saturdays and rendered so as to reach this Office by 12 noon on Sundays.

2. This Return will show under Column "A" the total number of Missing of all arms. Under Column "B" the total numbers included in the Missing (Column A) that are thought to have been taken alive. Due allowance must be made for those who were previously reported missing but who have since rejoined or whom it has been ascertained have been killed.

E. Weekly Nominal Rolls of Other Rank Casualties.

No separate Nominal Rolls of O/R Casualties other than those sent on the weekly A.Fs B. 213 are required. The utmost endeavour will be made to ensure that these Nominal Rolls are carefully and accurately compiled.

Lieut Colonel,
A.A.& Q.M.G. 74th (Yeo) Division.

3/6/18.

Copies to :- "G"   229th Inf. Bde. C.R.E.   A.D.M.S.   Signals. Train.
        War Diary. 230th Inf. Bde. C.R.A.   D.A.D.V.S.   M.G.Bn.   M.T.Coy.
                   231st Inf. Bde. 985 Emp. Coy. Camp Comdt. D.G.Officer

G.R.O. 3897. APPENDIX 1.

Casualties - Reporting of. G.R.O. 2485 is cancelled and the following instructions will be observed when reporting casualties:-

(1) All casualties caused by enemy weapons in use at the time as such, and all casualties caused by British or Allied weapons which are in action against the enemy will be reported as "Battle Casualties"

(2) The word "weapon" will be held to include Lethal Gas, Mustard Gas, Liquid Fire, high-tension currents, and enemy barbed wire, as well as all other instruments used in fighting.

(3) In reporting "Battle Casualties" the terms "Killed in action", "Died of wounds", "Wounded", "Wounded (at duty)" or "Missing" only will be used except in the case of Shell Shock and Lethal or Mustard Gas Casualties where the special nature of the Casualty will be indicated thus :-
"Killed in action (Gas)"
"Wounded (Gas)"
"Wounded (Shell Shock)"

(4) No report of "wounded (Shell Shock)" shall be made except on the authority of the Officer Commanding a Special Hospital inaccordance with G.R.O. 2384, nor will a report of "Wounded (Gas)" be made except in accordance with G.R.O's 3127 and 3128.

(5) In cases where it is considered desirable to enquire into the conduct of an officer or man who is believed to have been taken prisoner by the enemy, and a Court of Enquiry is held for that purpose, the casualty will be reported as "Missing, believed Prisoner of War (Court of Enquiry Case)"

See para 2 (b), S.S. 617, issued with G.R.O. 2884.

(6) A Casualty from Mine Gas poisoning sustained by an officer or man in the course of his duty, and which is not due in any way to neglect or disobedience of orders, will be reported as a "Battle Casualty"

7. A casualty arising from any other injury will be reported simply as "Injured", "Died of Injuries" or "Killed acc" (in the case of immediate death from injury). When, however, the injury is self-inflicted, it will in the first instance be reported as "Injured S.I.", "Died of Injuries S.I." or "Killed S.I." (in the case of immediate death from self-inflicted injury), until the case has been investigated and Army Form W.3428 completed, when the injury will be definitely classified as "Wilful", "Negligent", "Without Negligence", or "Accidental" as the case may be.

(8) When an Officer or Other Rank who is both "Wounded and Missing" and has previously reported (1) Missing, (2) Wounded, the second notification should read :-
(1) Wounded and Missing, previously reported Missing.
(2) Wounded and Missing, previously reported Wounded.

In the case where an Officer or Other Rank is reported "Wounded and Missing" and it is desired to correct the report, then it must be clearly shown whether it is desired to correct the report of Wounded as well as Missing thus:-
(1) Cancel report of Wounded and Missing, now reported Wounded.
(2) Cancel report both of Wounded and Missing.

(9) All casualties above mentioned, including Injuries, will be reported by Formations in the Daily Casualty Wire to Headquarters of Armies and L of C. Area, in precisely the same manner as Battle Casualties have been in the past. Headquarters of Armies and L. of C. Area will include in their Daily Lists to 1st and 3rd Echelons Casualties classified as "Injuries" in the same form as Battle Casualties.

APPENDIX 2.   Pro-forma "A"

DAILY CASUALTY RETURN.

...................Unit.   Due at D.H.Q. by 8 p.m.

Actual casualties from Noon............to Noon............

Unit.	KILLED		WOUNDED		MISSING		Died of Injuries.		Injured.		Remarks.
	Off.	O.R.	Off.	O.R.	Off.	O.R.	Off.	O.R.	Off.	O.R.	
TOTAL.											

Details of Officer Casualties are given on the Back.

Signed._____

P. T. O.

DETAILS OF CASUALTIES TO OFFICERS.

Unit to which Offr. is attached.	Unit.	Rank.	Initials & Name.	Casualty.		
				Nature.	Date.	Remarks.
12th Norfolks.	Norfolk Yeo.	2/Lt.	A.E.Brown.	Killed.	3rd	

NOTICES.

SECRET.

Appendix 3.   Pro-forma "B"

.... UNIT.

RETURN OF MISSING AND PRISONERS for week Ending ....

UNIT.	A. Missing.		B. Estimated Prisoners.		Remarks.
	Officers.	Other Ranks.	Officers.	Other Ranks.	

In the Column of Remarks should be stated briefly where the action occurred and the date.

War Diary / War Diary June Appendix IV CG 223

SECRET.   PROVISIONAL ENTRAINING INSTRUCTIONS.

12th June 1918.

1. In the event of the Division being ordered to move suddenly, entrainment will take place from 3 different stations according to attached provisional schedule.

2. Each Infantry Brigade Group will detail one Company with Cooker to load all Trains at each Station, these will be taken from trains Nos. 22, 23, and 24 and will travel on these Trains. Similarly, the Companies with Cookers on Trains Nos. 1, 2 and 3 will unload all trains at the detraining stations.

3. Parties for Trains Nos. 1, 2 and 3 should be held in instant readiness to entrain, and the Companies detailed from trains Nos. 22, 23 and 24 as loading parties should be at the entraining Station 3½ hours before the first train is due to start.

4. The entrainment of all Units must be completed half-an hour before the time of departure of the train, when it will be moved from the loading siding, it is therefore necessary that all vehicles and horses should be at the station 3 hours before the time of departure of the train, by which they are to proceed.

5. In order to avoid congestion in moving to the various stations the GIVENCHY - PENIN-TINQUES road and any roads west of it are allotted to the 229th Infantry Brigade Group.
The B.G.C. 230th Infantry Brigade group will arrange that the troops at VILLERS-SIR-SIMON and PENIN leave the GIVENCHY-PENIN TINQUES road clear for the passage of the 229th Infantry Brigade.

6. The 230th Infantry Brigade Group may use roads E. of GIVENCHY-PENIN-TINQUES road exclusive as far as the IZEL les HAMEAU - TILLOY road exclusive.

7. The 231st Infantry Brigade Group may use any roads E. of the IZEL les HAMEAU - TILLOY road exclusive.

Headquarters.
12th June 1918.

Lieut-Colonel
A.A. & Q.M.G.
74th (Yeo) Division.

P.T.O.

2

Copies to :-
- 229th Inf.Bde.
- 230th Inf.Bde.
- 231st Inf.Bde.
- "G"
- C.R.A.
- C.R.E.
- A.D.M.S.
- D.A.D.V.S.
- 74th Div.Train.
- 74th M.G.Battn.
- 74th Div.Signal Coy.
- D.A.D.O.S.
- A.P.M.
- Camp Commandant.
- 74th Div.Employ.Coy.
- War Diary.
- File.

ENTRAINING STATION - TINQUES.

Train.	UNIT.	VEHICLES. 4 whld.	2 whld.	ANIMALS. L.D.	H.D.	REMARKS.
1.	229th Inf.Bde.H.Q.	4	4	19	4	229th Inf.Bde and
	No.2 Sec.Div.Sigs.	-	3	6	-	Divl.Hdqrs.billeting
	No.4 Coy. 74 M.G.Bn.	-	28	49	2	parties with 1 Supply
	229th L.T.M.Bty.	-	-	-	-	officer and 1 A.S.C.
	12th Bn.S.L.I. ;-					N.C.O. will also
	1 Coy. with Cooker &					proceed on this
	Team.	-	2	-	2	Train.
4	12th Bn. S.L.I;- less 1 Coy. with Cooker & Team	4	30	46	15	
7	16th Devons less 1 Coy. with Cooker & Team	4	30	46	15	
10	12th Bn. R.S.F. less 1 Coy. with Cooker & Team	4	30	46	15	
13	14th Bn.R.H. less 1 Coy. with Cooker & Team	4	30	46	15	
16	Divl.H.Q. H.Q. & No.1 Sect.	4	3	61	8	
	Div.Signal Coy.	2	25	67	2	
	H.Q. R.E.	-	5	10	-	
19	16th Devons ;- 1 Coy. Cooker and Team	-	2	-	2	
	448th Coy.A.S.C.	4	3	13	12	
	439th Fld.Coy.R.E.	5	18	74	2	
22	12th Bn.R.S.F. 1 Coy. with Cooker and Team	-	2	-	2	
	14th Bn.R.H.;- 1 Coy. with Cooker & Team	-	2	-	2	
	229th Fld.Amb.	7	12	25	22	
	H.Q. Div.Train.	2	-	5	4	

NOTE :- The number of animals shown above are based on assumption that Units are up to establishment and include Divisional Train animals attached.

PTO

ENTRAINING STATION - SAVY.

TRAINS	UNITS	VEHICLES 4 whld.	VEHICLES 2 whld.	ANIMALS L.D.	ANIMALS H.D.	REMARKS
2	230th Inf.Bde.H.Q.	4	4	19	4	230th Inf.Bde. billeting party with 1 Supply Officer and 2 A.S.C. N.C.O's will also proceed on this Train.
	No.3 Sec.Div.Sigs.	-	3	6	-	
	209th Coy.M.G.Bn.	-	23	49	2	
	15th Suffolks ;- 1 Coy. with Cooker & Team	-	2	-	2	
	230th L.T.M.Bty.	-	-	-	-	
5	15 Suffolks less 1 Coy. with Cooker & Team.	4	30	46	15	
8	10th Bn.E.Kents less 1 Coy. with Cooker & Team	4	30	46	15	
14	12th Bn.Norfolks less 1 Coy. with Cooker & Team.	4	30	46	15	
14	16th Bn.Sussex less 1 Coy. with Cooker & Team.	4	30	46	15	
17	10th Bn.E.Kents ;-1 Coy.Cooker & Team.	-	2	-	2	
	449th Coy.A.S.C.	4	3	13	12	
	5th R.M.R.E.	5	18	74	2	
20	12th Norfolks ;- 1 Coy.with Cooker & Team	-	2	-	2	
	16th Sussex ;- 1 Coy with Cooker & Team.	-	2	-	2	
	230th Fld.AmB.	7	12	25	22	
	59th Mob.Vet.Section	2	4	23	2	
23	1/12th Bn.L.N.Lancs. (Pioneer Bn.)	10	24	72	15	

NOTE :- The number of animals shown above are based on the assumption that Units are up to strength and includes Divl. Train animals attached.

ENTRAINING STATION – AUBIGNY

Train.	UNIT.	VEHICLES. 4 whld.	2 whld.	ANIMALS. L.D.	H.D.	Remarks.
3	231st Inf.Bde.H.Q.	4	4	19	4	231st Inf.Bde.billeting
	No.4 Sec.Div.Sigs.	–	3	6	–	part with 1 supply off.
	231st L.T.M.Bty.	–	–	–	–	and 1 A.S.C. N.C.O. will
	210 Coy.M.G.Bn.	–	28	49	2	also proceed on this
	25th R.W.F.:- 1					Train.
	Coy.Cooker & Team	–	2	–	2	
6	25th Bn.R.W.F. less 1 Coy. with Cooker and Team.	4	30	46	15	
9	24th Bn.Welsh Regt less 1 Coy. with Cooker & Team.	4	30	46	15	
12	10th Bn.K.S.L.I. less 1 Coy. with Cooker & Team.	4	30	46	15	
15	24th Bn.R.W.F.less 1 Coy. with Cooker and Team.	4	30	46	15	
18.	24th Bn.Welsh Regt;- 1 Coy. with Cooker & Team.	–	2	–	2	
	H.Q. & 231 Coy.74th M.G.Battn.	–	54	71	3	
	No.5 Sec.Div.Sigs.	–	2	3	–	
21	450 Coy.Div.Train.	4	5	15	12	
	5th R.A.R.E.	5	18	74	2	
	Div.Employ.Coy.	–	–	–	–	
24	10th Bn.K.S.L.I.:- 1 Coy.with Cooker & Team.	–	2	–	2	
	24th Bn.R.W.F.;- 1 Coy. with Cooker & Team	–	2	–	2	
	231st Fld.Amb.	7	12	25	22	
	H.Q. R.A.	2	2	13	6	

NOTE :- The number of animals shown above are based on the assumption that Units are up to strength and includes Divl.Train animals attached.

War Diary June
Appendix V

SECRET.   C.A. 237

INSTRUCTIONS RE MOVE OF THE DIVISION BY TACTICAL TRAINS.
==

1. The Division may be moved by 4 methods.-

   A. Entirely by Road.
   B. A modified Strategical move.
   C. A complete strategical move.
   D. Tactical Trains.

2. Case A. explains itself.

3. In case B. (Modified Strategical move) the Infantry Brigades with their Transport and certain Divisional Troops move by Rail. The remainder of the Division moves by road. A special programme of entrainment will be issued in this case.

4. In case C. (Complete strategical move) the whole Division except Mechanical Transport will move by rail.

5. Case D. (Tactical Trains)

   (a) Tactical Trains are usually run in "Sets", a set consists of 2 "Coaching Stock" trains and either 1 or 2 "Omnibus Trains.
   (b) "Coaching Stock" trains take personnel only with their Lewis Guns, But NO TRANSPORT ANIMALS OR BAGGAGE.
   (c) "OMNIBUS Train" take a proportion only of 1st Line Transport, the remainder of the animals and transport proceeding by road.
   (d) "Omnibus Trains" are not always provided, in which case all Transport and animals proceed by road.
   (e) The whole idea of a "Coaching Stock" Train is to enable troops to entrain or detrain at any point on the line, irrespective of whether there is a station there or not, and that troops can be marched direct from the train into action.
   (f) It is therefore essential that Officers Commanding Units ensure that Officers and men take nothing with them on a "Tactical Train" except what they actually stand up in.
   (g) Camp Kettles and Officer's Valises etc, will on no account be taken on to "Coaching Stock" Trains.

                                                          H.J. Butchart

Headquarters.   Major for
                                                             A.A. & Q.M.G.
24th June 1918.   74th (Yeo) Division.

Copies to:- 229th Inf.Bde.   O.R.A.   O.C. 74th Div.Train.
             230th Inf.Bde.   C.R.E.   O.C. 74th Div.Signals.
             231st Inf.Bde.   A.D.M.S.   O.C. 74th M.T.Coy.
        Camp Commandant.   D.A.D.V.S.   O.C. 74th M.G.Bn.
        File & War Diary.   D.A.D.O.S.   A.P.M.
        "G"   O.C. Employ.Coy.

War Diary June
Appendix VI

SECRET.   G.Q. 238

ADMINISTRATIVE INSTRUCTIONS RELATIVE TO
OPERATION ORDER No. 63.

Headquarters,
24th June 1918.

The following instructions are issued relative to the move of 230th and 231st Brigade Groups by Tactical Trains to AIRE.

1. SUPPLY AND BAGGAGE.
Supply Wagons loaded with Rations and Forage for consumption on 26th inst, will report to Units tonight.
All personnel proceeding by Train will be in possession of rations for consumption on 26th.
Rations and forage for consumption on 26th will be carried in the Supply Wagons for the personnel and animals proceeding by road.
Baggage wagons will report to Units tonight, and will proceed loaded together with 1st Line Transport.

2. MOTOR TRANSPORT.
Four Motor Lorries will report at each Brigade Headquarters at 6 am. tomorrow to convey the Trench Mortars and Blankets of each Group to the new area. The M.G.Battalion blankets will be carried by the Lorries of the 230th Brigade Group.

3. SALVAGE.
All Salvage Dumps will be handed over to the Area Commandants. Salvage personnel will proceed under orders of the Unit by which they are rationed.

4. ENTRAINMENT.
The personnel of the 230th Brigade Group will entrain at LIGNY St. FLOCHEL on 25th inst, as follows:-

<u>1st "Coaching Stock" Train leaving at 1010 hours.</u>
230th Infantry Brigade Headquarters.
230th Light Trench Mortar Battery.
10th Bn.East Kent Regt.
15th Bn.Suffolk Regt.
5th Coy.R.M.R.E.
Supply personnel of 449th Coy.A.S.C.

<u>2nd "Coaching Stock" Train leaving at 1410 hours.</u>
13th Bn.Sussex Regt.
230th Field Ambulance.
74th M.G.Battalion.

The personnel of the 231st Infantry Brigade Group will entrain at TINCQUES on 25th inst as follows ;-

<u>1st "Coaching Stock" Train leaving at 1130 hours.</u>
231st Infantry Brigade Headquarters.
231st Light Trench Mortar Battery.
25th Bn.R.W.F.
24th Bn.Welsh Regt.
Supply personnel of 450th Coy.A.S.C.
5th Fld.Coy.R.A.R.E.

<u>2nd "Coaching Stock" Train leaving at 1550 hours.</u>
10th Bn.K.Shropshire L.I.
231st Field Ambulance.
1/12th Bn.Loyal N.Lancs.

P.T.O.

-2-

Attention is directed to paras 1 & 3 of Standing Orders for Entrainment forwarded under this office Q.H.4 of 15th inst, and Instructions regarding Moves by Tactical Trains issued under this office O.A. 237 of today's date.
Lewis Guns will be carried on 1st Line Transport.

5. ACKNOWLEDGE.

H.E. Butchart

Headquarters.
24th June 1918.

Major for
A.A. & Q.M.G.
74th (Yeo) Division.

Copies to :- 230th Inf.Brigade.   C.R.E. 74th (Yeo) Division.
              231st Inf.Brigade.   A.D.M.S.   -do-
              O.C.74th Div.Train.   D.A.D.V.S.   -do-
              O.C. 74th M.G.Battn.   Salvage Officer   -do-
              O.C. 74th Div.Signals. "G"
              Canadian Corps.   War Diary.
                                      A.P.M.   -do-

File War Diary June
Appendix VI

SECRET.
C.R. 241

ADMINISTRATIVE INSTRUCTIONS RELATIVE TO

OPERATION ORDER No. 63.

Headquarters
25th June 1918.

The following instructions are issued relative to the move of 229th Infantry Brigade Group, Divisional Artillery, and Headquarters Group to new Area.

1. SUPPLIES AND BAGGAGE.

All personnel proceeding by Train will be in possession of rations for consumption on 27th inst.

Supply Wagons will carry rations and forage only for personnel and animals proceeding by road for consumption on 27th.

Baggage Wagons will report to Units tonight, and will proceed loaded together with 1st Line Transport.

2. MOTOR TRANSPORT.

The following Motor Lorries will be provided.
(1) Seven Lorries at Divisional Headquarters at 6-30 am. Five of these, will be at the disposal of the Camp Commandant. Two will be under the direction of O.C. Divl. Employment Company for the conveyance of men unable to march to the new Area.
(2) Four Lorries at 229th Infantry Brigade Headquarters at 6-30 am, to convey the Trench Mortars and Blankets of the Brigade Group to the new Area.
(3) Sixteen Lorries at 229th Infantry Brigade Headquarters at 6-30 am; these are under the direction of the A.D.M.S. for the conveyance of Sick in billets.
(4) Five Lorries at Headquarters R.A. for the use of Headquarters R.A., and the two Medium Trench Mortar Batteries.

3. SALVAGE.

All Salvage Dumps will be handed over to the Area Commandant. Salvage personnel will proceed under orders of the Unit to which they are rationed.

4 ENTRAINMENT.

The personnel of the 229th Infantry Brigade Group and the Headquarters Group will entrain at LIGNY St. FLOCHEL and TINCQUES on the 26th inst as follows :-

<u>1st "Coaching Stock" Train leaving LIGNY St. FLOCHEL at 1010 hours.</u>
229th Infantry Brigade Headquarters.
229th Light Trench Mortar Battery.
16th Bn. Devon Regt.
14th Bn. Royal Highlanders.
Divisional Headquarters.
448th Coy. A.S.C. Supply Personnel.

<u>2nd "Coaching Stock" Train leaving TINCQUES at 1118 hours.</u>
12th Bn. Somerset L.I.
229th Field Ambulance.
985th Divl. Employment Company.
Traffic Control Police.
439th Fld. Company R.E.
H.Q. Divisional Train.
447th Coy. A.S.C. Supply Personnel.
H.Q. Royal Engineers.

P.T.O.

-2-

Attention is directed to paras 1 & 3 of Standing Orders for Entrainment forwarded under this office Q.M.4 of 15th inst, and Instructions regarding Moves by Tactical Trains issued under this Office C.A. 237 of 24th inst.

Lewis Guns will be carried on 1st Line Transport.

5. Railhead will be WITTERNESSE.

6. ACKNOWLEDGE.

H J Butchart

Headquarters.

25th June 1918.

Major for
A.A. & Q.M.G.
74th (Yeo) Division.

Copies to :—
229th Inf.Brigade.	C.R.A. 74th (Yeo) Division.
230th Inf.Brigade.	C.R.E. —do—
231st Inf.Brigade.	A.D.M.S. —do—
O.C. 74th Div.Train.	D.A.D.V.S. —do—
O.C. 74th M.G.Battn.	Salvage Officer.—do—
O.C. 74th Div.Signals.	Camp Commandant.—do—
O.C. Div.Employ.Coy.	A.P.M.
Can.Corps."Q"	"G"
Baths Officer.	War Diary.
D.A.D.O.S.	File.

SECRET

War Diary June Appendix VIII
CQ 243

28th June 1918.

229th Bde.	"G"	
74th Div. Train.	XI Corps.	For information.
74th Div. M.T. Co.	5th Division.	
74th Div. Signal Co.	61st Division.	

Reference this Office S.G.21/4 of 28th inst.

1. **BILLETS & CAMPS.**
   12th Devons & 2 Coy. Somersets will camp in J.19.c. and d. Transport lines in J.25.d.
   Tents will be drawn from dump in charge of 1/C Argyle & Sutherland Highlanders at J.25d8.8.
   The Coy. proceeding to ST VENANT will be billeted in the Asylum there. Particulars as to the billet will be given by the Staff Captain, 183 Infantry Brigade at Billet No 25 BERQUETTE.
   The Coy. proceeding to BUSNES will be shown their billets by the Area Commandant. The billeting party will meet the Area Commandant at the Cemetery P.25d 6.2 at 11 o'clock a.m. on 29th inst.

2. **BOUNDS**
   Troops are forbidden to approach within 200 yards of the Ammunition Dump in J.25a.

3. **MOTOR TRANSPORT.**
   A. Three lorries will report at the 12th S.L.I. headquarters RELY at 8 a.m. on 29th inst and will be used as follows:-
      1 lorry for blankets for 2 Companies proceeding to J.19 area.
      1 lorry for blankets for two Companies proceeding to ST VENANT and BUSNES.
      2 lorries for men who are unable to march.

   B. Two lorries will report at 12th Devon Regt. Headquarters at WITTERNESS at 8 a.m. on 29th inst and will be used as follows:-
      1 lorry for blankets.
      1 lorry for men unable to march.
   Os'C. Battns. will detail a guide to accompany each lorry.

4. **SUPPLIES.**
   Rations for consumption on 30th inst will be carried on Supply Wagons.
   Refilling Points on and after 30th inst will be as follows:-
      A. Troops in J.19 area at LA LACQUE (I.31.d.9.10) at 12 midday.
      B. Troops at ST VENANT and BUSNES at the church in GUARBECQUE (O.17.B.cen) at 1 p.m.
   On the 30th inst two days rations will be drawn from both LA LACQUE and and GUARBECQUE thus both parties will be in possession of one days reserve rations.
   Os'C. Battalions will ensure that representatives attend at both refilling points punctually at the hours stated as the rations will be transferred direct from the motor lorries to the Supply Wagons.

5. **ACKNOWLEDGE.**

   [signature]
   Major.
   for Lieut.Col.
   A.A. & Q.M.G.
   74th (Yeo) Division.

HO.C90.74 D
9/84

On His Majesty's Service.

CONFIDENTIAL

A. G.
3rd Echelon Base.

ANS/34

Ref. Sheet 36A 1/40,000   Administrator Brigadier 39 (2nd) Division
                            Headquarters 39 (2nd) Division
                            From 1st to 31st July 1915

Army Form C. 2118.

WAR DIARY
or
INTELLIGENCE SUMMARY.
(Erase heading not required.)

Instructions regarding War Diaries and Intelligence Summaries are contained in F.S. Regs., Part II. and the Staff Manual respectively. Title pages will be prepared in manuscript.

Place	Date	Hour	Summary of Events and Information	Remarks and references to Appendices
NORRENT FONTES	1.		Wickham of Animals regards organizing C.R.E reported as to what was required.	Appendix I
"	8.		Brigadier General A.A. KENNEDY C.M.G. assumed command of 230 in Left Bde. Intimation received that the Division would relieve the 61st Division in the Line on 10th July.	
"	9.		Instructions issued for "B" teams to proceed to Divisional Reception Camp at WITTERNESSE on 11th inst.	Appendix II
"			Administrative Instructions or move issued. It was decided that Divisional H.Q would take over H.Q of 61st Division. Intended move to LILLETTE Chateau as only 6 rooms were available in the Chateau arrangements were made to erect 2 NISSEN huts and two Marquees.	Appendix III
"	10		C.in.C 61st Division Command. Supply railhead for the Division Changes from WITTERNESSE to AIRE.	Appendix IV
"	12		Instructions issued for B teams to be organised into Brigade Wings.	
"	13		As 6½ Reserve Motor Veterinary Section are not to move from LAMBRES orders issued for the Divisional Mobile Veterinary Section to move to TREIZENNES.	Appendix V
LILLETTE N23 d&b	14		Divisional H.Q closed at NORRENT FONTES at 10am and opened at LILLETTE Chateau at Noon. 1pm.	
"	15.		A conference attended by D.A.A. & Q.M.G, B.Gen commander, C.R.E. + Bde Brigs was held at S.N.O. It was agreed, who also that Reinforcements for the Bdes in the Line would not to use through from the Bde Reception camp. must reach Thiluhez Orders. Also the Bde "B" teams & the Res in Reserve of the Pioneer Batalion should rejoin their units.	

Sig Auckinart Ging
D.A.D.Y.S 2nd Gen

Army Form C. 2118.

WAR DIARY
or
INTELLIGENCE SUMMARY.
(Erase heading not required.)

Ry Shed 36A 1/6 0.000
Administrator Branch
Headquarters 74 (Yeo) Division
July 1918

Instructions regarding War Diaries and Intelligence Summaries are contained in F.S. Regs., Part II. and the Staff Manual respectively. Title pages will be prepared in manuscript.

Place	Date	Hour	Summary of Events and Information	Remarks and references to Appendices
LILLETTE M33d88	16		All refilling points for the Division (except MAZINGHEM) considerable congestion was caused, the refilling points for XXII Corps Group the Left Div Bde. were changed to FONTE and N23 and G26 respectively. They are in order that from the new refilling points for the first aid	Appendix VI
	17		Instructions issued regarding forward arrangements for Bdes on the line	
	20		Appendix VII Shows the Administrator arrangements for troops at present occupied by the Division	Appendix VII
	23		Instructions issued to take over the 61st Div. Recepn D.A.A.G. 74 (Yeo) Div Camp at LINGHEM	
	24		229 Infy Bde. relieved the 230 Infy Bde. on the Right Sector of the line during the night. 1st Reception Camp moved from WITTERNESSE to LINGHEM.	Appendix VIII
	27		Commenced feeding the two Infantry Bdes in the line with rations transport from Railhead PIPE	
	29		"B" teams of the M.G. Battalion went up to the Battalion Transport lines from the Reception Camp to permit of their technical training in Reinforcements to the Division during the week are shown in Appendix IX	Appendix IX
	31		Casualties (Effective) on July 1st and July 31st and the strength of the Division (Effective) taken on also shown on the previous	

Andrew W Montgomery
For Major DAAG 74 (Yeo) Div.

War Diary Aug
Appendix 1

LOCATION	UNIT	DRINKING WATER Existing	HORSE WATER Existing	HORSE WATER Suggested
HOUMET FONTUN G. 35. b.	D. H. Q. I.O.F.S. 74th Div. Signal Coy 59th Mobile Vet. Sec.	Drawn from village wells, good condition.	Watering from Fontes. (B. 29.b.)	
LIETTE, I.29.c.	H.Q.229th Inf.Bde.	Spring liable to contamination by surface water in wet weather. Water is boiled before use.	Watering by buckets from spring below drinking water area.	That H.Q. at down the trough & pump of their equipment.
FONTES, B. 29. b.	14th R.H. 229th L.T.M.B. 349 Coy. A.S.C.	Running stream, chlorinated in water carts. The pump is in farmyard.	Water at troughs filled by buckets from stream below drinking water area.	Required - 1 pump from Div Trans extra 20 ft. trough by R.E.
TREIZENNES I. 6.b.	459 Field Coy R.E.	From well and hand pump.	Pumpsupplied from equipment of unit at running stream	Pumpsupplied from equipment of unit at running stream
LAMBRE.	229th Field Ambulance.	Hand pumps & bucket.	Watering horses into pond about into water cart from well a mile from horse lines.	Required a pump and trough at a convenient place clear of the Unit.
FLECHIN, S.14c.	H.Q. 229th Inf.Bde. 15th Hussars.	From well and hand pump	Stream.	1 pump and 1 trough, Edo equipment.
ELNES, S. 23 a.	10th Buffs.	ESTREE BLANCHE.	Stream.	1 pump and 1 trough 20 fe.t Required.
ENDY, R. 29.d.	1st Suffolks. 74th M.T. Coy.	WELL.	Stream.	
ROMCORT G. 14.c.230th L.T.M.B.		FLECHIN.		
ESTREE BLANCHE. R. 23. b.	R.H.R. 446th Coy A.S.C.		Stream.	trough supplied, R.E.R.can supply pump.

		WATER CARTS.	HORSES.	
QUERIEU. N.13.d.	M.G. Batn. 1 Company.	From well near Vittornesse. Water Carts.	From back of stream.	That M.G. Batn put down equipment pump and trough.
St. PILARE. T.5.d.	H.Q. 231 I.Bde 25th R.W.F. 10th E.S.L.I. 450th Dev Div Tn. 231st L.T.M.B.	Spring int water carts	Bad from a dirty pool.	That R.A. put this equipment pump and trough down.
BORENG. U.1.c.	24th Welch. R.A.R.B.	St. Hilare	By buckets from stream.	1 trough supplied 60 feet R.A.R.B. can supply pump.
PADQUEHEN.	Pioneer Batn. 251st F.A.	ST. HILARE of LESTRESSIN	From stream	Pioneer Batn are erecting pump and troughs.
FONTAINE LES ERPACH. A.12.b.	H.Q. Div R.A.	BENCH CHELLE.	BENCH CHELLE.	
ARDS. T.30.a.	117 Bde R.F.A.	FERFAY.	Troughs at stream Troughs out of order Pumps required.	That 117 Bde No increase equipment troughs to be repaired.
AMETTES. B.4.c.	44th Bde R.F.A.	From well.	Troughs at stream, troughs out of order Pumps required.	That 44th Bde. ditto.
HEPON. B.8.c.	H.Q. & 1 Section D.A.C.	BENCH CHELLE.	ditto.	That D.A.C. " troughs to be repaired.
BEROCHELLE. B.7.c.	2 Sects.D.A.C.	Spring	1 pump and 2 troughs, stream.	D.A.C. " pump to be repaired. Extra troughs are required.
BELLERY. B.5.a.	X and Y H.T.M.B. Wells.		Stream, no troughs.	Might water at H.Q.s of Bde.

CONTINUED.		WATER CAMPS.		HORSES.
LIGNY LES AIRES. S. 18. b.	2. Coys. M.G.Bqtn. ATRODROME H.Q. M.G. Battn.		Village, Pond, Dirty.	The water to be obtained from HEDON CHELLE or ESTREE BLANCHE.
AUCHI AU BOIS. T. 14. d.	447 Coy A.S.C.	WELLS.		ditto. AMETTES.
LA COULLE. N. 30. c.	935th D.F.Coy H.Q. Div. Train.	WELLS.		FORTES.
LEKITRES. N. 19. c.	230th F.A.	Pipe line.	Stream.	Trough supplied. M.W.R.S. own supply 1 pump and 1 trough required.
WESTREM. S. 24. c & d.	M. G. Battn. less one coy.	Wells.	Watering from HEDON CHELLE.	

War Diary   Appendix II

SECRET.   C.A.258   No. 9

INSTRUCTIONS re "B" TEAMS.

Reference Sheet 36 A 1/40,000   9th July, 1918.

1. The personnel referred to in Section XXX of S.S. 135 as amended by O.B. 1919 of 14th June of all Infantry Battalions (including Pioneers), Machine Gun Battalions, and Light Trench Mortar Batteries will move to the Divisional Reception Camp at WITTERNESSE on 10th inst, except the "B" team of 24th (Pembroke & Glamorgan Yeo) Battn. The Welsh Regt. which will move to WITTERNESSE on the 11th inst.

2. Officers i/c "B" Teams will hand to the O.C. Reception Camp on arrival, nominal rolls of all ranks under their Command.

3. Brigadier Generals and Officers Commanding are responsible that a proper proportion of camp kettles and blankets are sent with all "B" teams.

4. Rations for consumption on day subsequent to arrival at WITTERNESSE will be taken by all "B" Teams with the following exceptions:-

    (a) 231st Infantry Brigade less 24th Welsh Regt. Rations for consumption on 11th will be drawn by O.C. Divisional Reception Camp.
    (b) 24th Welsh Regt. Rations for consumption on 12th will be drawn by O.C. Divisional Reception Camp.

5. O.C. Divisional Reception Camp will intimate completion of moves to this Office.

6. Lorries will be provided as follows to convey blankets, Officers Kits etc to the Divisional Reception Camp on 10th July, 1918.

    (a) 1 Lorry for 231 Bde at Refilling Point St. Hilaire. *MAZINGHEM*
        1 Lorry for 230 Bde at Refilling Point Estree Blanche.
        1 Lorry for 229 Bde (less party in J.19) at Refilling Point FONTES.
        1 Lorry at Hd.Qrs. M.G.Battn. LIGNY LES AIRE.
        1 Lorry for L.N.Lancs and 229 Bde party in that Area at J.25 central.

    All the above lorries will report at 3.p.m.

    (b) On 11th July.
        1 Lorry at HAMET BILLET at 10.00 a.m. for 24th Battn. Welsh Rgt

7. Acknowledge.

                                        H.J. Butchart
                                                Major,
                        for A.A.& Q.M.G. 74th (Yeomanry) Division.

Issued at 6 p.m.

Copies to :-
1. "G"
2. 229th Bde.
3. 230th Bde.
4. 231st Bde.
5. C.R.E.
6. O.C. 74th M.G.Battn.
7. O.C. 74th Div.Reception Camp
8. O.C. 74th Div. Train.
9. War Diary.
10. File.
11-15. Spare.

War Diary July.
Appendix III

SECRET.   C.Q.260.

ADMINISTRATIVE INSTRUCTIONS RELATIVE TO
74th DIVISIONAL ORDER NO. 66.

                                                           9th July 1918.
Reference Sheet 36.A. 1/40,000.

1. <u>Trench and Area Stores.</u> All trench and area stores will be taken over by ingoing Units and a consolidated list forwarded to this Office as soon as possible.

2. <u>Ammunition, Reserve Rations and Water.</u> A statement showing the ammunition and reserve rations taken over will be forwarded to this Office as soon as possible. The list will show the location of each Ammunition, Ration and Water Dump.

3. <u>Divisional Train.</u> The Divisional Train will be located at MAZINGHEM. Each Company will move in on the day following the arrival of its Brigade Group in the new area.

4. <u>Baggage and Supply Wagons.</u> These wagons will be returned to the affiliated Train Companies by Units as soon as the Companies have moved into MAZINGHEM.

5. <u>Mobile Veterinary Section.</u> The Mobile Veterinary Section will move to LAMBRES on the 14th inst and take over billets etc from the 61st Divisional Mobile Veterinary Section.

6. <u>Supplies.</u> Refilling Point for all Units will be MAZINGHEM COMMENCING ON THE DATES AS SHOWN ON THE ATTACHED TABLE. Train Wagons will convey rations to Q.M.Stores which will be located at Units Transport Lines. Supplies will then be taken forward at night by 1st Line Limbers.

7. <u>Motor Transport.</u> Lorries will be provided for the conveyance of blankets as follows:-

Date.	Place reporting.	No. of lorries.	Time	Remarks.
10th July	230th Bde.H.Q.	4	9 am.	To include R.E.R.E.
"	231st Fd.Ambce.H.Q.	1	9 am.	
"	74th M.G.Battn.H.Q.	1	9 am.	
"	1/12 L.N.Lancs (Pioneers) J.25 cen.	1	9 am.	
"	24th Welsh Regt.H.Q.	1	2 pm.	
11th July	229th Bde.H.Q.	4	9 am.	To include 439 Fd.Coy.
"	230th Fd.Ambce.H.Q.	1	9 am.	

                                                H.J.Burkchart
Headquarters.   Major for
                                                       A.A. & Q.M.G.
9th July 1918.   74th (Yeo) Division.

Copies to:-
1. 229th Inf.Bde.   6. 74th Div.Signals.   11. 74th Div.M.T.Coy.
2. 230th Inf.Bde.   7. 74th M.G.Battn.   12. 61st Division.
3. 231st Inf.Bde.   8. A.D.M.S.   13. Camp Commandant.
4. C.R.A.   9. D.A.D.V.S.   14. "G"
5. C.R.E.   10. 74th Div.Train.   15. War Diary.
                          11. File.

Table showing dates Units will commence drawing supplies from MAZINGHEM.

Unit.	Date.	For consumption on.	Remarks.
231st Inf.Bde.	10.7.18.	11.7.18.	
230th Inf.Bde.	11.7.18.	12.7.18.	
74th M.G.Battn.	11.7.18.	12.7.18.	From 230th Brigade Dump.
1/12 L.N.Lancs.	11.7.18.	12.7.18.	From 231st Brigade Dump.
No.5 Coy. R.M.R.E.	11.7.18.	12.7.18.	
229th Inf.Bde.	12.7.18.	13.7.18.	
No.5 Coy. R.A.R.E.	10.7.18.	11.7.18.	
439 Coy. R.E.	12.7.18.	13.7.18.	
74th Div.H.Q.	12.7.18.	13.7.18.	
74th Div.Signals.	12.7.18.	13.7.18.	
Mob.Vet.Sect.	12.7.18.	13.7.18.	
229th Fd.Ambce.	12.7.18.	13.7.18.	
230th Fd.Ambce.	11.7.18.	12.7.18.	Drawing as soon after 10 am. as possible.
231st Fd.Ambce.	10.7.18.	11.7.18.	do.
Div.Amm.Col.	13.7.18.	14.7.18.	From 231st Brigade Dump on 13th only.
Div.Arty.less D.A.C.	14.7.18.	15.7.18.	

The hour of refilling on the 10th, 11th, 12th, 13th, and 14th will be at 10 am. and thereafter as follows:-

229th Bde Group.   7-30 am.
230th Bde Group.   8-30 am.
231st Bde Group.   9-30 am.
Div.Troops Group.   9-00 am.

War Diary JUS
Appendix IX

C.Q. 198/1.

Headquarters.
   229th Infantry Brigade.   O.C., 74th M.G.Battn.
   230th Infantry Brigade.   C.R.E.
   231st Infantry Brigade.   O.C., 74th Divnl. Reception Camp.

---

1.   "B" Teams will be formed in-to Brigade Wings to consist of the "B" Teams of their respective Brigades.
      The "B" Teams of the Machine Gun Battalion will form part of the Brigade Wing of the Brigade holding the Right Sector of the line. The "B" Teams of the Pioneer Battalion will form part of the Brigade Wing of the Brigade holding the left Sector of the line.

2.   The Senior Officer of each Brigade Wing will Command the Wing.

3.   O.C., Reception Camp will deal with Wing Commanders regarding all matters concerning "B" Teams.
      O.C., "B" Teams will not deal direct with O.C., Divisional Reception Camp.

4.   O.C., Reception Camp will have "B" Teams organised in accordance with the foregoing instructions and intimate to this office the names of the Officers Commanding the Three Brigade Wings.

Headquarters.

12th July. 1918.

Sd/ H.J.Butchart. Major for
A.A.& Q.M.G.,
74th (Yeomanry)Division.

Copy to:- "G".

War Diary July   Copy No 16.
Appendix V   CQ/260.

SECRET.

AMENDMENT TO ADMINISTRATIVE INSTRUCTIONS RELATIVE TO 74th DIVISIONAL ORDER NO. 66.

Para 5 is cancelled.
The 59th Mobile Veterinary Section will move to TREIZENNES on 14th instant.

ACKNOWLEDGE.

H. J. Butchart

13th July, 1918.

Major for,
A.A. & Q.M.G., 74th (Yeomanry) Division.

Copies to:-
1. 229th Inf.Bde.
2. 230th Inf.Bde.
3. 231st Inf.Bde.
4. O.R.A.
5. C.R.E.
6. 74th Div.Signals.
7. 74th M.G.Bn.
8. A.D.M.S.
9. D.A.D.V.S.
10. 74th Div.Train.
11. 74th Div.M.T.Coy.
12. 61st Division.
13. Camp Commandant.
14. "G".
15. War Diary.
16. File.

War Diary July
Appendix VI

O.C.,
74th Divisional Reception Camp.
————————————————

It has been decided that no Drafts will go up to Brigades in the Line unless specially asked for through this Office.

In future the procedure will be, that on the arrival of Drafts at the Divisional Reception Camp the Officer Commanding will immediately hand over those for Brigades in the Line to the "B" Teams of the Units concerned.

O's C. "B" Teams are responsible that Nominal Rolls of all Drafts received are forwarded to the Headquarters of their Units on the day following their arrival in order that they may be taken on the strength of their Battalions as from the day after their arrival at the Reception Camp.
Vide. this office A.T.11 dated 1.7.18.

Drafts for the Brigade in the Reserve and for all other Units of the Division will go forward as in the past, the procedure being the same i.e. O.C., Divisional Reception Camp will notify Divisional Headquarters the night before of the numbers going forward on the following day and a wire will be sent to the Formation or Unit concerned by Divisional Headquarters.

These instructions do not apply to personnel returning from Courses and Leave. These will go forward for all Units in the ordinary way unless they are on the Nominal Roll of the "B" Teams of the Unit.

Andrew M Montgomery
for
Major.
D.A.A.G.,
74th (Yeomanry) Division.

Headquarters.

17th July, 1918.

Copies to:-
    229th Infantry Brigade.
    230th Infantry Brigade.
    231st Infantry Brigade.
    C.R.A.
    C.R.E.
    A.D.M.S.
    "Q".

Appendix VII

74th (Yeomanry) Division Administrative Arrangements.

Instructions (under the headings given below) with regard to Administrative arrangements in the Area now occupied by the Division are attached.

Schedule No.
1. Agriculture.
2. Ammunition.
3. Areas and Area Commandants.
4. Baths & Laundry.
5. Burials.
6. Canteens.
7. Field Cashier.
8. Leave.
9. Medical arrangements for Normal Warfare.
10. Medical arrangements for Heavy Fighting.
11. Ordnance.
12. Police arrangements, Traffic Control and Prisoners of War.
13. Water Supply.
14. Reserve Rations and Water.
15. Salvage.
16. Supply Arrangements.
17. Veterinary Arrangements.
18. Reception Camp.

July 1918.

Schedule 1. - AGRICULTURE.

1. LIEUT. DOLLIMORE, Devon Yeomanry Battalion, is the Divisional Agricultural Officer. He has 100 Men provided by Corps to work the Divisional Agricultural Area. They are billeted at LA PIERRIERE and attached to the Reserve Battalion of the right Sector for rations.

2. The boundaries of the Divisional Agricultural area are -
V.1.a.0.1. - A Line drawn from V.1.a.0.1. - 500 yards W. of the BUSNES - ST. VENANT Road to P.3.d.0.0. - ST. VENANT - ROBECQ P.29.d.8.3. - V.1.a.0.1.

3. The Divisional Agricultural Officer works under the direction of the Corps Agricultural Officer.

Schedule II. - AMMUNITION.

A. Gun, Howitzer and T.M. Ammunition.

1. **Railheads.**

   BERGUETTE.

   GUARBECQUE Siding.

2. **Dumps.**

   GUARBECQUE SIDING Dump.

   BANNISTER Dump.

3. **Amounts maintained.**

Nature.	R.P.G. of Guns.	R.P.G. in Echelon.	R.P.G. at A.R.P.	R.P.G. Total.
18 pdr.	500	351	175	1,026
4.5"How.	200	82	100	382
TMG	'100 R.P.G. In reserve positions, and in normal positions as required.			
TMK	As required.			

   The above figures are maintained for 72 - 18 pdr. guns and 24 - 4.5" Howitzers, 12 Medium Trench Mortars, and Heavy Trench Mortars as ordered by Corps.

4. **METHOD OF SUPPLY.**

   Ammunition is demanded by wire from MULES, XITH CORPS as per G.H.84, who advises Staff Captain R.A. when and where it will arrive.

   Ammunition for GUARBECQUE SIDING Dump is sent by broad guage to GUARBECQUE where a narrow guage conveys same round the Dump.

   Trains arrive at night, are unloaded and depart before daylight.

   Ammunition for BANNISTER DUMP is sent:-

   (a) By Motor Lorry from Corps Dump.

   (b) By broad guage from to BERGUETTE where same is met by a Div. R.A. Railhead Officer who checks same. Lorries have to be demanded previously from the S.M.T.O. to load up at BERGUETTE and convey same to BANNISTER DUMP.

   The two A.R.Ps. are run by Nos. 1 & 2 Sections of the D.A.C. who draw from A.R.Ps and deliver to Battery Wagon Lines.

AMMUNITION (Contd).

B. S.A.A. and GRENADES.

1. Divisional Dump. The Divisional Dump is with the S.A.A.
   Section at BERTHUETTE (O.18.d.2.4.)

2. SYSTEM OF SUPPLY.
   Brigades indent direct on S.A.A. Section for requirements.
   S.A.A. Section send forward ammunition to where it is
   required, and apply to Division "Q" to be refilled.
   Refilling is carried out by Motor Lorry from SHELLS XIth
   CORPS.

NOTE. All grenades and T.M. Ammunition will be issued
undetonated from Divisional Dump. Formations will arrange
to detonate at Brigade Dumps.

Schedule No. 3.

AREAS.

Reference Map. Sheet. 36.a. 1/40,000

Boundaries of the Divisional Area are at present as follows:-

Northern Boundary. Line from Drawbridge H.30.a.0.3. - Canal D'Aire to
I.33.d.7.2. - I.35.d.4.8. along Canal to J.31.b.0.3.
J.33.a.0.0. - K.33 central.

Western Boundary. Line from H.30.a.0.3. - H.35.b.9.8. - U.8.a.9.6.

Southern Boundary. U.8.a.9.6. - U.8.b.7.5. - U.3.d.9.0. - U.5.d.3.0. -
P.28.c.9.8. - P.29.d.9.1. P.30 Central. -
Q.19.c.5.0. - Q.20.c.0.3. - Q.21.c.0.3.

Area Commandants.

1. For villages of GUARBECQUE   Located at.
   and BERGUETTE.   GUARBECQUE.

2. For villages of Ham-en-Artois,   Located at.
   MANQUEVILLE, la MIQUELLERIE   Ham-En-Artois.
   and adjacent areas.

3. For villages of MOLINGHEM   Located at.
   ISBERGUES, LA LACQUE, TREIZENNES   LAMBRES.
   and adjacent Areas.

Schedule. No. 4.

BATHS AND LAUNDRY.

1. The Division supplies Baths, clean socks and underclothing to all Units of the Division and to all Corps and Army Troops in the Divisional Area.

2. Capt. R.ARBUTHNOT LESLIE, Suffolk Yeomanry, is responsible for the supervision of all the Divisional Baths and for the supply of clean socks and underclothing.

3. | Divisional Baths. | Capacity. |
|---|---|
| 1. HAM EN ARTOIS. | 80 per hour. |
| 2. GUARBECQUE. | -do- |
| 3. LA MICHELLERIE. (not yet in working order) | |
| 4. LINGHEM. | 60 per hour. |

4. Small stocks of clean clothing are maintained at each bath but until authority is given for more sets to be held on charge it is not possible to give each man bathing a clean suit, unless the Unit hands in a dirty suit for each man to be bathed, to the baths the day before. Under no circumstances will clothing be delivered to Units.

5. The Infantry Brigade Group in Reserve has the first call on all Baths. On Friday the Staff Captain forwards his bathing programme for the following week to the Divisional Baths Officer who then allots the baths to the other Units of the Division and Army and Corps Troops within the Area, at the times left vacant.

6. It is of the utmost importance that Units bathing, ensure that batches of men according to the capacity of the baths arrive punctually every half hour, e.g. At HAM EN ARTOIS 40 should parade every half hour.

7. Casual Details and small parties of men who may be proceeding on courses or leave will be bathed at any hour.

8. A Divisional Clothing Store is maintained at AIRE where all dirty clothing is disinfected in a Foden Lorry and sorted into bundles before being taken to the Corps Laundry there. A Divisional Gas Oven is kept at Ham where outer clothing of men being bathed is disinfected.
   At GUARBECQUE and LINGHEM clothing is ironed, there being no disinfector there.

9. A Divisional Sock Laundry is being started at the Divisional Clothing Store. When in full working order it is hoped to be able to provide each Infantry Brigade with 1000 pairs of clean socks daily for the use of the Infantry Battalions, T.M.B's, and Machine Gun Companies in the Line. An equivalent number of dirty socks being handed into the Laundry the night before.

10. The Divisional Baths Officer provides a suit of clean underclothing in lieu of each suit of gassed clothing which is handed in to the Divisional Gas Clothing Store. The Gassed Clothing is specially treated under the supervision of the Divisional Gas Officer, and when innocuous is handed in to the Divisional Baths as ordinary dirty clothing.

Schedule No. 5.

BURIALS.

1. GENERAL INSTRUCTIONS.

1. Burials are divided into two classes viz:-
   (a) Burials under normal conditions e.g.,
       When the Division is holding a prepared line.
   (b) Burials during Heavy Fighting such as may be anticipated
       when the Division is making a rapid advance.

2. Os.C.Units are responsible for the burial of their own dead, and the dead in the Area occupied by them.

3. While in the present Area the Left Bde. in the line will be responsible for the upkeep of the Cemetery at LA HAYE P.11.a.9.2. and the Right Bde. for the Cemeteries at CARVIN P.24.d.8.7. and BUSNES RIVER P.18.d.9.5.

4. Bodies of Allied Troops should be buried as far as possible in separate lots by nationalities.

5. Indians should be buried in existing Indian Cemeteries.

6. Enemy Graves should be marked, registered and recorded in the same way as British and Allies. They will not however be buried in Cemeteries.

:11 DETAILED INSTRUCTIONS.

A. BURIALS UNDER NORMAL CONDITIONS.

1. All bodies will be buried in authorised cemeteries only. The following is a list with locations of authorised cemeteries in the Divisional Area.

    ST.VENANT. Communal Cemetery Extension.   Sheet.36 A.P.4.b.8.7.
    GUARBECQUE Military Cemetery.   -do-   O.17.b.7.4.
    LA HAYE Cemetery.   -do-   P.11.a.9.2.
    CARVIN Cemetery.   -do-   P.24.d.8.7.
    BUSNES RIVER Cemetery.   -do-   P.18.d.9.5.

2. Single Graves should be dug 5' deep, 2' wide, 6'6" long and not more than 12" apart.
    A Path not exceeding 5' in width should be left between rows of graves.

3. At the time of burial each grave must be marked either with a wooden peg with label attached, or a label placed in a bottle and the bottle fixed neck downwards in the earth. Os.C.Units are responsible that the particulars referred to in para A.5.(b) are entered on the labels in BLOCK CAPITALS with a hard black pencil. On no account are indelible pencils to be used for this purpose.

4. Graves Registration Labels (Army Form. W.5371) can be procured from the Stationery Depot BOULOGNE. A box containing pegs will be kept in each authorised Cemetery. A small supply of labels and pegs if required for immediate use may be obtained from the O.C. No. 9. Graves Registration Unit FONTES. It is pointed out that the bottle preserves the label much longer than when the label is attached to a peg.

5. Os.C. Units concerned are responsible that :-
    (a) The Identity Disc Red, Pay Book, (A.B.64.) and all personal effects of a sentimental value are removed from the body and forwarded through the O.C., of the Unit to which the deceased belonged direct to D.A.G., G.H.Q., 3rd Echelon with the least possible delay. The Green Identity Disc will be left on the body. If no Identity Disc or other definite proof of identity is found the following will be noted:-
       Regimental Badges, measurement and description of body.

5. (Continued)

(b) A return on A.F.W. 5814 is rendered in quadruplicate signed by the Officer or Chaplain conducting the burial showing:-

    Number.
    Rank.
    Name (with initials) in BLOCK CAPITALS.
    Battalion.
    Regiment.
    Date of Death.
    Exact place of burial by reference to:-

    i. The Official name of the Cemetery.
    ii. The 1/40,000 Map or,
    iii. An accurate description, with reference to Woods, Houses, Cross Roads, Kilometre stones etc.

The copies of the above return will be forwarded by the O.C. Unit as follows:-
1 copy direct to Director of Graves Registration and Enquiries War Office, Winchester House, St. James Square, London. S.W.1.
1 copy to D.A.G., G.H.Q., 3rd Echelon.
1 copy to D.A.D.G.R. and E. Fifth Army.
1 copy to Corps Burial Officer.

(c) Each Unit enters in a Book for that purpose the particulars given in the Burial Return mentioned in the foregoing sub para. The name of the Officer or Chaplain conducting the burial will be entered in every case.
It is of the utmost importance that these books be kept with meticulous care. Os.C. Units will have these books prepared forthwith.

B. BURIALS DURING HEAVY FIGHTING.

1. Where it is NOT possible to comply with para A.1. every endeavour will be made to collect bodies in convenient sites suitable for permanent acquisition by the French Government under the Law of 29/12/15. The suitability of a site depends among other things on its being 100 metres distant from groups of houses or ruins and NOT near a well.

2. It may be necessary to bury bodies in trenches. Where this is done each end of the trench should be clearly defined by a substantial mark.
Officers will be buried with the men except General Officers whose bodies will be disposed of as directed by the Senior Staff Officer on the ground. Trenches should, where possible be, 5' deep 6'6" wide and of a convenient length.

3. Para A.5. applies equally to burials during heavy fighting.

4. Where it is impossible to mark trenches with labels for each body in the Trench, Burial Discs and rods will be used.

5. A supply of Burial Discs and Rods will be held by each Field Ambulance. Each Disc will be marked with the Divisional Sign on one side and a number on the other. The number on the Disc will be known as the Trench Number. Each Trench will, at the time of burial, be marked with a rod and disc. The rod and disc will be placed in the middle of one of the long sides of the trench.
The Officer or Chaplain conducting the burial will mark on the right hand top corner of the burial return the Number of the Trench in which the bodies described in the return are buried. A separate Form will be used for each Trench. In order to fix the exact position of the bodies in each Trench a serial number will be given to each body. When alloting these numbers the Officer or Chaplain will stand on the opposite side of the Trench from, and facing, the rod and disc. He will then number the bodies from left to right. Every endeavour should be made to ensure that a Chaplain is present to conduct the burial in all cases.

Schedule No 6.

Divisional Canteens.

Divisional Canteens have been opened at:-

MOLINGHEM with a branch at LILETTE CHATEAU.

GUARBECQUE.

LA PIERRIERE.

LINGHEM.

The Divisional Canteen Officer is Lieut. H.BROWN, Sussex Yeomanry. His Office is at Divisional Headquarters.

Schedule No. 7.

Field Cashier.

The Field Cashier attends at Divisional Headquarters every Monday from 10 a.m. to 12 noon.

In addition, the Field Cashiers Office at XI. Corps Headquarters is open daily as follows:-

    Week days 9-30 a.m. to 12-30 p.m.
                        2 p.m. to 4-30 p.m.
    Sundays.   9-30 a.m. to 12-30 p.m.

Schedule No. 8.

Leave Arrangements.

All ranks proceeding on leave travel by the leave train on the day preceding the day of embarkation, entraining at AIRE.

Parties for CALAIS report to R.T.O. at 4-30 p.m. and Parties for BOULOGNE at 8.a.m.

The returning leave trains arrive at AIRE, from CALAIS about 12-30 p.m. and from BOULOGNE about 3-30 p.m.

All personnel returning from leave spend at least one night at the Divisional Reception Camp.

Divisional Guides are attached to the R.T.O. AIRE for conducting parties to the Divisional Reception Camp.

Schedule No. 9.

MEDICAL ARRANGEMENTS.

DURING NORMAL WARFARE.

The following are the Field Ambulance Posts for the evacuation of sick and wounded :-

Map Reference - Sheet 36a.   1/40,000

1. **Car Loading Posts.**   Right Sector.   Left Sector.
                             F.24.b.3.5.   P.5.c.1.9.
                             P.17.c.4.2.
                             P.26.b.6.0.

2. **R.A.M.C. BEARER POSTS**
                             P.31.b.8.7.   P.5.c.1.9.
                             P.17.c.4.5.
                             P.27.b.1.3.
                             P.15.a.0.3.

3. **ADVANCED DRESSING STATIONS.**
                             P.18.b.1.4.   P.2.o.6.1.

For both Sectors.

4. **MAIN DRESSING STATION, & H.Q. Field Ambulance.** O.16.c.6.7.   (BERGUETTE)

5. **WALKING WOUNDED COLLECTING POST.** O.17.b.6.5.   (GUARBECQUE)

6. **H.Q. FIELD AMBULANCE.** P.13.b.9.6.   (MOLINGHEM)

7. **RESERVE BRIGADE.** is served by the Field Ambulance at Molinghem O.13.b.9.6. but wounded from the Reserve Brigade are passed to the nearest A.D.S. or the M.D.S. at BERGUETTE.

    The Field Ambulance at Molinghem has three extra Motor Ambulances attached to it from the F.A. in Reserve.

8. **FIELD AMBULANCE IN RESERVE.**

    Is stationed at LIGNE as a Corps Rest Station.

Schedule No. 10.

MEDICAL ARRANGEMENTS FOR HEAVY FIGHTING.

1. Immediately on information being received of impending or active operations all sick and ~~wou~~ will be evacuated under arrangements of D.D.M.S. XI Corps.

2. The existing arrangements as to evacuation from the front line will hold good with the following modifications:-

- (a) All Motor Ambulances of 229 and 231 Field Ambulances, less one to be retained by each, will report to O.C. 230th Field Amboe. at main dressing station BERGUETTE who will be responsible for transport of wounded from both A.D.S's.
- (b) O.C. 229th Field Ambulance will detail two Bearer Sub-Divisions to report to, one to 230th and one to 231st Field Ambulances for work in the forward area if required.
- (c) 231 Field Ambulance will receive walking wounded cases at its present location at MOLINGHEM and O.C. 231 Field Ambulance is responsible that ;-
    - (1) The route from A.D.S's to the Walking Wounded Station at MOLINGHEM is sufficiently indicated by directing boards
    - (2) The walking wounded collecting post at GUARBECQUE is equipped with dressings and refreshments.
    - (3) Sufficient personnel is posted to act as guides to the walking wounded.

3. Field Medical Cards and A.F.W. 3210 will be filled in at the Main Dressing Station and Walking Wounded Station and each of these stations will register the cases with which it ~~deals~~ deals and will administer A.T.S.

4. In the event of a retiral on to the LES AMUSOIRES-HAVERSKERQUE line the following changes will be made :-

- (a) The M.D.S. at BERGUETTE will close down and the Walking Wounded Station at MOLINGHEM will become the M.D.S.
- (b) The left A.D.S. will close down as soon as O.C. 231 Field Amboe has opened newb A.D.S. at O.11. Central.
- (c) The right A.D.S. will remain as at present.
- (d) The personnel and equipment of the M.D.S. at BERGUETTE will be moved back to WITTERNESSE.

Schedule No. 4.

ORDNANCE.

Ordnance Railhead   AIRE.

The Office of the D.A.D.O.S. the Divisional Ordnance Store, Divisional Armourers Shop and Ordnance Refilling Point for all groups are situated at MOLINGHEM.

Stores are conveyed by motor lorry from AIRE station to the Divisional Ordnance Store.

Schedule 12.

SECRET.   C.A. 311.

POLICE ARRANGEMENTS.

Reference:
   Sheet 36A. 1/40,000.

1. **STRAGGLERS POSTS & COLLECTING STATIONS.**

   1. Line of Stragglers Posts for the present Front Line System.

No. of Post.	MAP REFERENCE.	UNIT PROVIDING.	STRENGTH.
1.	Bridge J.26.c.5.1.	Traffic Control.	1 N.C.O. 3Men.
2.	X Roads. P.2.a.3.2.	-do-	-do-
3.	X Roads. P.2.c.4.0.	-do-	-do-
4.	Drawbridge. O.12.c.1.9.)	Left Inf. Bde.	1 N.C.O. 3Men*
5.	Rlybridge. P.13.a.3.4.)	Left Inf. Bde.	1 N.C.O. 3Men*
6.	Footbridge. P.20.a.5.6.	Right Inf. Bde.	1 N.C.O. 3Men*
7.	Drawbridge. P.20.central.	Right Inf. Bde.	1 N.C.O. 3Men*
8.	X Roads. P.26.c.1.2.	Traffic Control.	1 N.C.O. 3Men
9.	X Roads. P.32.a.3.9.	-do-	-do-

   * Infantry Relieve Traffic Control Posts on the order "Man Battle Stations". At the same time an M.M.P. will report at each of these posts.

   Collecting Stations for the above Stragglers Posts are situated as follows:-
   A. P.1.c.8.2.   for Nos. 1, 2, 3, 4, and 5 Posts.
   B. P.31.b.9.9.   for Nos. 6, 7, 8, and 9 Posts.

   On the order "Man Battle Stations" the Infantry Brigade in reserve will detail 1 Officer and 2 N.C.O's and 15 men to report forthwith to A.P.M. at the P. of W Cage to act as P. of W Escort and Guard.

2. Disposal of Stragglers.
   (a). <u>Unarmed</u> will be collected into parties at the Stragglers Posts and escorted back to the Collected Station where they will be rearmed from Casualties and marched back to their Transport Lines. The O i/c Units Transport Lines will send them forward to rejoin their respective Units.

   (b). <u>Armed.</u> will be collected at Stragglers Posts and marched back to their Brigade or Unit Headquarters.

   (c). The names, numbers and Units of all Stragglers will be taken before they are despatched to rejoin their Units.

   (d). Stragglers returning to their Units should be used to carry up material etc.

11. TRAFFIC CONTROL.
    1. The Traffic Control Officer is stationed at P.5.d.7.1.
    2. The following are the permanent Traffic Control Posts in the Divisional Area.

No. of Post.	MAP REFERENCE.	UNIT PROVIDING.
1.	H.30.c.0.3.	No. 1 Traffic Control Squadron.
2.	H.30.c.8.2.	No. 1 Traffic Control Squadron.
3.	P.3.a.central.	Divisional Traffic Control Police
4.	P.2.a.3.2.	-do-
5.	P.2.c.4.0.	-do-
6.	P.29.central.	-do-
7.	P.26.c.1.2.	-do-
8.	P.32.a.3.9.	-do-

No. of Post.	Map Reference.	Unit Providing.
9	O.17.b.Central.	Divisional Traffic Con.Police.
10.	O.16.b.7.7.	-do-
11.	O.14.a.Central.	-do-
12.	D.27.c.3.6.	-do-
13.	I.32.a.3.4.	-do-
14.	O.27.d.9.8.	-do-

3. Circuits are shown on X1 Corps Traffic Circuit Map. Order of preference on "UP" Roads during operations is:-

    i. Road Material for immediate repairs.
    ii. Ammunition.
    iii. Supplies and Water.
    iv. R.E.Stores and Road Material other than shown in i.

Ambulance Cars will have precedence on "DOWN" Roads.

111. The personnel of Stragglers and Traffic Control Posts are rationed by the A.P.M..
A Wagon is detailed from the Train to enable him to deliver the Rations at the various Posts.

1V PRISONERS OF WAR.

1. All unwounded Prisoners of War will be sent to the Divisional Prisoners of War Cage. Brigades are responsible for the custody of Prisoners until they are handed over to the A.P.M. or his representative
    Prisoners of War will be taken over by the A.P.M. from Infantry Brigades at the P.of W.Cage at O.5.d.7.1.
2. Wounded Prisoners of War will be evacuated through the Advanced Dressing Stations.
3. Prisoners will be accompanied by a statement giving the following particulars.
    i. Nos.of Prisoners showing officers and other ranks separately.
    ii. Location of capture.
    iii. Unit by whom captured.

This statement will be handed over to the Officer or N.C.O. i/c of the P.of W.Cage.
4. A receipt will be obtained for all Prisoners of War handed over.

Schedule No. 15.

Water Supply.

The supply and maintenance of water points in the Divisional Area are controlled by two Water Patrols, each of 1 N.C.O. and 4 men.

The following are the locations of the main sources of water supply.

Location.	Remarks.
N.5.d.9.2.	Artesian Wells.
S.19.a.2.4.	-do-
O.10.a.8.0.	-do-
O.10.c.5.4.	-do-
O.35.b.2.5.	-do-
O.35.b.1.6.	-do-
O.35.b.1.9.	-do-
O.34.d.5.6.	-do-
O.35.c.3.0.	-do-
O.34.b.0.6.	-do-
O.29.d.5.5.	-do-
O.29.c.7.6.	-do-
O.29.c.5.0.	-do-
O.18.c.4.9.	-do-
O.16.b.1.5.	-do-
O.16.b.50.7.	-do-
O.10.c.2.4.	-do-
O.4. d.5.5.	-do-
O.11.d.9.1.	-do-
O.17.b.8.8.	-do-
O.24.d.8.7.	-do-
U.6. b.6.2.	-do-
P.32.a.4.5.	-do-
P.26.c.5.8.	-do-
P.26.c.1.7.	-do-
P.20.a.5.5.	-do-
P. 9.b.2.5.	-do-
P. 8.a.8.4.	-do-
P.20.c.4.5.	-do-
P.20.b.9.5.	-do-
S.19.c.9.0.	Spring.
O.13.d.7.7.	-do-
O.14.b.8.0.	-do-
N.32.c.8.1.	-do-
N.31.d.8.8.	-do-
U.25.b.5.6.	Water Cart Filling Point.
O.25.c.5.7.	-do-
U. 6.c.0.0.	-do-
P.32.b.5.7.	-do-

Schedule 14 - RESERVE RATIONS AND WATER.

The following table shows the composition and location of Reserve Rations and Water maintained.

Right Sector - Ration and Water Dumps.

DETAIL.	Right Sub-Sector. P.29.b.5.3.	Left Sub-Sector. P.17.d.5.1.	RESERVE AREA.	
			*P.27.b.2.3.	*P.19.a.7.2.
Petrol tins of water.	50.	50.		
Corned Beef Tins.	600 Rations.	600 rations.		
Biscuits, Tins.	600 rations.	600 rations.		
Iron Rations.			1000.	1000.

* Corps Dump.

Left Sector - Ration and Water Dumps.

DETAIL.	Right Sub-Sector. P.11.a.9.2.	Left Sub-Sector. P.5.c.1.9.	RESERVE AREA. *P.1.d.8.1.
Petrol tins of water.	40.	40.	20.
Biscuits.	560 rations.	560 rations.	1000 rations.
Preserved Meat.	576 rations.	576 rations.	1000 rations.

* Corps Dump.

Schedule No. 15.

SALVAGE.

1. **Salvage.** In the present area all Units are responsible for collecting salvage in and around the camps or areas occupied by them.

   A small Salvage dump will be formed in every areas and notice boarded so that all ranks may know where any salvage collected by them is to be deposited.

2. Divisional Salvage Dumps are located as follows:-

   Main Divisional Dump.   MOLINGHEM.
   Advanced Dump.   GUARBECQUE.

3. Transport of Salvage.

   All empty wagons returning from the front will stop at any salvage dump they may pass, load up with salvage and deposit at the Divisional Salvage Dump nearest to the route they are taking.

   The Divisional Salvage Officer will apply to Division "Q" for transport to convey salved material from the Divisional Dumps to the Corps Dump at AIRE.

   The Ammunition Salvage Dump is located at I.25.a.1.8.

4. Solder recovery plant.

   Solder recovery plants are located at GUARBECQUE and MOLINGHEM.
   All empty tins of every description are to be delivered by units at these Dumps.

Schedule No. 16.

SUPPLY ARRANGEMENTS.

Supply Railhead.   AIRE.

Refilling points.

    Reserve Brigade.   FONTES.

    Right Brigade and Divisional Troops - MAZINGHAM.(N.17.c.6.2.)

    Left Brigade N.23.a.4.9.

Divisional Train draws direct from Railhead and delivers to Units Transport Lines except in the case of the Reserve Brigade and Divisional Artillery whose supplies are conveyed from Railhead to Refilling Points by Motor Lorry and thence to Transport and Wagon Lines by Supply Wagons of Divisional Train.

Reserve of rations retained in forward areas is shown in appendix.

Divisional Fuel Dumps are maintained at each Supply Refilling Point.

Schedule No. 17. - VETERINARY.

Animals are evacuated from the 59th Mobile Veterinary Section TREIZENNE by road to X1 Veterinary Evacuating Station, GLOMINGHEM.

Animals unable to walk are removed in horse ambulance wagon.

The most convenient V.E.S. is always used so it is liable to change with a move of the Division.

Veterinary Evacuating Stations are G.H.Q. troops.

Schedule No. 18.

Divisional Reception Camp.

The Reception Camp is located at LINGHEM.

The Camp provides accommodation for reinforcements, casuals, leave ment etc. proceeding to and from their Units and in addition the personnel left out of action under the provisions of Section 19 of S.S. 135 as amended by G.H.Q. letter O.W. 1919

Personnel posted to Battalions in excess of 900 other ranks will remain at the Reception Camp until required to replace losses.

The personnel left out of action ("B" Teams) are formed into Brigade Wings. The "B" Teams of the Pioneer Battalion forms part of the Brigade Wing of the Brigade holding the Left Sector in the Line.

The Senior Officer of each Brigade Wing commands the Wing. Wing Commanders are responsible for the training and instruction of the "B" Teams of their Brigade.

Drafts of Reinforcements for all Units in the Division except for Brigades in the line remain at the Reception Camp for 36 hours after arrival, during which time they are ~~given~~ bathed and given a rest.

Reinforcements Drafts for Brigades in the line join their respective "B" Teams. "B" Teams join the Reception Camp on the day preceeding the Brigade Relief and rejoin their Units on the day the latter withdraw into reserve.

Officers and Other Ranks who are reinforcements, leave the Reception Camp in possession of 48 hours rations.

All men returning from leave are rationed up to the night of their arrival with their Units only.

Guides from each Infantry Battalion, Pioneer Battn, M.G.Battn. and the D.E.C., are attached to the Reception Camp to act as guides for reinforcements to their Units.

The guide from the D.E.C. is provided for the Divisional Headquarters.

SECRET.   C.Q.306.

ADMINISTRATIVE INSTRUCTIONS Reference to
74th Division Order No. 69.

                                                            21st July 1918.

TRENCH AND AREA STORES.

1. The 230th Infantry Brigade will hand over all Trench and Area Stores to the 229th Infantry Brigade, and receive a receipt therefor.

AMMUNITION AND SUPPLY DUMPS.

2. The 230th Infantry Brigade will hand over to the 229th Infantry Brigade all Ammunition, Reserve Ration and Water Dumps within the sector. The 229th Infantry Brigade will forward a statement to this Office showing the composition and Location of these Dumps, as taken over.

BAGGAGE WAGONS.

3. The O.C. Train will arrange for the Baggage Wagons to report at the Transport Lines of the Units concerned by 10 a.m. on the 23rd inst.

TRANSPORT.

4. One Motor Lorry will report at the Headquarters of each of the three Battalions of the 229th Infantry Brigade at 9 a.m. on the 23rd inst, to convey the blankets etc, of the "B" Teams to the Divisional Reception Camp WITTERNESSE.
These lorries will thereafter convey the blankets etc of the 230th Infantry Brigade "B" Teams from the Divisional Reception Camp WITTERNESSE to the Divisional Reserve Area - One lorry being allotted to the "B" Team of each Battalion.

SUPPLIES.

5. Refilling Points will remain as at present.

6. ACKNOWLEDGE.

                                                    Lieut-Colonel.
                                                    A.A. & Q.M.G.
                                                 74th (Yeo) Division.

Copies:-
1. 229th Infantry Brigade.   7. A.D.M.S.
2. 230th Infantry Brigade.   8. 74th Div. Train.
3. 231st Infantry Brigade.   9. A.P.M.
4. C.R.A.   10. File.
5. C.R.E.   11. Diary.
6. 74th Div. Signal Coy.   12. "G".

Army Form C. 2118.

WAR DIARY
INTELLIGENCE SUMMARY.
(Erase heading not required.)

Appendix "X"

Place	Date	Hour	Summary of Events and Information	Remarks and references to Appendices

Effectives strength of 74th (Geo) Div. on July 1st 670 Officers and 14175 ORs on 2ly

Battle
Total Number of Casualties in the Division in July:- Killed Officers 1
OR. 24
Wounded Officers 10
OR. 147.
Accidental Injuries OR. 1
Injured OR. 8

Total Number of Reinforcements received total July 28th:-
Officers 4
Other Ranks 317.

Total Number of Sick evacuated during month:
Officers 11
Other Ranks 415.

Prisoners taken during month:
Unwounded Off. 2
OR's 12.
Wounded Off. 1
OR. 1.

Andrew M Montgomery Lt
for Major DAA & QMG 74 (Geo)Div.

War Diary
A.P.R. Branch
Head Qrs 74th (Yeo) Divn
from 1st to 31st August /18

VOLUME XVIII

Army Form C. 2118

WAR DIARY
or
INTELLIGENCE SUMMARY
(Erase heading not required.)

Administrative Branch
7A (Secondary) Div. H.Q.

Reference Sheet
36 A 1/40 000

Place	Date	Hour	Summary of Events and Information	Remarks and references to Appendices
LILETTE CHATEAU M33d 88	Aug 3rd		Brig. Gen. A. KENNEDY C.M.G. Cmdg 230 Inf. Bde. assumed temporary command of 7A (Sec) Div. during the absence of the G.O.C. on short leave to the U.K.	
Do	Aug 4th		"B" Teams (i.e. those comprising left out of action) of 230 Inf. Bde. moved into Rest Respite Camp LINGHEM.	
Do	Aug 4th–5th		"B" Teams of 231 Inf. Bde. moved into 230 Inf. Bde. Rest Respite Camp. Administration instructions 230 Inf. Bde. relieved 231 Inf. Bde. in the line. Copy of administrative instructions attached marked Appendix I.	Appendix I
Do	Aug 6th		Relieving 74th Bde. Gr. No. 70 dated Aug 1st = Appreciation of the stores required for relief of 27th Bde. R.F.A. by 308 Bombdrs in the line commenced Aug 6th & 7th Aug.	
Do	Aug 7th		Relief of 27th Bde. R.F.A. 305 Bde. R.F.A. completed. Refilling Point of Left Supply Coln. =	
Do	Aug 8th		Group changed from M23 a 4.9. to BUSNES. Main train movement came into force i.e. 70 per day for the divisional supply situation reduced to normal i.e. M.T. from Railhead to the R.P. My A.P.O. Supply began to unite transport line forward to intake 1st line wagons & from Canal Gp Refilling Pt. "B" teams of 231 Inf. Bde. reported to Reception Camp prior to being withdrawn and concentrated moved forward 7 231 Inf. Bde.	
Do	Aug 10th		229 and 230 and 231 Inf. Bde. troops all refilled at BUSNES.	
Do	Aug 10th		Div. Troops at HAM EN ARTOIS. Two Ind. Harvesting Officers appointed to work under Corps Agricultural Officer. One working area bounded by BUSNES – ROBECQ – ST. VENANT – BUSNES. The working parties of 200 men p.a. Inf. supplied by support Bn. One working area in advance of that line work of 16–17 miles. 231 Inf. Bn. moved forward and took over whole line. 230 Inf. Bn. withdrew into support and 229 Inf. Bn. into Reserve area	
Do	Aug 15th		About HAM EN ARTOIS. GUARNEQUE – ARMIQUELLERIE. Administration instructions for more attacks issued. Copy attached Appendix II. New Police Instructions for the area issued.	Appendix II Appendix III

Capt A.D. Montgomery (?) by Major, 7 A (Sec) Div.

WAR DIARY or INTELLIGENCE SUMMARY

Army Form C. 2118

Administrative Branch Page 2
74 (Yeo) Div. M.D.

Place	Date	Hour	Summary of Events and Information	Remarks and references to Appendices
LILLETTE CHATEAU N33d88 P.3.I.C. Cachy.	Aug. 16th		Field Ambulance detachment relating to the Reporting of Casualties, etc. Copy attached & marked Appendix IV	Appendix IV
	Aug 18		The G.O.C. Fifth Army attended a Brigade Church Parade. Corps visit at CORPS BOARD his Orders Clerk 36A (two bay) rebuilding the 229 I.f. Bde. address to the house & visited the house, Brigade and main street. Several stations inspected after. Arrival of Main Street Stations inspected the 162nd (N. Somerset Yeo) Bn. & SLB and	
	Aug 19		G.O.C. Eleventh Corps inspected Her 162nd (A. Devon Yeo) St. Devon Regt. Her 14th (Fife and Forfar Yeo) BLRH.	
	Aug. 20th		G. O.C. Eleventh Corps inspected the line changed to GUARBECQUE. Refilling Point for I.f. Bn. Lorries in the line. 23, I.f. Bde. in the line by the 229 I.f. Bde. from Div. orders issued for the relief of the 23, I.f. Bde. in the line by the 235 I.f. Bde - relief carried on night 23/24.	
BUSNES CHATEAU P.3.I.C. Cachy.	Aug. 24		Div. H.Q. moved to BUSNES Chateau and known round 229 I.f. Bde. & Divnl. 231 Train in HYME 23/24. 231 I.f. Bde. moved to Support with Res. H.Q. at LA HAYE P.11.6.6. 230 I.f. Bde. moved into Div. Reserve with Bn. in BUSNES, LA MERRIEREAD HAMET BULLET and 2/I Res. H.Q. at P.7.C.0.5. Orders to relief of the 59th Division by the 59th Division received. Eleventh Corps administrative instruction QM.23 with reference to this relief received. Copy attached marked Appendix V	Appendix V
	Aug. 25		230 I.f. Bde. relieved by 176 I.f. Bde.-moved to billets in ST.HILAIRE—BOURECQ area. 231 I.f. Bde. relieved by 177 I.f. Bde. moved to billets in LACOQUE-LAMBRES area. 44th Bn. R.F.A. carried out of the line and moved to billets in LA MIQUELLERIE. Administration instructions relative to move issued. Copy attached & marked Appendix VI	Appendix VI
	Aug. 27		Entraining Programme received. Copy attached, marked Appendix VII. 229 I.f. Bde. relieved in the line by 177 I.f. Bde. Moved to billets in HAM EN ARTOIS— MOLINGHEM area.	Appendix VII

Army Form C. 2118

WAR DIARY or INTELLIGENCE SUMMARY

(Erase heading not required.)

Administration Branch Pages 2
74= Division Div H.Q.

Place	Date	Hour	Summary of Events and Information	Remarks and references to Appendices
BUSNES CHATEAU P.31 Q Sh.36d.	Aug 27 /18		R.E. Thield Companies reinforcements Infantry troops Field Ambulances relieved and reported affiliated Posts. 117 Bn. R.F.A. moved to FONTES M.35. D.A.C. and Machine Transport Reports. WITTERNESSE. Camp handed over to 59= Division. 'B' team reported unit. First Reception Camp temporarily attached to 2nd Iny Bde. and remained staff temporarily as reported at MORBENT FONTES at the D.H.Q. Closed at BUSNES CHATEAU at 6 pm. and reopened at MORBENT FONTES at 7 pm. Copy of Administration Instruction Relative to Div. Order No. 79 attached marked Appendix. Division commenced entraining. D.A.Q.M.G. proceeded to Victoria by motor.	Appendix VIII
	Aug 28.			
	Aug 29.		Entries commenced entraining as follows:— 2.20 If Bn. troops for CORRIE and proceeded to billet in FRANVILLERS and LA HOUSSOYE. Rec H.Q. BEHENCOURT CHATEAU. 230 Iny Bde HEILLY troops in locality. Rec H.Q. BAIZIEUX. 231 Iny Bde. MERICOURT SUR ANCRE billeted thereabouts RISEMONT with Rec H.Q. at the latter. DHQ at BEHENCOURT CHATEAU.	
BEHENCOURT CHATEAU Sheet 57E.			R.Ps. at LA HOUSSOYE, HEILLY and RISEMONT respectively. Supply railhead CORRIE. Instructions issued for forwarding Div. Reports Camp at FRANVILLERS. Div. Artillery commenced entraining at 11 am to plan 9 Infantry Batteries detraining. "B" teams and Div. Employment and all Transport Bn. Vio Reception Camp Div. Arty. Parties detraining to MARICOURT Area. Personnel heard marched overnight for immediate move of Division to MARICOURT. Rations 2 Cav. Regt. carried. 1000. Rations for Sept 1 being carried on man, pack & 1 Cav. Supply waggons. Bull Bread party on approx. and 12.0 p.m. forward	
	Aug 30.			
	Aug 31.		A Statement made to Appendix IX is attached showing total casualties and Strengths, effectives and Ration-Strengths and number of P. Count taken.	Appendix IX

Andrew Allen Ayrsmith
for Major D.A.A.G. 74 (Yeo) Dn.

Draft Appendix I

C.Q.244/1.

SECRET.

Administrative Instructions relative to 74th Divisional Order

No. 70.

1st August, 1918.

1. **Trench and Area Stores.**
   The 231st Infantry Brigade will hand over all Trench and Area Stores to 230th Infantry Brigade and obtain a receipt therefor. The 230th Infantry Brigade will forward to this Office as soon as possible a list of the stores as taken over.

2. **Ammunition and Supply Dumps.**
   The 231st Infantry Brigade will hand over to the 230th Infantry Brigade all Ammunition and Reserve Ration and Water dumps within the Section. The 230th Infantry Brigade will forward a statement to this Office as soon as possible showing the composition and location of these dumps as taken over.

3. **Baggage Wagons.**
   The O.C. Divisional Train will arrange for the Baggage Wagons to report at the Transport Lines of the Units of both Brigades at 9.a.m. on the 4th inst.

4. **Transport.**
   Three Motor Lorries will report at Headquarters 230th Inf. Bde at 9 a.m. on the 4th inst to convey the blankets of the "B" Teams to the Divisional Reception Camp at LINGHEM. On arrival at the Divisional Reception Camp these lorries will wait and convey the blankets etc of the 231st Inf. Bde. "B" Teams to the Divisional Reserve Area.

5. **Supplies.**
   On and after the 5th inst the 231st Inf. Bde. will refil at FONTES at 8 a.m. and the 230th Inf. Bde. at MAZINGHEM at 6-30 a.m.

6. **Acknowledge.**

Lieut Colonel,
A.A.& Q.M.G. 74th (Yeomanry) Division.

Copies to:- No. 1. "G"   8 74th Div. Train.
            2. File.   9 229th Inf. Bde.
            3. Diary.   10 230th Inf. Bde.
            4. O.R.B.   11 231st Inf. Bde.
            5. O.R.E.   12 A.P.M.
            6. A.D.M.S.   13 O.C. Reception Camp.
            7. 74th Div.Sigs. 14. XI Corps.

SECRET.
Copy No. 2

ADMINISTRATIVE INSTRUCTIONS RELATIVE TO   C.Q. 383/2
74TH DIVISION ORDER No. 75.

1. **TRANSPORT.** The O.C. Divisional Train will arrange for the baggage wagons of the 3 Infantry Brigades to report at the Transport Lines of the respective Units at 9 a.m. on the 16th inst. These wagons will be returned to the Train Companies on the 17th inst.

2. **TRENCH AND AREA STORES.** The 229th and 230th Infantry Brigades will hand over all Trench and Area Stores in their possession including the additional issue of Packsaddles and message carrying rockets, and in the case of the 230th Infantry Brigade, the unexpired portion of the weekly issue of Solidified Alcohol. The 230th and 231st Infantry Brigades will forward a list of the stores taken over by them to reach this office by the 20th inst.

3. **SUPPLIES.** On and after the 17th inst, the following will be the Refilling Points :-
   229th Inf. Brigade Group - MOLINGHEM at 8-30 a.m.
   230th Inf. Brigade Group.- BUSNES P. 31.b.3.2 at 8-30 a.m.
   231st Inf. Brigade Group.- BUARBECQUE O.17.b.3.1 at 8-30 a.m.
   Divl. Artillery Group. - BUARBECQUE Church at 8.a.m.
Owing to the necessary economy in the use of Motor Lorries, the Divnl. Train will draw Supplies from Railhead.
Units will send their 1st Line Transport to these Refilling Points at the hours stated to draw rations, with the exception of the Divisional Artillery. O.C. Train will arrange for the conveyance of the Artillery rations and forage forward from the Refilling Point.

4. **BLANKETS.** Three Motor Lorries will report at 74th Divisional Reception Camp at 2-30 p.m. on the 16th inst to convey Blankets etc of the "B" Teams of the 229th Infantry Brigade to the Reserve Brigade Area.

5. **AMMUNITION AND SUPPLY DUMPS.** The 229th Infantry Brigade will hand over to the 230th Infantry Brigade the instructions issued from this office regarding the checking and allocation of all Dumps in the Divl. Sector. The 230th Infantry Brigade will forward a report to this office as soon as possible, in terms of the above instructions.

6. **AGRICULTURE.** The 229th Infantry Brigade will arrange for Lieut. HAWKINS, West Somerset Yeomanry to remain in the forward area to supervise the Agricultural scheme as laid down in this office Q.P.5 of the 12th inst. The 230th Infantry Brigade will be responsible for harvesting the Area East of the ROBECQ-ST VENANT Road. The 229th Infantry Brigade will detail 200 men to report to Lieut. LOLLIMORE at 9 a.m. daily at LA PERRIERE for Agricultural duties in the back area commencing on 18th inst.
Officers and men detailed for Agricultural work will as far as possible be detailed from those with agricultural knowledge, otherwise a lot of work is wasted.

7. **ACKNOWLEDGE.**
Headquarters

15th August 1918.

Lieut-Colonel.
A.A. & Q.M.G.
74th (Yeo) Division.

Copies to :-
No. 1. "G"
2. File.
3. Diary.
4. C.R.A.
5. C.R.E.
6. A.D.M.S.
7. 74th Signals.
8. 74th Div. Train.
9. 229th Inf. Bde.
10. 230th Inf. Bde.
11. 231st Inf. Bde
12. A.P.M.
13. O.C. Rstep Cmp
14. XI Corps.
15. D.A.D.V.S.
16. O.Comdt.

Appendix III

SECRET.   POLICE ARRANGEMENTS.   OA/311

Reference Sheet 36 A 1/40,000

1. STRAGGLERS POSTS & COLLECTING STATIONS.

1. Line of Stragglers Posts for the present Front Line System.

No of Post.	Map Reference	Unit Providing.	Strength. N.C.O. O/R.
No 1.	P.5.a.2.0.	Divnl.Traffic	{ 3
No 2.	P.5.c.6.1.	Control Police	1 { 5
No 3.	P.11.a.6.8.	"	{ 3
No 4.	P.24.c.3.7.	"	{ 5
No 5.	P.29.b.8.1.	"	1 { 3

In the event of Active Operations 1 M.M.P. will be detailed to take charge of each of the above Posts.
Collecting Stations for the above will be :-

No 1. M.M.P. Post ST. VENANT for No 1,2.& 3 Posts.
No 2. P.29.b.1.7. for Nos. 4 and 5 Posts.

Central Collecting Stations will be at P.26.c.1.2.

On the order "Man Battle Stations" the Infantry Brigade in Reserve will detail 1 Officer and 15 Other Ranks to report to A.P.M. at the P.of W. Cage to act as P. of W. Escort & Guard which is also at P.26.c.1.2.

2. Disposal of Stragglers.
(a) Unarmed will be collected into Parties at the Stragglers Posts and escorted back to the Collecting Station where they will be reformed from Casualties and marched back to their Transport Lines. The O.i/c of Units Transport Lines will send them forward to rejoin their respective Units.

(b) Armed will be collected at Stragglers Posts and marched back to their Brigade or Unit H.Q.

(c) The names, numbers and Units of all Stragglers will be taken before they are despatched to rejoin their Units.

(d) Stragglers returning to their Units should be used to carry up material etc.

II. TRAFFIC CONTROL.

1. The Traffic Control Officer is stationed at P.26.c.1.2.
2. The following are the permanent Traffic Control Posts in the Divisional Area:-

See Over.

No. of Post.	Map Reference.	Unit Providing.
No 1.	O.9.d.6.1.	
2.	O.17.b.central.	
3.	P.20 central.	
4.	P.26.c.1.2.	
5.	P.32.a.3.9.	
6.	P.3.d.8.0.	
7.	O.2.a.4.0.	Divisional Traffic Police.
8.	P.5.a.2.0.	
9.	P.5.c.6.1.	
10.	P.11 a.6.8.	
11.	P.24.c.3.7.	
12.	P.29.b.8.1.	
13.	P.29.b.0.9.	
14.	P.29.a.8.0.	

3. Circuits are shewn on XIth Corps Traffic Circuit Map.
Order of precedence on "UP" Roads during operations is:-
    i.   Road Material for immediate repairs.
    ii. Ammunition.
    iii. Supplies and water
    iv. R.E. Stores and Road Material other than shewn in i.

Ambulance Cars will have precedence on "DOWN" Roads.

III. The personnel of Stragglers and Traffic Control Posts are rationed by the A.P.M.
A wagon is detailed from the Train to enable him to deliver the Rations at the various Posts.

IV. **PRISONERS OF WAR.**
1. All unwounded Prisoners of War will be sent to the Divisional Prisoners of War Cage. Brigades are responsible for the custody of Prisoners until they are handed over to the A.P.M. or his representative.
Prisoners of War will be taken over by the A.P.M. from Infantry Brigades at the P. of W. Cage at P.26.c.1.2.
2. Wounded Prisoners of War will be evacuated through Advanced Dressing Stations.
3. Prisoners will be accompanied by a statement giving the following particulars.
    i.   Nos. of Prisoners showing Officers and Other Ranks
    ii. Location of capture. (separately.
    iii. Unit by whom captured.

This statement will be handed over to the Officer or N.C.O. i/c of the P. of W. Cage.
4. A receipt will be obtained for all Prisoners of War handed over.

                                     Owens Lieut.-Colonel.
                       A.A.& Q.M.G., 74th (Yeomanry) Division.

13/8/18.
Copies to:

229th Bde.			
230th Bde.	M.G.Bn.	Div.M.T.Coy.	
231st Bde.	A.D.M.S.	Div.Recptn.Camp.	
C.R.A.	D.A.D.V.S.	Div.Emp.Coy.	
C.R.E.	D.A.D.O.S.	C.Commdt.	
XIth Corps "A"	A.P.M.	"G"	
A.P.M. XI Corps.	Div.Train.	File & Diary.	

Appendix IV — War Diary

74th (YEOMANRY) DIVISION.

INSTRUCTIONS ON REPORTING CASUALTIES.

A 11

Owing to the large number of Amendments and Additions to the Method in which Casualties have to be reported, all previous Instructions issued by this Office are cancelled and should be destroyed forthwith.
The following Instructions will be followed from this date.

ORDINARY CASUALTY REPORTS.

To be rendered by all Units and Formations.

Return.	For which Period.	When due at DHQ.
(a) Casualties to General Officers, Staff Offrs & Commdg. Officers. By WIRE.	As they occur.	As they occur.
(b) do On Casualty Pro forma.	do.	Within 12 hours of Casualty.
(c) Accurate Daily Wire Including names of Officers.	24 hours. 12 noon to 12 noon.	3 pm. Daily.
(d) Accurate Daily Return. Including Names of Officers.	do.	7.30 pm. Daily Pro forma A Appendix 2. Issued with AII dated 6/6/18.
(e) Weekly Return of Missing & Prisoners.	Weekly 12 noon Saturdays to 12 noon Saturdays.	6.p.m. Saturday Pro forma B. Appendix 3. Issued with AII dated 6/6/18.
(f) Weekly Nominal Rolls of Casualties, on A.F.B 213.	Weekly 12 noon Saturday to 12 noon Saturday.	6.pm. Sundays.

INSTRUCTIONS ON REPORTING CASUALTIES.

A 11.

1. **DESCRIPTION OF CASUALTIES.** The attention of all concerned is particularly directed to the "Instructions regarding the Reporting of Casualties" issued under G.R.O. 3887 of 25th April 1918 as amended by G.R.O. 4695 of Aug. 6th 1918. (Appendix 1.)

2. **MISSING OFFICERS & OTHER RANKS.** In all cases where an Officer or Other Rank is reported Missing a brief statement explaining the circumstances should be rendered without delay. A brief account will be given in the Daily Casualty Wire and full particulars stated in the daily Casualty Return.

3. **CASUALTIES EXCEEDING 10 PER UNIT.** During periods when no special operations are taking place, if casualties of any one Unit exceed 10 on any one day, a brief explanation will be added e.g., "Mine Explosion", "Heavy Shelling", "Hostile Raid", as the case may be.

---

1. **ORDINARY CASUALTY REPORTS TO BE RENDERED BY ALL UNITS & FORMATIONS.**

   A. CASUALTIES TO GENERAL OFFICERS, STAFF OFFICERS & CMDG. OFFICERS.

   1. **WIRE.** Casualties to General Officers, Staff Officers and Commanding Officers will be wired to D.H.Q. immediately they occur, giving a brief statement showing how the casualty occurred.

   2. **WRITTEN REPORT.** A written report will be rendered to reach this Office within 12 hours of the casualty, confirming same and giving fuller particulars.

   3. Those Casualties will be included in the Casualty Return and Wire in addition to being dealt with as above.

   4. Information will also be wired when any of the above Officers are evacuated sick.

   B. ACCURATE DAILY WIRE.

   1. All Units and Formations will render through the usual Channels an accurate Daily Casualty Wire.

   2. This Wire will be made up to 12 noon for the preceding 24 hours and will be forwarded to reach D.H.Q. at 3 p.m. on the same day, thus Casualties occuring between 12 noon 2nd May and 12 noon 3rd May must reach D.H.Q. 3 pm. 3rd May and will be termed Casualties for 3rd May. NIL Wires WILL be rendered.

   3. Casualties will be shewn by Units (in CLEAR as distinct from the Estimated Wire) showing the Numbers KILLED, Wounded, MISSING, DIED OF INJURIES, INJURED, distinguishing Officers and Other Ranks. In the case of Officers the Unit, attached Unit, Rank, Initials and Name, will be stated, but in the case of Other Ranks the numbers only will be given.

/4.

4. In the case of Officers the actual date on which the casualty occurred will be added after the Name of the Officer. (In the same way Officers Commanding Units when reporting Other Rank Casualties on A.Fs B 213 will endeavour to give the exact date on which the casualty occurred.)

5. SPECIMEN WIRE (ACCURATE)

74th Division.
"Casualties for 3rd May AAA 10th E.Kents KILLED 2/Lt. A.B. BROWN R.E.K.M.R. 3rd O/R.3. WOUNDED O/R 8 INJURED Capt. F.P.WHITE 3rd Bn.E.Kents Rgt. 2nd at duty revolver AAA 15th Suffolks KILLED O/R.2 WOUNDED 2/Lt. G.GREEN Lovat Scouts 3rd O/R. 6 includes 4 at duty MISSING O/R 3 on patrol AAA 16th Sussex DIED OF INJURIES O/R 3 bomb explosion."

6. Before reporting Names of Officers these must always be verified in the Army List to ensure that the correct Unit, Initials and Spelling are given. Carefully compiled Nominal Rolls of Officers should always be kept up to date by each Unit.

7. When an Officer who has been previously reported "wounded at duty" is subsequently admitted to hospital on account of the wound, a notice will be inserted in the Daily Casualty Return as follows:-
"Capt. "A" (Unit) reported wounded at duty 1/2/18 in List No. admitted to Hospital on account of wounds 6/2/18."

He will then be immediately struck off the Strength of his Unit and a reinforcement demanded in the usual way.

8. Officers who are wounded, but who rejoin within a few days should be reported in the Return as follows:-
"Capt."B" (Unit) reported wounded 2/3/18 in List No ... rejoined on 8/3/18."

9. Besides reporting Casualties to this Office Casualties occurring in Labour Companies will be reported by the Company concerned direct to Corps by Wire who will report them to Fifth Army "A" as Corps Troops in their Daily Casualty Wire.

10. Casualties occurring amongst Military Police will be reported by the A.P.M. to D.H.Q. in the usual manner. This information with the added detail of Number Rank and Name and whether M.F.P. or M.M.P. will be wired by the A.P.M. to the P.M. FIFTH ARMY and repeated to Corps. This is in no way to affect the weekly reporting of Casualties at present in vogue in the Provost Branch
(A.R.O. 1706 of 17/9/17.)

11. Reports of Deaths from Wounds or injuries in Base Hospitals or Casualty Clearing Stations will not be included in the Daily Casualty Wires.
Deaths, which, however, occur in the Regimental Dressing Stations or Field Ambulances will be notified in the Daily Casualty wires sent by Units. Os C. Field Ambulances are responsible that all such deaths are reported to the Units concerned at the earliest possible moment.

/C.

4.

C. ACCURATE DAILY RETURN.

1. All Units and Formations will render through the usual Channels an Accurate Daily Casualty Return, on Pro forma A (Issued with A/11 of 6/6/18.

2. This Return will be made up to 12 noon for the preceding 24 hours and will be rendered so as to reach this Office by 7.30pm each day.

3. This Return will confirm the Daily Wire and will give any further particulars not included in the Wire.

4. When a man is evacuated to the Field Ambulance as a result of Gas and classified under (N.Y.D.Gas) Units will not report this in the Daily Reports. The Medical Authorities will send intimation to the Unit as soon as the case has been diagnosed as "Wounded Gas". On receipt of such intimation the Unit will include the casualty in the Casualty Report of that day and at the same time give the date on which he was originally evacuated to the Field Ambulance, e.g., what might appear in the Daily Return on 4/8/18 is "Wounded(Gas) on 2/8/18".

D. WEEKLY RETURN OF MISSING.

1. Units and Formations will render a Weekly Return of Missing made up to 12 noon on Saturdays to reach this Office by 6 pm Saturdays.

2. This Return will show under Column "A" the total number of Missing of all arms. Under Column "B" the total numbers included in the Missing Column "A" that are thought to have been taken alive. Due allowance must be made for those who were previously reported Missing but who have since rejoined or whom it has been ascertained have been killed.

E. WEEKLY NOMINAL ROLLS OF OTHER RANK CASUALTIES.

No separate Nominal Rolls of Other Rank Casualties other than those sent on the weekly A.Fs B.213 are required. The utmost endeavour will be made to ensure that these Nominal Rolls are carefully and accurately compiled.

METHOD OF REPORTING ESTIMATED CASUALTIES WHEN HEAVY FIGHTING IS IN PROGRESS.

This applies only to Infantry(including Pioneer) Bns. and Machine Gun Bns. and Coys. Copies of Circular Memorandum No. A.G.214 (O) giving full instructions in the matter have been circulated to all concerned.

Owens

15/8/18.
Lieut.-Colonel.
A.A. & Q.M.G. 74th (Yeomanry) Division.

Copies to:-

229 Bde.	C.R.E.	A.P.M.	Div.M.T.Coy.	"G"
230 Bde.	A.D.M.S.	Div.M.G.Bn.	Div.Emp.Coy.	File
231 Bde	D.A.D.V.S.	Div.Sigs.	Div.Recp.Camp.	Diary.
C.R.A.	D.A.D.O.S.	Div.Train.	C.Commdt.	

P.T.O.

G.R.O. 38 as amended by G.R.O. 4693. APPENDIX 1.

CASUALTIES REPORTING OF.
G.R.O. 2485 is cancelled and the following Instructions will be observed when reporting Casualties:-
(1) All Casualties caused by enemy weapons in use at the time as such and all casualties caused by British or Allied Weapons which are in action against the enemy will be reported as "Battle Casualties".

(2) The word "Weapon" will be held to include Lethal Gas, Mustard Gas, Liquid Fire, High-tension currents, and enemy barbed wire, as well as all other instruments used in Fighting.

(3) In reporting "Battle Casualties" the terms "Killed in action", "Died of Wounds", "Wounded", "Wounded (at duty)" or "Missing" only will be used except in the case of Lethal or Mustard Gas casualties where the special nature of the casualty will be indicated thus:-
" Killed in action (Gas)"
" Wounded (Gas)"
(4) The report "Wounded (Gas)" will only be made in accordance with G.R.Os 3127 and 3128.

(5) In cases where it is considered desirable to enquire into the conduct of an Officer or man who is believed to have been taken prisoner by the enemy, and a Court of Enquiry is held for that purpose, the casualty will be reported as "Missing, believed Prisoner of War (Court of Enquiry Case)".
See para 2 (b) S.S.617, issued with G.R.O. 2884.
(6) A Casualty from Mine Gas poisoning sustained by an Officer or Man in the course of his duty and which is not due in any way to neglect or disobedience of orders, will be reported as a "Battle Casualty".
(7) A Casualty arising from any other injury will be reported simply as "Injured", "Died of injuries", or "Killed acc." (in the case of immediate death from injury). When, however, the injury is self-inflicted it will in the first instance be reported as "Injured S.I." "Died of Injuries S.I." or "Killed S.I." (in the case of immediate death from self inflicted injury), until the case has been investigated and Army Form W 3428 completed, when the injury will be definitely classified as "Wilful", "Negligent", "Without Negligence" or "Accidental" as the case may be.
(8) When an Officer or Other Rank who is both "Wounded and Missing" and has been previously reported (1) Missing, (2) Wounded, the second notification should read:-
(1) Wounded and Missing, previously reported missing.
(2) Wounded and Missing, previously reported wounded.
In the case where an Officer or Other Rank is reported "Wounded and Missing" and it is desired to correct the report, then it must be clearly shewn whether it is desired to correct the report of Wounded as well as Missing thus:-
(1) Cancel report of Wounded & Missing, now reported Wounded.
(2) Cancel report both of Wounded and Missing.
(9) All Casualties above mentioned, including injuries, will be reported by Formations in the Daily Casualty Wire to Headquarters of Armies and L.of C.Area, in precisely the same manner as Battle Casualties have been in the past. Headquarters of Armies & L.of C. Area will include in their Daily Lists to 1st and 3rd Echelons Casualties classified as "Injuries" in the same form as Battle Casualties

SECRET.

XI Corps Q.M. 23
Copy No. 4

XI Corps Administrative Instructions
reference XI Corps Order No. 390 dated 25.8.18. (Relief of 74th Division by 59th Division).

1. The administrative arrangements as now organised by 74th Division will be continued by 59th Division.

2. 59th Division will put corresponding Units into billets as previously occupied by 74th Division.

3. Supply Railheads will remain as at present; change will be notified later.

4. All trench, area and R.E. stores (including tip carts and pontoons in excess of Mob. equipment) will be handed over, receipts being given and taken. List of Special Area Stores is attached.

5. All tents and shelters in excess of those authorised on the Mobilization Equipment of Units will be handed over. Divisions to report to Corps Headquarters the numbers handed over and taken over.

6. 74th Division will hand over the Corps Administrative Table complete to 59th Division. All Corps and attached Troops now administered by 74th Division will be taken over by 59th Division, details to be arranged between Divisions.

7. All institutions, baths, etc. complete with all furniture, accessories, etc. will be handed over, including stock of clothing at Baths.

8. All transport details for the Corps now found by 74th Division will be taken over by 59th Division, details to be arranged between Divisions.

9. All ammunition echelons will move full.

10. 74th Division will settle their account with Corps Clothing Exchange prior to leaving the Corps Area.

11. The 74th Divisional Agricultural Officer will remain in the area until the harvest has been completed.
    All personnel of 74th Division employed on harvesting will remain at work until relieved by personnel of 59th Division. Work must not be allowed to lapse.

12. 59th Division will report in due course if the taking over has been satisfactorily completed.

13. Acknowledge.

Lieut. Colonel,
A.Q.M.G. XI Corps.

XI Corps,
R 25. 8.18.

Distribution:-

Nos. 1 - 5 74th Division.
6 - 10 59th Division.
11 G.S.
12 - 13 G.O.C. R.A.
14 C.E.
15 AQ.
16 S.L.
17 A.D.O

No.18. D.D.M.S.
19. A.D.V.S.
20. "Shells"
21. A.P.M.
22. Labour Comdt.
23. Corps Agric. Offr.
24. Forward A. Cmdt.
25. Back Area Cmdt.
26. Camp Cmdt. LA JAUQUE
27. O.i/c Corps Laundry.
28. Fifth Army Q.

List of Special stores to be handed over by 74th Division.

GLOVES Leather 20 pairs.)   To be returned to O.O.C.T.
        Cotton   40 pairs.)   Corps Stores under G.R.O.4475.

PACKSADDLERY G.S.   60 sets.

BOOTS GUM THIGH.   prs. 24 for C.R.E. 74th Divn. To be returned
                                                  to O.O.C.T.

SERVICE DRESS CLOTHING. for exchange of clothing gassed.
        Any remaining from this issue to be returned to O.O.C.T.
            Jackets 500.   Trousers 500.   Puttees 500.

ANTI-GAS CLOTHING.

	Suits Combination.	Suits Anti-gas.	
		Coats Long.	Trousers.
	200	40	40
	200	100	100
	400	200	200
Total.	800	340	340

All CHAFF CUTTERS, STOVES FOYERS, YUKON PACKS, and
TARPAULINS which belong to the Corps area will be handed over.

GRENADE DISCHARGERS.   To be returned under G.R.O. 4781.

SECRET.   Copy No. 3......

ADMINISTRATIVE INSTRUCTIONS RELATIVE TO
74th DIVISION ORDER No. 79.   C.Q. 420/1

DIVISIONAL RECEPTION CAMP.

Reference 1/40,000 Map 36A.

1. **MOVE OF PERSONNEL.** The Staff of the Reception Camp will join the 230th Infantry Brigade Group at ST HILAIRE on 27th. Attached is a statement of the numbers in the Reception Camp by Units.

2. **AREA STORES.** All Area, and R.E. Stores together with all Tents and shelters will be handed over to the 59th Division. O.C. Reception Camp will obtain receipts for all stores handed over and forward complete lists to this office.

3. **SUPPLIES.** All Details, "B" Teams and Reception Camp Staff will carry rations for 27th and 28th when reporting. Rations for 29th for "B" Teams and Details will be drawn by their respective Units, and by a Unit of the 230th Infantry Brigade for the Reception Camp Staff. 230th Infantry Brigade will detail the Unit to which the Staff will be attached for rations, accommodation, and transport including entrainment. All Rum held by the Reception Camp will be handed over to the 59th Division and receipts forwarded to this office by O.C. Reception Camp.

4. **TRANSPORT.** Motor Lorries for conveyance of Blankets and Officer's Kits will report at the Divisional Reception Camp at 1.p.m. on 27th and will be distributed as follows :-

   229th Inf.Brigade "B" Teams and Details.   2 Lorries.
   231st Inf.Brigade "B" Teams and Details.   2 Lorries.
   Reception Camp Staff and other Details.   1 Lorry.

5. **ACKNOWLEDGE.**

Headquarters,   Lieut-Colonel
26th August 1918.   A.A. & Q.M.G.
                                                 74th (Yeo) Division.
Issued at ...... p.m.

Copies to :-
   No. 1 "G"   9. A.D.M.S.
      2. File.   10. D.A.D.O.S.
      3. War Diary.   11. D.A.P.M.
      4. 229th Inf.Bde.   12. Baths Officer.
      5. 230th Inf.Bde.   13. 59th Division.
      6. 231st Inf.Bde.   14. Divl.Train.
      7. C.R.A.   15. Div.Signals.
      8. C.R.E.
                         P.T.O

74th DIVISIONAL RECEPTION CAMP.

Detailed statement by Units of "B" Teams and Reinforcements.

UNIT.	"B" TEAMS.		REINFORCEMENTS.		Remarks.
	Offs.	O.R.s	Offs.	O.R.s	
16th Devons.	2	51	-	3.	
14th Bn. B.H.	3	74	-	1.	
12th Bn. Somerset L.I.	2	118	1	9.	
10th Bn.K.S.L.I.	4	114	-	2.	
24th Bn.Welsh Regt.	5	89	-	23	
25th Bn. R.W.F.	1	81	-	7.	
10th Bn. Bn.Fus.	-	-	-	44 *	* Includes 16 men Isolated.
15th Suffolks.	-	-	-	30	
16th Sussex.	-	-	-	18.**	**Includes 3 men Isolated.
74th Div.Train.	-	-	-	5	
74th M.G.Bn.	-	-	-	15	
R.A.P.D.	-	-	-	18.	
2/42nd B.N.Lancs.	-	-	-	2	+ Posted to 14th Bn.R.W.F. Brig. Bomber.
117th Bde. R.F.A.	-	-	-	1	
44th Bde. R.F.A.	-	-	-	2	
230th Bde.Signals.	-	-	-	2	
261st Fld. Amb.	-	-	-	5.	
985 Div. Employ.Coy.	-	-	1+	-	
R.C.Chaplain.	-	-	2	13 %	%Includes 1 Q.M.S. and 2 Batmen.
Recept. Camp Staff.					
TOTALS.	17	527	4	202.	

Appendix VII

MOVE OF 74th DIVISION with ARTILLERY.

Courant N. 211

FIRST AREA
Entraining Stations:-
LILLERS
BERGUETTE
AIRE

FOURTH ARMY
Detraining Stations:
HEILLY
CORBIE
MERICOURT L'ABBE.

Trn. No.	LILLERS	Mche	Date & Dep. Time	Trn. No.	BERGUETTE	Mche	Date & Dep. Time	Trn. No.	AIRE	Mche	Date & Dep. Time
1	230th Bde. H.Q. Bde. Sig. Sect. Bde.T.M.Bty.(Light) 230th Fld.Ambce. 1 Co.Cooker & teams of 10th E.Kent Rgt.	HT 72	28* 22.41	2	229th Bde. H.Q. Bde. Sig. Sect. Bde.T.M.Bty.(Light) 229th Fld.Ambce. 1 Co.Cooker & teams of 14th R.Highrs.	HT 73	28* 23.30	3	231st Bde. H.Q. Bde. Sig. Sect. Bde.T.M.Bty.(Light) 439th Fld.Co. R.E. 1 Co.Cooker & teams of 25th R.W.F.	HT 74	28* 24.00
4	10th E.Kent Rgt. less 1 Co.Cooker & teams		29th	5	14th R.Highrs. less 1 Co.Cooker & teams		29th	6	25th R.W.F. less 1 Co. Cooker & teams		29th
7	15th Suffolk Rgt. less 1 Co.Cooker & teams		29th	8	12th Somerset L.I. less 1 Co.Cooker & teams		29th	9	24th Welsh Rgt. less 1 Co.Cooker & teams		29th
10	16th R.Sussex Rgt. less 1 Co.Cooker & teams		29th	11	16th Devon Rgt. less 1 Co.Cooker & teams		29th	12	10th Shrops.L.I. less 1 Co.Cooker & teams		29th
13	Div. H.Q. (less Employmnt Coy.) H.Q.& No.1 Sec.Sigs.	HT 60	29th 10.41	14	H.Q. M.G. Bn. "A" & "B" Coys.M.G.Bn.	HT 61	29th 11.30	15	12th N.Lancs.Rgt. (Pioneers)	HT 62	29th 12.30
16	H.Q. R.E. No.5 Fld.Co.Roy Monmouth R.E.	HT63	29th 13-41	17	"C" & "D" Coys.M.G.Bn.		29th 14-30	18	231st Fld.Ambce. No.4 Co. Div. Train. 1 Co.Cooker & teams of 24th Welsh Rgt.	HT65	29th 15-00
19	No.3 C4. Div. Train 1 Co.Cooker & teams of 15th Suffolk Rgt.	HT66	29th 16-41	20	No.5 Fld.Coy. Royal Anglesey R.E. No.2 Co. Div. Train 1 Co.Cooker & teams of 12th Somerset L.I.	HT67	29th 17-30	21	985th Employmt.Co. H.Q. Div. Train 59th Mob. Vet. Sect. 1 Co.Cooker & teams of 10th Shrops.L.I.	HT70	29th 18-00
22	½ S.A.A.Sect. 1 Co.Cooker & teams of 16th R.Sussex Rgt.	HT69	29th 19-41	23	½ S.A.A.Sect. 1 Co.Cooker & teams of 16th Devon. Rgt.	HT70	29th 20-30	24	Bde. H.Q. (474) No.1 Sec. D.A.C. less 4 G.S.16 limbd.ammun. wgns.& teams "X" T.M.Btty.	HT71	29th 21-00
25	"A" Battery 1 G.S. 4 limbd.ammun. wgns.& teams of No.2 Sec. D.A.C.										

(2)

Trn. No.	LILLERS	Mche	Date & Dep Time	Trn. No.	BERGUETTE	Mche	Date & Dep Time	Trn No.	AIRE	Mche	Date & Dep. Time
25	"B" Battery 1 G.S. 4 limbd.ammun. wgns.& teams of No.2 Sec. D.A.C.	HT72	29th 22-41	26	"A" Battery 1 G.S. 4 limbd.ammun. wgns.& teams of No.1 Sec. D.A.C.	HT73	29th 23-30	27	Bde. H.Q.(117£) No.2 Sec.D.A.C.less 4 G.S.16 limbd.ammun. wgns.& teams "Y" T.M.Batty.	HT74	29th 24-00
28	"C" Battery 1 G.S. 4 limbd.ammun. wgns.& teams of No.2 Sec. D.A.C.	HT51	30th 1-41	29	"B" Battery 1 G.S. 4 limbd.ammun. wgns.& teams of No.1 Sec. D.A.C.	HT52	30th 2-30	30	H.Q. R.A. H.Q. D.A.C. H.Q.Co.Div.Train.	HT53	30th 3-00
31	"D" Battery 1 G.S. 4 limbd.ammun. wgns.& teams of No.2 Sec. D.A.C.	HT53	30th 4-41	32	"C" Battery 1 G.S. 4 limbd.ammun. wgns.& teams of No.1 Sec. D.A.C.	HT55	30th 5-30	33	"D" Battery 1 G.S. 4 limbd.ammun. wgns.& teams of No.1 Sec. D.A.C.	HT56	30th 6-00

Composition of trains:- 1 Coach, 30 Covereds, 17 Flats.
Transport to be at station 3 hours before departure of train, personnel 1 hour.

C. Ashmley
Major,
Traffic Officer.

SACHIN,
26/8/18. Copies to:- D.D.R.T.(F). 5. Q.M.G.,G.H.Q. 1. Fifth Army Q. 3. Fourth Army Q. 1.
A.D.G.T.(5) 1. A.D.G.T.(4) 1. XI Corps 2. 74th Div. 6. Traffic,LONGPRE 4.
R.T.O=LILLERS,HERGUETTE,AIRE,AIRE DISTRICT 1 each. O.C.,R.O.D.,BURBURE 5.
O.C.,R.O.D. 1. O.C.,R.O.D.,AIRE 3. O.C.,R.O.D.,DOULLENS 1. M.Plot 2.
Capt.Hartopp,C.R.N.,4. Capt.MacBeth,C.R.,ROKESCAMPS 3.

SECRET.

Appendix VIII (handwritten: "8 am all three dumps")

Copy No. 48

ADMINISTRATIVE INSTRUCTIONS RELATIVE TO
74th DIVISION ORDER No 79.

CQ 420/3

27th August 1918.

Reference Map 1/40,000 Map 36A.

1. **STANDING ORDERS.** Attention is directed to Divisional Standing Orders for Entrainment and Detrainment. The last para (No 11.) of which is hereby cancelled. Particular attention is directed to paras 3 re handing of Entraining States to R.T.O.

2. **LOADING & OFF-LOADING PARTIES.** Each Infantry Brigade will detail one Company to load all Trains, and one Company to off-load all Trains. Off-loading Companies will proceed on Trains 1, 2 & 3. and loading Companies will proceed on Trains 20, 21, and 22.

3. **DIVISIONAL ENTRAINMENT OFFICERS.** The following Officers are appointed Divisional Entrainment Officers at the Stations mentioned:-

   Captain H.A. BLUNT Sussex Yeomanry at BERGUETTE.
   Captain R.G. SEYMOUR R.North Devon Hussars at AIRE
   Lieut. H. BROWN, Sussex Yeomanry at LILLERS.

   These Officers will be in charge of the Entrainment at the Stations mentioned and will assist the R.T.O., wire the state of Entrainment in accordance with G.R.O. No 4743 dated 11/4/18 and ensure that standing orders are carried out.

4. **ADVANCE PARTIES.** Advance Parties composed as under will proceed on trains No 1, 2, 3.

	TOTAL.	
	Offs.	O.Rs
Divisional Headquarters- D.A.D.M.S. D.A.P.M., C.Commdt 4 Police, 4 Batmen	3	8
Each Inf.Bde.H.Q. Staff Captain & Batman,	1	1
Each Inf.Bn. M.G. & Pioneer Bn. 1 Off. 4 CQMS and 1 rep. of Bn. P.Q and 1 Batman.	1	6
Each Field Co. R.E., F.Amb., 1 Off. 1 Sergt., 1 Batman and Div.Signals.	1	2
74th Div.Train. 4 Supply Officers 4 NCOs & 4 Batmen	4	8

   1 Bicycle will be taken by each Officer
   Total Party - 28 Officers, 99 O/Rs. and 28 Bicycles.

5. **DETRAINING OFFICERS.** The O.C. the offloading Coys. will act under the A/D.A.A.G. as Divisional Detraining Officers and wire the state of Detrainment in accordance with G.R.O's 4743 dated 11/6/18. Brigades will on receipt of these instructions wire names and Units of O.'s C. these Companies.

6. **ENTRAINMENT.** Units will entrain in accordance with attached schedules. B.C's C. Infantry Brigade Groups will be responsible for issuing orders for the entrainment of their Groups, as detailed in attached schedules.

7. **SUPPLY AND BAGGAGE WAGONS.** Supply and Baggage Wagons of the Divisional Train will be entrained with the Units to which they are affiliated.

P.T.O.

8. **SUPPLIES.** Refilling Points on 28th inst will be as follows:-

229th Infantry Bde.Group,including S.A.A.
Section Divnl.Ammunition Column. — HAM EN ARTOIS at 2 p.m.
250th Infantry Bde.Group.including S.A.A.
Section Divl.Ammunition Column. — ST HILAIRE at 2 p.m.
231st Infantry Bde.Group. — — TREIZIENNES at 2 p.m.
Divnl.Artillery less S.A.A. Section D.A.C. at FONTES at 7 a.m.&
4 p.m.

Refilling Point on 29th inst, for Divl.Artillery only at FONTES at 2pm.
The Division less Artillery will carry rations for consumption 29th inst, on the man and for 30th inst, except as undernoted, on the Supply Wagons.
Units entraining after 12.00 a.m. on 29th will carry breakfast for 30th inst on the man.
The Divisional Artillery less S.A.A. Section D.A.C. will carry rations for 30th on the man and for 31st inst on the Supply Wagons.

9. **MOTOR TRANSPORT.** Motor Lorries are allotted on the following Scale :-

No. of Lorries.	To whom to report.	Location.	Hour	Date.
7	H.Q. 229 Brigade.	HAM EN ARTOIS.	2 p.m.	28th.inst.
8	H.Q. 250th "	ST HILAIRE.	2 p.m.	28th. "
7.	H.Q. 251st "	LAMBRES	2 p.m.	28th. "
7.	Divl.Headquarters.	NORRENT FONTES.	2 p.m.	28th. "
11.	Headquarters R.A.	NORRENT FONTES.	2 P.m.	29th. "

B.G's Commanding Divnl.Artillery and Infantry Brigade Groups will issue the necessary instructions regarding the move of the Lorries allotted to the Units in their respective Groups to the new area.

10. **DETRAINMENT.**
Units entraining at LILLERS will detrain at HEILLY.
Units entraining at BERGUETTE " detrain at CORBIE.
Units entraining at AIRE will detrain at HERICOURT L'ABBE.

11. **ACKNOWLEDGE.**

Cousens
Lieut-Colonel
A.A. & Q.M.G.
74th (Yeo) Division.

Issued at 4 p.m.

Copies to :- No. 1. G.O.C.
2-3 . File.
4. 229 Bde.
5. 250 Bde.
6. 231 Bde.
7. 74th M.G.Bn.
8. C.R.A.
9. C.R.E.
10. O.C.Train.
11. O.C.Signals.
12. A.D.M.S.
13. D.A.D.V.S.
14. D.A.D.O.S.
15. D.A.P.M.
16. C.Comdt.
17. Salvage Off.
18. S.C.F.
19. Baths Off.
20. O.C.Emp.Coy.
21. O.C.M.T.Coy.
22. XI Corps.
23. 59th Divn.
24. R.T.O.LILLERS.
25. R.T.O.BERGUETTE.
26. R.T.O. AIRE.
27. R.T.O. HEILLY.
28. R.T.O.CORBIE.
29. HERICOURT L'ABBE.
30. Traffic PENNES.
31. Fourth Army.
32-34 Div.Entrain. Officers.
35-37 Div.Detrain. Officers.
38. Diary.
39-41 "G"
42-50. Spare.

DISTRIBUTION OF MOTOR LORRIES.

C.Q. 420/3/1

Reference this office C.Q. 420/3 Administrative Instructions relative to 74th Division Order No.70, the following is the distribution of Motor Lorries :-

Divl.H.Q. (including Employ.Coy)			6.
Gas Services.			1.
Headquarters R.A.			1.
Each Arty.Brigade.	2	=	4.
Each M.T.M.Battery.	3.	=	6.
Each Inf.Bde.H.Q.	1	=	3.
Each L.T.M.B.	1	=	3.
Each Inf.Battn.	1	=	9.
M.G.Battn.			1.
Pioneer Battn.			1.
Each Field Amb.	1	=	3.
	TOTAL =		38.

Sourens
Lieut-Colonel.
A.A. & Q.M.G.
74th (Yeo) Division.

Copies to :-

No. 1.	G.O.C.	15.	D.A.P.M.	28.	R.T.O.CORBIE.
2-3.	File.	16.	C.Comdt.	29.	R.T.O.MERICOURT
4.	229 Bde.	17.	Salvage Off.		L'ABBE.
5.	230 Bde.	18.	S.C.F.	30.	Traffic PERNES.
6.	231 Bde.	19.	Baths Officer.	31.	Fourth Army.
7.	74th M.G.Bn.	20.	O.C. Emp.Coy.	32.-34	Div.Entrain.
8.	C.R.A.	21.	O.C. M.T.Coy.		Officers.
9.	C.R.E.	22.	XI Corps.	35-37.	Div.Detrain.
10.	O.C.Train.	23.	59th Divn.		Officers.
11.	O.C. Signals.	24.	R.T.O.LILLERS.	38.	Diary.
12.	A.D.M.S.	25.	R.T.O. BERGUETTE.	39-40	"G"
13.	D.A.D.V.S.	26.	R.T.O. AIRE.	42-50	Spare.
14.	D.A.D.O.S.	27.	R.T.O. HEILLY.		

229th INFANTRY BRIGADE GROUP

ENTRAINING STATION – BERGUETTE.

Train No.	Marche.	Hour of Depart.	Date.	Contents.
2	H.T. 73	23.30.	28/8/18.	229th Bde.H.Q. 229th L.T.M.B. 229th Sig. Section 229th F.Amb. 1 Coy., Cooker and Team of 14th Bn. R.H. Advce.Party of 229th Bde.Group.
5.	H.T. 52.	2.30.	29/8/18.	14th Bn.R.H., less 1 Coy., Cooker and Team.
8.	H.T.55	5.30	29/8/18.	12th Bn.Somerset L.I. less 1 Coy., Cooker and Team.
11.	H.T. 58	8.30	29/8/18.	16th Bn.Devon Regt. less 1 Coy., Cooker and Team.
14.	H.T.61	11.30	29/8/18.	74th M.G.Bn.H.Q. and 2 Coys.
17.	H.T.64	14.30	29/8/18.	2 Coys.74th M.G.Battn.
20.	H.T.67	17.30	29/8/18.	439th Fld.Coy.R.E. 448th Coy. Div.Train. 1 Coy., Cooker & Team of 12th Bn.Somerset L.I.
23.	H.T.70.	20.30.	29/8/18.	½ S.A.A. Section 74th D.A.C. 1 Coy., Cooker and Team of 16th Bn.Devon Regt.

Composition of Trains :- 1 Coach. 30 Covereds. 17 Flats.
Transport to be at Station 3 hours before departure of train, personnel 1 hour.

230th INFANTRY BRIGADE GROUP.

ENTRAINING STATION - LILLERS.

Train No.	Marche.	Hour of Depart.	Date:	Contents.
1	H.T. 72	22.41	28/8/18.	230th Bde.H.Q. 230th Signal Sec. 230th L.T.M.B. 230th F.Amb. 1 Coy., Cooker & Team of 10th Bn. E.Kent.Regt. Advce Party 230th Bde.Group, D.H.Q. and Signals.
4.	H.T. 51	1.41	29/8/18.	10th Bn.E.Kent Regt, less 1 Coy., Cooker and Team.
7.	H.T. 54	4.41	29/8/18.	15th Bn.Suffolk Regt less 1 Coy., Cooker and Team.
10.	H.T. 57	7.41	29/8/18.	16th Bn.Sussex Regt.less 1 Coy., Cooker and Team.
13.	H.T. 60	10.41	29/8/18.	74th Div.H.Q.,H.Q. Emp.Coy. H.Q. & No.1 Sec.Div.Signals. Headquarters R.E.
16.	H.T. 63	13.41	29/8/18.	5th Fld.Coy.R.M.R.E. 449th Coy.Div.Train. 1Coy., Cooker & Team.of.15th Bn.Suffolk Regt.
19.	H.T. 66	16.41	29/8/18.	½ S.A.A. Sect.74th D.A.C. 1 Coy., Cooker and Team of 16th Bn.Sussex Regt.

Composition of Trains :- 1 Coach. 30 Covereds. 17 Flats.
Transport to be at Station 3 hours before departure of train, personnel 1 hour.

231st INFANTRY BRIGADE GROUP.
ENTRAINING STATION AIRE.

Train No.	Marche	Depart.	Date.	Contents.
3	H.T. 74	24.00	28th.	231st Bde. H.Q. 231st Sig.Sect. 231st L.T.M.B., 5th F.Co.R.A.R.E. 1 Coy., Cooker & Team of 25th Bn. R.W.F.. Adv. Party 231st Inf.Bde.Group.
6.	H.T. 53	3.00	29th.	25th Bn.R.W.F. less 1 Coy., Cooker & Team.
9.	H.T.56.	6.00	29th.	24th Bn.Welsh Regt.less 1 Coy., Cooker and Team.
12.	H.T.59.	9.00	29th.	10th Bn.K.Shropshire.L.I. less 1 Coy., cooker and Team.
15.	H.T.32.	12.00	29th.	1/12th L.N.Lancs. (Pioneers.)
18.	H.T.65.	15.00	29th.	231st Fld.Amb. 450th Coy.Div.Train. 1 Coy., Cooker and Team of 24th Bn. Welsh Regt.
21	H.T. 70.	18.00	29th.	H.Q. Divl.Train. 59th Mob.Vety.Section. 1 Coy., Cooker and Team of 10th Bn.K. Shropshire L.I.

Composition of Trains :- 1 Coach. 30 Covereds. 17 Flats.
Transport to be at Station 3 hours before departure of Train, personnel 1 hour.

DIVISIONAL ARTILLERY.

ENTRAINING STATION - LILLERS.

Train No.	Marche.	Date and Time of depart.	Contents.
22	H.T.69	29th. 19.41.	"A" Battery. 44th Bde. R.F.A. and teams 1 G.S. & 4 Limb. Amm. Wagons of No.2 Section D.A.C.
25.	H.T.72.	29th. 22.41.	"B" Battery 44th Bde. R.F.A. 1 G.S. 4 Limb. Amm. Wagons and teams of No.2 Sec. D.A.C.
28.	H.T.51.	30th. 1.41.	"C" Battery 44th Bde. R.F.A. 1 G.S. 4 Limb. Amm. Wagons and Teams of No.2 Sec. D.A.C.
31	H.T.53.	30th. 4.41	"D" Battery. 44th Bde. R.F.A. 1 G.S. 4 Limb. amm. wagons and teams of No.2 Sec. D.A.C.

ENTRAINING STATION - BERGUETTE.

Train No.	Marche.	Date & Time of Depart.	Contents.
26	H.T.50. H.T.73.	29th. 30.30. 29th. 23.30.	"A" Battery 117th Bde. R.F.A. 1 G.S. 4.Limb. Amm. Wagons & Teams of No.1 Sec. D.A.C.
29.	H.T.52.	30th. 2.30	"B" Battery. 117th Bde. R.F.A. 1 G.S. 4 Limb. Amm. Wagons and Teams of No.1 Section D.A.C.
32.	H.T.55	30th. 5.30.	"C" Battery. 117th Bde. R.F.A. 1 G.S. 4 Limb. Amm. Wagons & Teams of No.1 Section D.A.C.

ENTRAINING STATION - AIRE.

Train No.	Marche.	Date & Time of depart.	Contents.
24	H.T.71	29th. 21.00	44th Bde. R.F.A. H.Q. No.1 Sect. D.A.C. less 4 G.S. 16 Limb. Amm. Wagons & Teams. "X" T.M. Battery.
27	H.T.74.	29th. 24.00.	117th Bde. H.Q. No.2 Sec. D.A.C. less 4 G.S. 16 Limb. amm. Wagons & Teams "Y" T.M. Battery.
30.	H.T.53.	30th. 3.00.	H.Q. R.A. H.Q. D.A.C. 447 Coy. Div. Train.
33.	H.T.56.	30th. 6.00	"D" Battery. 117th Bde. R.F.A. 1 G.S. 4 Limb. amm. Wagons and Teams of No.1 Sec. D.A.C.

Composition of Trains :- 1 Coach. 30 Covereds. 17 Flats.
Transport to be at Station 3 hours before departure of train., personnel 1 hour.

DISTRIBUTION OF MOTOR LORRIES.

O.Q. 420/3/1

Reference this office O.Q. 420/3 Administrative Instructions relative to 74th Division Order No.70, the following is the distribution of Motor Lorries :-

Divl.H.Q. (including Employ.Coy)			6.
Gas Services.			1.
Headquarters R.A.			1.
Each Arty.Brigade.	2	=	4.
Each M.T.M.Battery.	2.	=	6.
Each Inf.Bde.H.Q.	1	=	3.
Each L.T.M.B.	1	=	3.
Each Inf.Battn.	1	=	9.
M.G.Battn.			1.
Pioneer Battn.			1.
Each Field Amb.	1	=	3.
		TOTAL =	38.

(signed) B. Surens
Lieut-Colonel.
A.A. & Q.M.G.
74th (Yoo) Division.

Issued at 4 p.m,

Copies to :-

No.1.	G.O.C.	15.	D.A.P.M.	28.	R.T.O.CORBIE.
2-3.	File.	16.	O.Condt.	29.	R.T.O.MERICOURT L'ABBE.
4.	229 Bde.	17.	Salvage Off.		
5.	230 Bde.	18.	S.C.F.	30.	Traffic PERNES.
6.	231 Bde.	19.	Baths Officer.	31.	Fourth Army.
7.	74th M.G.Bn.	20.	O.C. Emp.Coy.	32.-34	Div.Entrain. Officers.
8.	C.R.A.	21.	O.C. M.T.Coy.		
9.	C.R.E.	22.	XI Corps.	35-37.	Div.Detrain. Officers.
10.	O.C.Train.	23.	59th Divn.		
11.	O.C. Signals.	24.	R.T.O.LILLERS.	38.	Diary.
12.	A.D.M.S.	25.	R.T.O. BERGUETTE.	39-40	"G"
13.	D.A.D.V.S.	26.	R.T.O. AIRE.	42-50	Spare.
14.	D.A.D.O.S.	27.	R.T.O. HEILLY.		

Appendix IX

74th (Yeomanry) Division.

AUGUST SUMMARIES of RETURNS.

1. Total Casualties.

	Officers	Other Ranks
KILLED	3	95
WOUNDED	25	510
MISSING	3	81
DIED OF INJURIES	–	2
INJURED	–	7
	31	695

2. FIGHTING STRENGTH.

	Off.	O.R.
Aug 3rd.	248	7901
10th.	253	7636
17th.	253	7380
24th.	244	7110
31st.	255	7254

3. EFFECTIVE & RATION STRENGTH.

	Effective Strength.		Ration Strength.	
	Off.	O.R.	Off.	O.R.
Aug. 3rd.	637	14801	541	14452
10th	636	14727	562	14735
17th	644	14570	535	14199
24th	642	14227	531	13548
31st	640	14268	571	12980

4. PRISONERS TAKEN.

Unwounded.		Wounded.	
Off.	O.R.	Off.	O.R.
–	19	–	2

6/9/18

A & Q
74th Division
September
1918

War Diary
"A" & "Q" Branch
74th (Yeomanry) Division
From 1st to 30th September 1918.

VOLUME XIX.

WAR DIARY or INTELLIGENCE SUMMARY

Army Form C. 2118

Headquarters
¼ (Jat) Division
A & Q Branch September 1918

Place	Date	Hour	Summary of Events and Information	Remarks and references to Appendices
BEAUCOURT	1	11.00	Divisional Headquarters closed at BEAUCOURT CHATEAU at 11.00 and opened at same hour at H.36.b.6. by Rly. to attach in Q. not supplying 230 Inf Bde with Orders issued for 230 Inf Bde to attack in Q. not supplying 230 Inf Bde with 1 Bn. 1.4.7. for in advance. Orders for supply columns.	Appendix I
H.36.b.61 (HEM)	2		Water ano brought forward by Motor Lorry to Cauley at A.19.b.31, A.24.c.0.0.& H.3.a.28 Sheet 62c. 1/40,000 (map) Instructions for water supply on 3 notices Instructions issued for each Bde. carrying 98 Point-Cans a water point for forward Bdes established at H.12.c.14 Instructions forwarded Bdes established at H.4. not the Refilling Point Count to Sheet that this was necessary to take back the Refilling point Count of Chebut	Appendix II Appendix III Appendix IV Appendix V
"	3		Refilling Point established at H.5.d central Sheet 62c 1/40,000	
"	6		Div H.Q. opened at J.10.b central Sheet 62c 1/40,000	
J.10.b central (HAUT ALLAINES)	7		Water Carts erected TEMPLEUX LA FOSSE for personal Animals watered from HAUT ALLAINES and COLOGNE RIVER at TINCOURT	
"	8		Refilling point moved to TEMPLEUX LA FOSSE Water being developed at J.3.a.11 and E.13.a central	
"	9		Watering arrangements Personnel from motor from water at LONGAVESNES for Animals guard and support Bde Reserve Bde & R.A. at TEMPLEUX LA FOSSE Horses at LIERMONT for armour Bde. K.15.d.8.8 for support R.F.A. Bde. Reserve Bde & D.A.C. at J.24.b.3.5. Remainder ¾ Division at HAUT ALLAINES Bois de BOIRC & outbuild	
D.H.Q. J.11.c.3.5	10		Divisional Headquarters moved to J.11.c.35	

W.J. Rickard, Major
A.A. & Q.M.G. ¼ (Jat) Divd

Army Form C. 2118.

WAR DIARY
or
INTELLIGENCE SUMMARY.
(Erase heading not required.)

Headquarters
74 (Yeo) Division
A.T.Q. (Branch)
September 1918.

Instructions regarding War Diaries and Intelligence Summaries are contained in F.S. Regs., Part II. and the Staff Manual respectively. Title pages will be prepared in manuscript.

Place	Date	Hour	Summary of Events and Information	Remarks and references to Appendices
J.H.Q. 35	15		Gestionne (Reviewed Change) & PERONNE (CHAPELETTE) STADIA Camp Linear leaving Guard.	Appendix VI
	16		Divisional Reception Camp moved to TEMPLEUX LA FOSSE. Orders received for Division to attack with a view to seizing a line affording good observation on the HINDENBURG LINE on the ground between Divisions ALL RIGHT and LEFT. ROISEL TEMPLEUX LE GUERARD all included. Two new arrangements made. Administrative instructions issued giving arrangements for carrying supplies etc.	Appendix VII
			B26 c 53 Supplies drawn from Rail Head by Divl Transport. Main Dressing Station established at BRIENCOURT J3 d 9.1 Advanced Dressing Station + Corps Post at LONGAVESNES E25 6.3.4 Advanced Collecting Station Car Post VILLERS FAUCON E26 a 9.5. Attack successfully carried at 18 officers 667 O.R. wounded & 110 wounded prisoners taken.	
	18		Engineer Dumps installed at VILLERS FAUCON & working by 12.00. Div RA H.Q. moved to VILLERS FAUCON + ROISEL Battery wagon lines forward at VILLERS FAUCON	
	20		Div Supply Rail Head moved to E29 b Advance Supply Dump + Animals watering at ROISEL + HAMEL	
	21		Division attacked & gained objectives on RIGHT but withdrew owing to no fire from LEFT. Orders received for relief of Division in the early 27 American Division on night 23/24.	
	23		Cst Post attached & relief completed 11.30 prisoners Orders issued for advance Divl H.Q. to Railway Farm E. Kennedy C.R.E. Cmg D30 D2/C30 Ordz Regs being left Capt all wounded ASC Staff Ordnance wpg remaining at duty.	Appendix IX

H G Rutherford Major
B G.S H.Q. 74 Div.

Army Form C. 2118.

WAR DIARY
or
INTELLIGENCE SUMMARY.
(Erase heading not required.)

Headquarters
7th (Ind) Division
Army Corps September 1918

Instructions regarding War Diaries and Intelligence Summaries are contained in F.S. Regs., Part II. and the Staff Manual respectively. Title pages will be prepared in manuscript.

Place	Date	Hour	Summary of Events and Information	Remarks and references to Appendices
J11c35	24		Orders issued for move of Division less RA to CORBIE area relieving 47th Divn Section.	Appendix X
	25		D.H.Q. closed at J11c47. Bois de BUIRE at 10am & opened at CORBIE at 11am. Staff officer advance to meet XIII Corps proceeds to FERFAY. Refilling point for Corps Supps CORBIE. MERICOURT & HEILLY. Orders issued for Division to move by rail & Lullers/CROQUES area detraining at BERGUETTE LILLERS/CROQUES.	
	26			Appendix XI
	27	8 A.M. 2 P.M.	Closed at CORBIE 10am & opened at NORRENT FONTES at 2pm.	Appendix XII
Norrent Fontes	28		Supply rail head changed to ALLOUAGNE. Personnel railhead CHOCQUES. Refilling points at BOURECQ, Y30A17, BURBURE.	Appendix XIII
	29		Orders issued for Divn to relieve 19 Division in the line commencing on 1st October. Communication received thanking 1st Division for the work done while the IV Army. Strength – The effective strength of the Division on 31st August was 640 Officers and 14,268 other ranks on 28 September 570 " 12042 "	Appendix XIV

Per Casualties received during the month 71 Officers and 1696 other ranks Wounded during the month Killed 32 off + 430 O/R Wounds 143 " + 1242/2 Missing 8 " 182 " Gas/Syph - 1 " 7 " Total Cas = 186 off + 3343 O/R

A.J. Bulcalph Major
7 R.R. Staff 7 (Inf) Divn
Casualties in action during...

Army Form C. 2118.

WAR DIARY
or
INTELLIGENCE SUMMARY.
(Erase heading not required.)

Troops 3rd
3rd (?) Division
1st of Front September 1918

Place	Date	Hour	Summary of Events and Information	Remarks and references to Appendices
NORRENT FONTES	30		Fighting Strength Infantry of the Division excluding M.G. Bn including Pioneers 31st August 1918. 253 Officers and 4234 OR. 1st September 1915. 275 with 2430 Officers 5143 OR. Letter received from Lt Gen R.H.K BUTLER. K.C.M.G, C.B, Commanding III Corps	Appendix XV

Signatures

SECRET. *War Diary September Appendix I* Copy No.........

C.Q. 437/2

ADMINISTRATIVE INSTRUCTIONS RELATIVE TO 74th DIVION ORDER No. 81.

Reference Map 1/40,000 Sheet 62c.   1st September 1918.

1. SUPPLIES.

Supplies for consumption on 2nd September have already been drawn by 231st Inf. Brigade Group, Div. Headquarters Group and Mobile Veterinary Section - those for the remainder of the Division will be drawn as follows :-

    229th Inf.Bde.Group from Refilling Point A 20b 5.9.) both at
)
    230th Inf.Bde.Group from Refilling Point A 20b 4.9.) 10 a.m.

   by Trains Supply Wagons. Supply Wagons to return to their respective Train Coys. after delivery of rations.

   Divisional Artillery. - from Refilling Point BONNAY at 8 a.m. by Supply Wagons. Supply Wagons will remain with their Train Coys. and march as a Supply Convoy under orders of the C.R.A. Representatives of Units will remain with their Supply Wagons and take them to their affiliated Units on arrival in the new area.

2. ORDERS.
B.G's C. Infantry Brigades will inform the Units comprising their respective Groups of the foregoing instructions.

Headquarters.

                                                               Lieut-Colonel
                                                               A.A. & Q.M.G.
                                                             74th (Yeo) Division.

Copies to ;- 229 Brigade.   C.R.A.
             230 Brigade.   War Diary.
             O.C. 74th Div. Train.

War Diary **September Appendix II**

Q.E. 26.

Headquarters
 229th Inf.Bde.   C.R.A.   O.C. 74th M.G.Bn.
 230th Inf.Bde.   C.R.E.   O.C. 74 Div.Signals.
 231st Inf. do.   A.D.M.S.   O.C. 74th Div.Train.
War Diary & File.   D.A.D.V.S.   Camp Commandant.
"G"

Reference Sheet 62c. Map 1/40,000

1. SUPPLIES.

Supplies for consumption on 3rd inst, will be drawn by Train Transport tomorrow 2nd inst from Refilling Point at A.20.b.5.9. as under :-

 229th Inf.Bde.Group   at 5-45 a.m.
 230th Inf.Bde.Group   at 6-15 a.m.
 231st Inf.Bde.Group   at   6-45 a.m.
 Div.Arty.Group   at 7-15 a.m.

Supply Wagons will be returned to the Train Coys. after the delivery of rations and forage.

2. WATER.

The following are the Water Points in this area :-

  Drinking Water.
  A.19.b.1.1.
  A.24.a.1.1.
  H.3.a.

  Horse Water.
  L.10 a.
  A.29 Central MOULIN DE FARGNY.
  H.9.a.4.6.

Headquarters,   Lieut-Colonel
1st September 1918.   A.A. & Q.M.G.
                74th (Yeo) Division.

War Diary Appendix III

Q.L. 27.

Headquarters
    229th Inf. Brigade.   C.R.A.   O.C. 74th M.G. Bn.
    230th Inf. Brigade.   C.R.E.   O.C. 74th Div. Signals.
    231st Inf. Brigade.   A.D.M.S.   O.C. 74th Div. Train.
Camp Commandant.   D.A.D.V.S.   "G"

---

1. Petrol Tins should be held by Battalions, L.T.M.B's and Inf. Brigade Headquarters on the following scale and carried as stated :-

    Battalions.
    4 on each of 10 Limbers   = 40
    25 " " : 2 Water Carts = 50
    4 " " " 2 Baggage Wgns. = 8
                Total Battn = 98.

    L.T.M.B.   = 8
    Inf. Bde. Headquarters   = 8

2. Each Battalion is at present in possession of 80 Petrol Tins.

Additional Tins to complete to above scale may be drawn from Camp Commandant at Divisional Headquarters.

    Applications by Units not mentioned above, may be submitted to this office.

    The greatest care must be taken to conserve these tins. Water will be scarce in the forward areas and further issues cannot be made.

Headquarters.

1st September 1918.

H.J. Butchart
Major
D.A.Q.M.G.
74th (Yeo) Division.

War Diary

Appendix IV

Q.L. 31.

Headquarters
   229th Inf. Brigade.   C.R.A.   O.C. 74th M.G. Battn.
   230th Inf. Brigade.   C.R.E.   O.C. 74th Div. Signals.
   231st Inf. Brigade.   A.D.M.S.   O.C. 74th Div. Train.
Camp Commandant.   D.A.D.V.S.   War Diary.
"G"   A.P.M.   File.

---

1. **SUPPLIES.**
Rations for consumption on 4th inst. will be drawn tomorrow, 3rd inst, by all Units by Train Supply Wagons from :-

   Refilling Point   CLERY SUR SOMME H.5.d.Central
as follows :-

   229th Inf. Bde. Group   at 6 a.m.
   230th Inf. Bde. Group   at 6-30 a.m.
   231st Inf. Bde. Group   at 7-0 a.m.
   Div. Arty. Group   at 7-30 a.m.

Supply Wagons will be returned to their Train Companies after delivery of rations.

2. **WATER.**
A Drinking Water Point has been established at H.4.c.1.4.

Water is reported at the following places :-
   Shallow Well.   C.12.d.2.5.
   Deep Well   C.17.b.6.1.   MOISLAINS.
   Borehole.   C.29.b.1.1.   40' to water, 150' deep.
   Borehole.   I.5.b.0.5.   HAUT ALLAINES.
   Spring.   H.11.b.5.5.   CLERY.

Headquarters.
2nd September 1918.

                                                   Lieut-Colonel
                                                  A.A. & Q.M.G.
                                                 74th (Yeo) Division.

War Diary

Appendix V

Q.L. 49.

Headquarters
- 229th Inf. Brigade.
- 230th Inf. Brigade.
- 231st Inf. Brigade.
- Camp Commandant.
- "G"

- C.R.A.
- C.R.E.
- A.D.M.S.
- D.A.D.V.S.
- D.A.P.M.

- O.C. 74th M.G. Bn.
- O.C. 74th Div. Signals.
- O.C. 74th Div. Train.
- O.C. S.A.A. Section D.A.C.
- File & Diary.

---

1 SUPPLIES.

Rations for consumption on 8th inst, will be drawn tomorrow, 7th inst, by all Units by Train Supply Wagons from

Refilling Point at H.5.d. Central (OLLRY) as follows :-

229th Inf. Brigade Group	at 8 a.m.
230th Inf. Brigade Group	at 7.0 a.m.
231st Inf. Brigade Group	at 7.30 a.m.
Div. Artillery Group	at 8.30 a.m.

Supply Wagons, except those of the Div. Artillery Group will be returned to their respective Train Coys. immediately after delivery of rations.

Headquarters.
6th September 1918.

for Lieut-Colonel
A.A. & Q.M.G.
74th (Yeo) Division.

Appx VI   O.Q. 68/5

Headquarters
 74th Division.

A device known as "Stadia Range Indicator" has been introduced with a view to ascertaining whether a hostile aeroplane is within or out of range and 32 of these instruments have been allotted to you. Each instrument will be issued with a card giving description.

If required, these can be drawn on application to the Ordnance Officer 3rd Corps Troops.

H.Q. 3rd Corps.
9/9/18.
                    (sgd) A.C.Gibson, ? Lieut-Colonel
                    A.O.D. for D.A. & Q.M.G.

D.A.D.O.S.
 74th (Yeo) Division.   Q.D. 30

Reference minute 1, please arrange to draw these instruments and distribute in the following order, notifying compliance to this office in due course :-

        Each Infantry Battalion   2 = 18.
        Each Battery R.F.A.   1 = 8
        Div. Ammunition Column   1 = 1
        Divnl. Train.   1 = 1
        Each Field Company R.E. 1 = 3
        Machine Gun Battalion   1 = 1
                            Total = 32

Headquarters.
13th September 1918.   H.J. Butchart
                                                Major
                                        for D.A.Q.M.G.
                                        74th (Yeo) Division.

Copies to :- 229th Inf.Bde.   C.R.A. 74th (Yeo) Division.
            230th Inf.Bde.   C.R.E.   -do-
            231st Inf.Bde.   O.C. 74th Divnl.Train.
            O.C. M.G.Battalion. "G"
            File.
            Diary

Diary CQ 461 Appendix VII

SECRET

ADMINISTRATIVE INSTRUCTIONS

Copy No. 55

RELATIVE TO 74th DIVISION ORDER No. 90.   C.Q. 461

Reference 1/20,000 Map. Sheet 62 N.E.

1. **TRANSPORT.**
   (a) *Baggage Wagons.* Train Baggage Wagons will report to the Transport Lines of their affiliated units by 10 a.m. on 17th inst, and remain attached until further orders.
   (b) *Packsaddlery and Water tin carriers.* Packsaddlery and water tin carriers will be drawn from D.A.D.O.S. Store TEMPLEUX LA FOSSE forthwith on the following scale :-

C.R.A. for R.F.A. Bdes.	20 Sets Saddlery.	40 Water Tin Carriers
230th Inf.Bde. & attd.Troops.	65 " "	130 " " "
231st Inf.Bde. & "	65 " "	130 " " "

   The Infantry Brigades mentioned are responsible for supplying whatever Transport may be necessary for getting forward R.E. Stores from the forward R.E. Dump.

2. **SUPPLIES.**
   (a) *Rations & Fodder.* Rations for consumption on 18th inst, will be drawn on 17th inst, at the usual hours and places. Rations for consumption on 19th will be drawn as follows :-

Div.Arty.Group.	at D.28.d.6.8. at 8-30 a.m on 18th inst.
229th Inf.Bde.Group.)	at Docauville Siding at D.28.c.2.5
230th Inf.Bde.Group.)	on the PERONNE - NURLU Road at
231st Inf.Bde.Group.)	3 p.m, on 17th inst.

   Supply Wagons will be returned to their respective Train Companies after delivery of rations.

   (b) *Solidified Alcohol.* 230th and 231st Infantry Brigades will draw 200 "Tommy Cookers" for each of the 4 Battalions comprising their respective Brigades.
   74th M.G.Battalion will draw 100 "Tommy Cookers"

   (c) *RUM.* 1 Ration of Rum per man may be drawn on 17th for consumption on 18th inst, by all R.A., R.E, Infantry and M.G. Units.

   (d) *Peasoup and Oxo.* Infantry Battalions and M.G. Coys. working under 230th and 231st Infantry Brigades will draw on 17th for consumption on 18th, one issue of peasoup or oxo per man.

3. **AMMUNITION AND FIREWORKS.:** Table "A" shows what each man will carry into action.
   Two forward ammunition and firework Dumps will be formed as under :-

   For the RIGHT Brigade   at F.25.a.4.7.
   For the LEFT Brigade.   at F.25.a.2.8.
   Table "B" shows the composition of each of these Dumps. Infantry Brigades will ensure that each Battalion reconnoitres the routes to the forward Dump from which it is to draw. Infantry Brigades will make all arrangements for drawing from these Dumps and for transporting the ammunition forward. *Less T.M.*
   Table "C" shows the ammunition to be carried by the 230th and 231st Infantry Brigades, each Trench Mortar Battery and Infantry Battalions

P.T.O.

4. WATER.

(a) Personnel. A Reserve Supply of Water amounting to 800 Gallons (400 Petrol tins) per Infantry Brigade and attached Troops will be placed in the forward ammunition Dumps at F.25.a.4.7. and F.25.a.2.8. under Divisional arrangements on X/Y night. The 230th and 231st Infantry Brigades are responsible for posting Guards over their respective Dumps and for the proper distribution of the water.

Water Tanks which will be filled by Motor Lorry will be moved up to E.27.b.9.1. as soon as the situation permits. The 230th & 231st Infantry Brigades and attached Troops and R.F.A. Brigades attached Division will draw Drinking Water from those Tanks.

All other Units of the Division will draw water from LONGAVESNES tanks and TEMPLEUX LA FOSSE.

(b) Animals.
"Z" day. All water which has been developed at VILLERS FAUCON and K.10.c. will be reserved for the R.F.A. Brigades attached to this Division.
Animals of 230th Infantry Brigade and attached troops will be watered at J.24.central.
231st Infantry Brigade and attached Troops will water at J.5.a.1.1. and J.10 central.
229th Infantry Brigade group and all other Troops of the Division will water at TEMPLEUX LA FOSSE.
"Z" plus 1 day.
If the situation permits 231st Infantry Brigade and attached Troops and all R.F.A. Units of the Division less D.A.C. will water at VILLERS FAUCON.
229th and 230th Infantry Brigades and attached Troops will water at K.10.
D.A.C. will water at Borehole in E.25.c.7.6.
In the event of VILLERS FAUCON being heavily shelled, Units will water as for "Z" day.

(c) Water Party. The Burial party will cease to act as such on 16th inst. The Burial Officer will arrange to move his party to the vicinity of LONGAVESNES on the 17th inst and will notify this Office of his new location.
He will detail 2 N.C.O's and 18 men to relieve the pumping party of the 1/12th L.N.Lancs at J.5.a.1.1. at 10 a.m. on 17th inst and will relieve Guard on the Water points at TEMPLEUX LA FOSSE J.10.a. LONGAVESNES and J.24 central by parties of 1 N.C.O. and 3 men at the same hour.
On the morning of the 18th inst he will detail a party of 3 N.C.O's and 18 other ranks to act as pumping party at K.10.c., this party will report there not later than 5 a.m. Further pumping parties, strength to be detailed later, will relieve parties of R.E. at wells in VILLERS FAUCON at 7 a.m. on 18th inst. Detailed orders for Water Guard have been issued direct to Divisional Burial Officer.

It is essential that Units should draw Drinking Water and water animals only at the places mentioned, otherwise some Units will go short. All animals must be taken to water in formed bodies under the charge of an Officer.

(d) Table "D" attached shows water in forward Area in 1917.

5. MEDICAL AND POLICE ARRANGEMENTS. will be issued separately. The fullest use will be made of German prisoners for the purpose of bringing back our wounded to R.A.P's and thence to VILLERS FAUCON. Each R.M.O. will be provided with extra stretcher bearers to make up a total number of 40. 8 of these per Battalion will be looked upon as a reserve and will be called upon only when required.

6. Acknowledge.

H.J. Butchart
Lieut Colonel,
A.A.& Q.M.G. 74th (Yeomanry) Division

Headquarters
16th September, 1918.
Issued at 2.p.m.

P.T.O.

#3#

Copies to :-

No.			
1.	G.O.C.	41-42	D.A.D.V.S.
2.	"G"	43-45	Div. Train.
3.	3rd Corps.(2)	46-48	D.A.D.O.S.
4-9	C.R.A.	49-50	D.A.P.M.
10-14	C.R.E.	51	1st Aust. Division.
15-	Signals.	52	18th Division.
16-	74th M.G.Bn.	53-54	Burial Officer.
17-22	229 Bde.	55-57	War Diary.
23-28	230 Bde.	58-60	File.
29-34	231st Bde.	61-70	Spare.
35-40	A.D.M.S.		

#3#

Copies to :-

No. 1.	G.O.C.	41-42	D.A.D.V.S.
2.	"G"	43-45	Div. Train.
3.	3rd Corps.(2)	46-48	D.A.D.O.S.
4-9	C.R.A.	49-50	D.A.P.M.
10-14	C.R.E.	51	1st Aust. Division.
15	Signals.	52	18th Division.
16	74th M.G.Bn.	53-54	Burial Officer.
17-22	229 Bde.	55-57	War Diary.
23-28	230 Bde.	58-60	File.
29-34	231st Bde.	61-70	Spare.
35-40	A.D.M.S.		

-5-

Copies to:-

No. 1.	G.O.C.	41-42	D.A.D.V.S.
2.	"G"	43-45	Div. Train.
3.	3rd Corps. (2)	46-48	D.A.D.O.S.
4-9	C.R.A.	49-50	D.A.P.M.
10-14	C.R.E.	51	1st Aust. Division.
15	Signals.	52	18th Division.
16	74th M.G. Bn.	53-54	Burial Officer.
17-22	229 Bde.	55-57	War Diary.
23-28	230 Bde.	58-60	File.
29-34	231st Bde.	61-70	Spare.
35-40	A.D.M.S.		

TABLE "A".

Kit to be carried on the man.

	lbs.	ozs.
Rifle, Bayonet, oil bottle etc.	10	8½
*Web Equipment, less haversack but with Pack.	6	4
Water Bottle Full.	4	0
2 Sandbags.	1	0
Entrenching Tool complete.	2	4
Small box respirator.	3	3
170 Rounds S.A.A.	10	10
	37	13½

Carried in Pack.	Lbs.	Ozs.		
Cardigan & Cap Comforter.	1	11		
Mess Tin & Cover.	1	12		
Holdall.	1	2		
=			4	9

Rations.				
Iron.	1	4		
Mobile.	4	0		
Unexpired.	5	12		
=			9	0

2 Grenades, Hand No. 36.	3	0		
2 " Smoke.	3	0		
1 Aeroplane Flare.		3		
1 Ground Sheet.	2	8		
=			8	11
Total =			60	1½

* Haversack may be carried in lieu at the discretion of B.G's C. Infantry Brigades.

TABLE "B".

Each of "A" and "B" Dumps will contain :-

100 Rnds. S.A.A. per man. 4 Bns. at 500 each.	= 200,000 rounds.
500 No.36. Grenades per Bn. 4 Bns.	= 2,000 Grenade.
Flares Red.	= 500 Flares.
Stokes Gun Shells. at 160 per gun. 4 Guns.	= 640 Shells.
Very Lights. White D.I. 1 inch.	= 2 Boxes.

TABLE "C".

Each Trench Mortar Battery of 4 Guns will carry 40 rounds per Gun.

Each Battalion will carry :-

        2 Boxes S.O.S. Grenades.   = 24 Grenades.
        1 Box Message Carrying Rockets - 10 Rockets.
        2 Boxes Very Lights 1" D.I. White.

230th and 231st Infantry Brigades will each be issued with:-

        2 Boxes Very Lights Red. 1 inch.
        2 Boxes Very Lights Green. 1 inch.

TABLE "D".

Notes on known sources of water in the Forward area of this Division, as they existed in 1917.

1. **F.21.c.0.3.**   Large Sugar Factory well about 7' in diameter and probably 200' of water.
It is believed a POTTER Pump was installed in 1917.

2. **F.27.c.6.6.**   Borehole in TEMPLEUX Quarries, just outside the entrance to a large dugout. This dugout contains a complete compression plant for raising water.

3. **L.2.B.6.6.**   Village Well. 72' to water. Worked by a Band Elevator in 1917.

4. **L.2.d.1.a.**   As No 3.

5. **K.11.c.2.4.**   Well 8' in diameter. 80' to water.
Pump in position in good working order and can be worked by hand crank now fitted.

6. **F.26.d.3.6.**   Well depth 99' good yield. worked by hand windlass.

7. **L.2.b.**   Well depth 80'. good yield. Hand chain helice.

8. **L.2.d.**   Well depth 120'. depth to water 14'. Petrol Pump installed.

Diary CQ461/1 Appendix VIII

SECRET   ADMINISTRATIVE INSTRUCTIONS   Copy No.

RELATIVE TO 74th DIVISIONAL ORDER No. 90.   CQ 461/1

PROVOST ARRANGEMENTS.

1. **ROADS.** The following Roads have been allotted to the Division:-

   VILLERS FAUCON - TEMPLEUX LE GUERARD - RONSSOY.
   VILLERS FAUCON - ST. EMILIE - RONSSOY - F.30.a.

II. **TRAFFIC CONTROL.** Additional Posts will be established as under:-

   E.23.a.8.5.   E.23.c.1.3.
   E.23.d.4.0.   F.21.c.4.8.
   E.30.c.1.9.   L.2.C.Cent.
   L.2.b.4.7.

   Forward Posts will be established as the situation demands. The Roads allotted to the Division will be patrolled as far forward as practicable by M.M.P.

   It is of the utmost importance that Roads be kept as clear as possible to allow of the uninterrupted passage of guns and M.T. All Mounted Troops, H.T. and Infantry will use Side Tracks wherever possible.

   Notice Boards are being placed in position where such Tracks are already in existence, but all Units can help to ease the congestion of roads by utilising every available "short cut" and roadside Track.

   The attention of all concerned is directed to FOURTH ARMY Traffic Orders, copies of which have been circulated.

III. **STRAGGLERS POSTS.** These will be established at:-

   F.21.c.4.8.,   L.2.b.4.7.,   L.2.c.Central.

IV. **PRISONERS OF WAR.** The P.O.W.Cage will be situated at E.27.d.8.8. A screen of M.M.P. will be placed along the Main EPEHY - ROISSEL Road from E.24.c.8.8. - K.5.b.4.2. to X Tracks at K.6.c.5.0. to cover all routes from the Front Line to the Divisional Area.

   Battalion Escorts will be instructed to take P.O.W. to the rear and deliver them to the first 74th Div.M.M.P. they meet who will hand the escort a receipt. Escorts will be instructed to proceed direct to Divisional Cage at E.27.d.8.8. should they miss the M.M.P. screen. Notices directing the route to the P.O.W. Cage will be placed at frequent intervals along all roads.

V. **ACKNOWLEDGE.**

H.J. Butchart Major.

Lieut.-Colonel.
A.A. & Q.M.G. 74th (Yeomanry) Division.

D.H.Q.
16/9/18.
Issued at:
Copies to:-

No 1   G.O.C.   9. 230th Bde.
   2   "G"   10. 231st Bde   17. 18th Divn.
   3   III Corps.   11. A.D.M.S.   18. Burial Off.
   4   C.R.A.   12. D.A.D.V.S.   19 & 20 War Diary.
   5   C.R.E.   13. Div.Train.(2)   21 & 22 File.
   6   Div.Sigs.   14. D.A.D.O.S.   23 - 28 Spare.
   7   M.G.Bn   15. A.P.M.
   8   229th Bde.   16. 181st Divn.

War Diary Appendix IX

SECRET.   Copy No. 39

INSTRUCTIONS FOR ADVANCED BILLETING PARTIES

REFERENCE 74th DIV. ORDER No. 93.

CA.473/1

1. Advanced Billeting Parties will move to CORBIE on 24th inst, by Motor Lorries as follows :-

2. Composition of Paty.

	Offs.	O/Rs.	Bicycles.
Divisional Headquarters.			
Traffic Control Officer.			
4 Police.			
4 Other Ranks.			
Total D.H.Q.	1	8	2
Each Infantry Bde.H.Q.			
Staff Captain.			
Interpreter.			
1 Other Rank.			
Total for 3 Inf.Bde.H.Q's.	3	6	3
Each Infantry Bn.(Inc.Pioneers & M.G.Battn.)			
1 Officer.			
4 C.Q.M.S.			
1 Representative Bn.H.Q.			
Total for 11 Battalions.	11	55	11
Each F.Coy.R.E., F.Amb. & Div.Sigs.			
1 Officer & 1 Sgt.			
3 Fld.Coys.R.E.	3	3	3
3 F.Ambs.	3	3	3
Div.Sig.Coy.	1	1	1
74th Divisional Train.			
3 Supply Officers. and			
4 N.C.O's.	3	4	3
S.A.A. Section D.A.C..			
1 Officer & 1 C.Q.M.S	1	1	1
Total =	26	81	27

3. A Bicycle will be taken for each Officer proceeding.
4. 7 Lorries will report at VILLERS FAUCON at E.28.a.6.4 at 10 a.m. on 24th inst.
On arrival at CORBIE, the party will report to Captain D.S. CAMPBELL West Kent Yeomanry at the Church CORBIE Q.5.a.6.8. Sheet 62d.
5. Rations for 48 hours will be carried by each Officer and O.R.
6. Captain Lord Victor PAGET, M.C. will be in command of the party.
7. ACKNOWLEDGE.

Headquarters.   Lieut-Colonel.
                                                           A.A. & Q.M.G.
23rd September 1918.   74th (Yeo) Division.

Copies to :- Nos. 1-5. 229 Bde.   16-20 A.D.M.S.   31-   D.A.D.V.S.
              6-10 230 Bde.   21-25 C.R.E.   32-   Div. Sigs.
              11-15 231 Bde.   26-30 Train.   33-   C. Comdt.
                                   Section D.A.C.   34-   A.P.M.
                                   R.A   41-   M.G.Bn

Diary

Appx IX

SECRET.   Copy No.......

AMENDMENTS TO INSTRUCTIONS FOR ADVANCED   C.Q. 473/2
BILLETING PARTIES REFERENCE 74th DIV ORDER No.93.

———

Reference C.A. 473/1 of today, please make the following alterations :-

Para 1. for 24th read 25th. Delete 2nd line.
Para 4. delete whole para and substitute "parties will
        proceed by first train on 25th inst, and report
        on arrival to Captain D.S. CAMPBELL West Kent
        Yeomanry at detraining station."

                                          H.J. Butchart Major
                                          for Lieut-Colonel
Headquarters.   A.A. & Q.M.G.
23rd September 1918.   74th (Yeo) Division.

Copies to :- 1 - 5   229 Bde.   21-25 C.R.E.   33-   C. Comdt.
              6 -10   230 Bde.   26-30 Train.   34-   D.A.P.M.
             11 -15   231 Bde.   31-   D.A.D.V.S. 35-   S.A.A.Sec.
             16 -20   A.D.M.S.   32-   Div. Sigs.   D.A.C.
             41-   C.R.A.   42-   M.G.Bn.   36-40 Spare.
             43-   "G"

War Diary   Appendix X

SECRET.   Copy No......... 38

ADMINISTRATIVE INSTRUCTIONS RELATIVE TO C.A. 473/3
OPERATION ORDER No. 93.

Reference 1/40,000 Sheet 62c.

1. **Supplies.** All personnel whether proceeding by Train or Road, will carry on the man rations for 25th and 26th and the Iron Ration.
Forage for 25th and 26th will be carried for all animals.

2. **Water Party.** O.C. Reception Camp will collect Water Party tonight, and dispatch the men to join their respective Units along with "B" Teams and Reinforcements.

3. **Burial Party.** will report to O.C. Reception Camp tonight and rejoin Units with "B" Teams and Reinforcements.

4. **Entrainment.** Personnel will entrain as follows :-

1st Train leaving TINCOURT at 11-15 a.m.
229th Inf. Bde. Headquarters.
229th L.T.M.B.
14th Bn. R. Highlanders.
439th Fld. Coy. R.E.
Supply Personnel of 448th Coy. A.S.C.
16th Bn. Devon Regt.
H.Q. Div. Reception Camp.
229th Field Ambulance.
Advanced Billeting Parties detailed in C.A. 473/1 of 23rd inst.

2nd Train leaving TINCOURT at 11-30 a.m.
12th Somerset L.I.
15th Bn. Suffolk Regt.
Div. Employ. Company.
Div. Headquarters.
Headquarters Div. Train.
H.Q. Signal Coy. & No.1 Section.

1st Train leaving PERONNE at 11-45 a.m.
230th Inf. Brigade Headquarters.
230th L.T.M.B.
10th Bn. E. Kent Regt.
5th Fld. Coy. R.M.R.E.
Supply personnel of 449th Coy. A.S.C.

2nd Train leaving PERONNE at 12 noon.
13th Bn. Sussex Regt.
230th Field Ambulance.
74th M.G. Battalion.

3rd Train leaving PERONNE at 12-30 p.m.
231st Inf. Brigade Headquarters.
231st L.T.M.B.
25th Bn. R.W.F.
24th Bn. Welsh Regt.
Supply personnel of 450th Coy. A.S.C.
5th Fld. Coy. R.A.R.E.

4th Train leaving PERONNE at 12-45 p.m.
10th Bn. S.L.I.
1/15th Bn. L.N. Lancs.
231st Field Ambulance

P.T.O.

5 Entrainment contd.

"B" Teams and Reinforcements at the Reception Camp will entrain with their respective Units. O.C. Reception Camp will ensure that all personnel report to their respective Units at the Entraining Station not less than one hour before the Train is due to leave.
The Officer or N.C.O. in charge of the "B" Teams and Reinforcements of each Unit will hand to his O.C. on arrival at the Entraining Station, a State showing the number of Officers and Other Ranks reporting.

5. STANDING ORDERS. Attention is directed to Standing Orders for Entrainment as amended by G.Q. 426/3 of 27th August 1918, particular attention is directed paras 1 & 3.
Officers in charge of Trains will send forward an Officer in advance to report to the R.T.O. at the Entraining Station, and ascertain the exact time at which the troops may be entrained. Until the advance Officer has reported, troops will remain clear of the Station and off the roads as far as possible.
Every precaution will be taken to ensure that Troops who are waiting to entrain do not block the approaches to the Station.

6. Divisional Entrainment and Detrainment Officers. The following will act as Divisional Entrainment and Detrainment Officers at the Stations mentioned :-

TINCOURT - Major J.B. DODGE. D.S.O. M.G.C.
PERONNE. - Lieut. W. Scott. 14th Bn. R. Highlanders.
VILLERS BRETONNEUX - Capt. D.S. CAMPBELL. West Kent.Yeo.

These Officers will be in charge of the Entrainment and Detrainment at the Stations mentioned, and will assist the R.T.O's, wire the state of Entrainment and Detrainment in accordance with G.R.O. No. 4743 dated 11/8/18 and ensure that Standing Orders are carried out.

7. Baggage & Supply Wagons. *of the supply wagons affiliated to* Baggage Wagons are already with Units, and will march with Transport. Supply Wagons with the exception of 50% Infantry, M.G. and Pioneer Battalions will remain with Units for transport of Forage.
O.C. Divisional Train will detail 10 G.S. Wagons to report to O.C. Divisional Reception Camp at 8.p.m. on 24th inst. These will be loaded with Kits etc. of "B" Teams and will then march to new Area with Divisional Transport under orders to be issued by O.C. Train. All Baggage Wagons will be returned to their respective Companies immediately after arrival in the new area.

8. Mobile Veterinary Section will march in rear of Divisional Transport and join it at BUSSU.
Head of Column passes ROISEL K.16.a. at 8.p.m.

9. S.A.A. Section D.A.C. will march with 229th Infantry Brigade Transport and join it at BUSSU. It will bivouac night 24/25th at HEM and pick up surplus baggage from old Reception Camp there.

10. SALVAGE. O.C. Salvage will hand over to Salvage Officer 27th American Division.

11. POLICE. The A.P.M. will detail 5 M.M.P. for attachment to each Brigade Group who will accompany 1st Line Transport by March route. He will also detail 5 Traffic Control Police to be attached to each Brigade Group for duty at Entraining and Detraining Stations. The T.C. Police will proceed by Train.

see 3.

3

12. **Camp Kettles.** 80 Camp Kettles per Infantry Brigade Group will be taken. They will be dumped under orders of B.G's C. concerned as follows :-

    229th Inf.Bde.Group at K.11.a.5.2.
    230th Inf.Bde.Group at D.29.d.2.2.
    231st Inf.Bde.Group at D.29.d.2.2.

One man will be placed in charge of the Camp Kettles of each Inf. Brigade Group.
A Motor Lorry will collect the Kettles from K.11.a.5.2 at 8 a.m. and from D. 29.d.2.2. at 9 a.m. on 25th inst. Kettles and men in charge will be taken to entraining Station where they will be taken over by Units as they arrive.

13. ACKNOWLEDGE.

Headquarters.
24th September 1918.
Issued at ..... p.m.

Lieut-Colonel
A.A. & Q.M.G.
74th (Yeo) Division.

Copies to :-

1 - 5	229 Bdo.	37-	"G"
6 -10	230th Bdo.	38-	War Diary.
11 -15	231 Bde.	39-41	File.
16 -20	A.D.M.S.	43-	O.C. Div.Emp.Coy.
21 -25	C.R.E.	44-46	Div.Recept.Camp.
26 -30	Train.	47-	C.R.A.
31 -	D.A.D.V.S.	48-	Major Dodge.
32 -	Div.Signals.	49-	Capt.Campbell.
33 -	C.Comdt.	50-	Lieut.Scott.
34 -	D.A.P.M.	51-	Div.Burial Officer.
35 -	S.A.A. Sec.D.A.C.	52-	Div.Baths Officer.
36 -	M.G.Battn.	53-	27th Amer.Division.
		54-	3rd Corps.
		55-	Traffic CORBIE
		56-	R.T.O. PERONNE.
		57-	R.T.O. TINCOURT.
		58-	R.T.O. VILLERS BRETONNEUX.

SECRET.   Copy No. ..4..

ADMINISTRATIVE INSTRUCTIONS RELATIVE TO
74 DIVISION ORDER No. 94.

O.Q. 480/1

26th September 1918.

Appendix XI

1. **ENTRAINMENT.** Units will entrain in accordance with attached schedules. B.G's C. Infantry Brigade Groups will be responsible for issuing orders for the entrainment of all Units within their Groups. The personnel of 74th Divisional Reception Camp will travel on Train No. 4.

2. **LOADING AND OFFLOADING PARTIES.** B.G's C. Infantry Brigade Groups will make their own arrangements for loading and offloading parties at the respective entraining and detraining stations. In addition, the O.C. 1/12th Bn. L.N.Lancs will detail one Officer and fifty Other ranks to report at each Entraining Station 3 hours before the departure of the first train. The parties detailed for HEILLY and MERICOURT will rejoin their Unit at CORBIE Station on the departure of Trains Nos. 14 and 15 respectively. B.G's C. are responsible that all Transport is at the Station 3 hours and personnel one hour before the departure of the Train.

3. **ENTRAINING AND DETRAINING OFFICERS.** B.G's C. Infantry Brigade Groups will detail one Officer for each entraining and detraining Station to act as Entraining and Detraining Officer. The attention of each Officer will be directed to the Divisional Standing Orders for Entrainment and Detrainment, and to the instructions laid down in G.R.O. No. 4743, dated 11/8/18., which will be strictly complied with. Names of Officers detailed to be wired to this office as soon as possible.

4. **SUPPLIES & BAGGAGE WAGONS.** Supply and Baggage Wagons of the Divisional Train will be entrained with Units to which they are affiliated and returned to the Train Companies after Refilling on the 29th inst.

5. **SUPPLIES.** Rations for consumption on the 29th inst, will be taken on the Train in the Supply Wagons after being drawn on the 27th inst, as follows :-

Div. Headquarters and Units on No. 1 Train.	CORBIE Station at 8-30 a.m.
229th Bde. Group	MERICOURT at 9 a.m.
230th Bde. Group	HEILLY at 8-30 a.m.
231st Bde. Group	CORBIE Station at 9-30 a.m.

In order to avoid congestion, representatives of Units will be sent at the times stated above to take over these rations which will be loaded on to Supply Wagons after the rations for consumption 28th have been placed on the Train.

6. **REFILLING POINTS.** Refilling Points on and after 29th inst, will be as follows :-

GROUP.	PLACE.	TIME.
229th Inf. Bde. Group.	HAM EN ARTOIS.	11. a.m.
230th Inf. Bde. Group.	BURBURE.	11. a.m.
231st Inf. Bde. Group.	GONNEHEM	11. a.m.

P.T.O.

7. MOTOR TRANSPORT.

Motor Lorries will be allotted as follows :-

	No.	Place.	Hour.
Div.Headquarters, including Employ.Coy, and Gas Services.	7	CORBIE.	7-30 am.
229th Inf.Bdo.Group. (Bde.H.Q. 1 / L.T.M.B. 1 / Each Bn. 1.	5	CORBIE.	6-30 am.
230th Inf.Bde.Group. including M.G.Bn., (Bde.H.Q. 1 / L.T.M.B. 1 / Each Bn. 1	6	FOUILLY.	6-30 am.
231st Inf.Bde.Group. including Pioneer Bn. (Bde.H.Q. 1 / L.T.M.B. 1 / Each Bn. 1	6	VILLERS BRETONNEUX	6-30 am.
74th Div.Train.	1	CORBIE.	6-30 am.

The Lorries will report at Brigade Headquarters for each Group, and B.G's. will distribute them within the Group. The Lorries must be released as soon as possible after arrival at the destinations as they are required for another purpose.

8. ACKNOWLEDGE.

Lieut-Colonel
A.A. & Q.M.G.
74th (Yeomanry) Division.

Issued at....3-30...p.m.

Copies to :-
- 1 - G.O.C.
- 2 - "G.s."
- 3-4 F110.
- 5-7 229 Bdo.
- 8-10 230th Bdo.
- 11-13 231st Bdo.
- 14 - M.G.Bn.
- 15 - O.C.S.A.A. Sec.
- D.A.C.
- 16 - C.R.E.
- 17 - Div.Train.
- 18 - Div.Signals.
- 19 - A.D.M.S.
- 20 - D.A.D.V.S.
- 21 - D.A.D.O.S.
- 22 - D.A.P.M.
- 23 - C. Comdt.
- 24 - S.O.F.
- 25 - Div. Emp. Coy.
- 26 - M.T. Coy.
- 27 - 3rd Corps.
- 28 - 13th Corps.
- 29-30 Spare.

SECRET.

TABLE "D" FOR MOVE OF 74th DIVISION, LESS ARTILLERY.

UNIT.	Serial No.	DESCRIPTION.
DIVISIONAL UNITS.	7401	Divisional H.Q.
	7403	H.Q. Divisional R.E.
	7404	12th Loyal N.Lancs. (Pioneers)
	7406	H.Q. and No.1 Section Divnl Signal Coy.
	7407	Area Employment Coy.
	7409a	M.G.Battn H.Q. and "A" and "B" Coes.
	7409b	"C" and "D" Coes. M.G.Battn.
229th INFANTRY BRIGADE.	7410	Brigade H.Q.
	7411	16th Devons.
	7412	12th Somerset Light Infantry.
	7413	14th Royal Highlanders.
	7416	Brigade Signal Section.
	7417	Light T.M. Battery.
230th INFANTRY BRIGADE.	7420	Brigade H.Q.
	7421	10th Buffs.
	7422	15th Suffolk Regt.
	7423	16th Sussex Regt.
	7425	Brigade Signal Section.
	7427	Light T.M. Battery.
231st INFANTRY BRIGADE.	7430	Brigade H.Q.
	7431	10th King's Scottish Light Infantry.
	7432	24th Welsh Regt.
	7433	25th Royal Welch Fusiliers.
	7435	Brigade Signal Section.
	7437	Light T.M. Battery.
DIVISIONAL AMMUNITION COLUMN	7473a	½ S.A.A. Section.
	7473b	½ S.A.A. Section.
DIVISIONAL TRAIN.	7475	H.Q. Divisional Train.
	7476	448th Coy., A.S.C.
	7477	449th Coy., A.S.C.
	7478	450th Coy., A.S.C.
DIVISIONAL ENGINEERS.	7481	439th Field Coy., R.E.
	7482	R.M. Field Coy., R.E.
	7483	R.A. Field Coy., R.E.
MEDICAL UNITS.	7486	229th Field Ambulance.
	7487	230th Field Ambulance.
	7488	231st Field Ambulance.
VETERINARY UNIT.	7490	Mobile Veterinary Section.

SECRET.

ENTRAINMENT PROGRAMME FOR MOVE OF 74th DIVISION, LESS ARTILLERY, SEPTEMBER 27th and 28th, 1918.

FROM FOURTH ARMY.   COURANT No.W.289.   **TO FIRST ARMY.**

ENTRAINING STATIONS:
- (A) CORBIE.
- (B) HEILLY.
- (C) HERICOURT.

DETRAINING STATIONS:
- (A) CHOCQUES.
- (B) LILLERS.
- (C) BERGUETTE.

Station and Train No. A.	B.	C.	SERIAL NOS.	Mche	Dept time	Date	Time due arr. detrn. statn.	Date	Remarks.
1	-	-	7401, 7405, 7403	T.57	11:51	27/9			
-	2	-	7420, 7425, 7467, 7427.	T.58	12:50	27/9			
-	-	3	7410, 7416, 7486, 7417.	T.59	13:33	27/9			
4	-	-	7430, 7435, 7488, 7437.	T.60	14:51	27/9			
-	5	-	7421.	T.61	15:40	27/9			
-	-	6	7411, 7475	T.62	16:38	27/9			
7	-	-	7431.	T.63	17:51	27/9			
-	8	-	7422.	T.64	18:40	27/9			
-	-	9	7412.	T.65	19:38	27/9			
10	-	-	7483, 7478, 7407.	T.66	20:51	27/9			
-	11	-	7482, 7477.	T.67	21:40	27/9			
-	-	12	7481, 7476.	T.68	22:38	27/9			
13	-	-	7432.	T.69	23:51	27/9			
-	14	-	7409a.	T.70	0:40	28/9			
-	-	15	7473a.	T.71	1:38	28/9			
16	-	-	7433.	T.72	2:51	28/9			
-	17	-	7423, 7490.	T.73	3:40	28/9			
-	-	18	7473b.	T.74	4:28	28/9			
19	-	-	7404.	T.51	5:51	28/9			
-	20	-	7409b.	T.52	6:15	28/9			
-	-	21	7413.	T.53	7:38	28/9			

SECRET. War Diary   Appendix XII   Copy No. 18

ADMINISTRATIVE INSTRUCTIONS RELATIVE TO   C.Q.483/4

74th DIVISION ORDER No. 95.   29th September 1918.

Reference Sheet. 36A. and 44B.

1. **TRENCH AND AREA STORES.** All trench and area stores will be taken over from outgoing units. Receipts will be given and forwarded to this Office by the 4th inst on the pro-forma previously issued.

2. **DUMPS.** All dumps of R.E.Stores, salvage, S.A.A. fireworks, petrol tins etc, will be taken over by relieving Units. Receipts will be given and a copy giving the composition and location of each Dump forwarded to this office by the 4th inst.

3. **BAGGAGE & SUPPLY WAGONS.** O.C. 74th Divnl.Train will arrange for these to be handed over to Units at the present Refilling Points at 11.a.m. tomorrow. These Wagons will be returned to the Divnl.Train Companies on the day following arrival in the new area.

4. **TRANSPORT LINES.** Units will take over the Transport Lines of the Units which they relieve. These will not be altered when inter Brigade reliefs take place.

5. **S.A.A. SECTION. D.A.C.** The O.C. S.A.A. Section will arrange to relieve the S.A.A. Section of the outgoing Division on the 3rd proximo.

6. **SUPPLIES.** The 74th M.G.Battalion will draw Supplies for consumption on 2nd October at ALLOUAGNE Church at 4.p.m. tomorrow. Remainder of the Division will draw Rations for consumption on 2nd October at 7.a.m. on 1st October and 229th Infl.Brigade Group for 3rd October at 7.a.m. on 2nd October.
Refilling Points will change as follows :-

	Date.	Place.	For.consumption.	Time.
229th Bde.Group.	3rd.	X.13.a.0.6.	4th.	9 a.m.
230th Bde.Group.	2nd.	X.13.a.0.6.	3rd.	8.a.m.
231 Bde. Group.	2nd.	X.13.a.0.6.	3rd.	7.a.m.

7. **MOBILE VETERINARY SECTION.** The D.A.D.V.S. will arrange to relieve the Mobile Veterinary Section of the outgoing Division on the 2nd prox.

8. **ACKNOWLEDGE.**

M.Owens
Lieut-Colonel
A.A. & Q.M.G.
74th (Yeo) Division.

Copies to :- No. 1. G.O.C.   9.   A.D.M.S.   17.   C.Comdt.
             2-3.   File.   10. D.A.D.V.S.   18.   Diary.
             4.   "G.S."   11. D.A.D.O.S.   19.   S.C.F.
             5.   229 Bde.   12. D.A.P.M.   20.   Div.Emp.Coy.
             6.   230 Bde.   13. Div.Train.   21-25. Spare.
             7.   231 Bde.   14. Div.Signals.   26.   C.R.E.
             8.   M.G.Bn.   15. M.T.Company.   27.   XI Corps.
                                   16. O.C.S.A.A. Sec.D.A.C.
                                                          28.   1st Divn.

War Diary September Appendix XIII

FOURTH ARMY NO. G.S.2/17.

74th Division.

The 74th Division has taken a prominent part in the successful advance of the Fourth Army during the past month and much to my regret has been ordered to another part of the British front.

The work of this Division during a period of severe and continuous fighting is worthy of the best traditions of the Yeoman stock of Great Britain.

Brought to this country from a hot climate, where they took part in a very different method of warfare, the 74th Division has quickly adapted itself to the altered conditions and has fought with a determination and courage which is beyond praise.

In the capture of AIZECOURT, DRIENCOURT, TEMPLEUX LA FOSSE, LONGAVESNES, VILLERS FAUCON and TEMPLEUX LE GUERARD the Division has made a name for itself which ranks with the best Division fighting in the British Army and I desire to offer to all ranks my warmest thanks for their gallantry and self sacrifice.

In addition to the considerable area of ground gained the Division has captured over 1,700 prisoners.

I greatly regret that the Division is leaving the Fourth Army and in wishing all ranks every good fortune I trust I may at some future time find the 74th Division once more under my command.

H. Rawlinson

H.Q., Fourth Army,
28th September, 1918.

General,
Commanding Fourth Army.

Appendix XIV

A/18.

File.

74th (YEOMANRY) DIVISION.

CONSOLIDATED LIST OF CASUALTIES FOR PERIOD 1st - 30th Sept.

UNIT.	KILLED Off.	KILLED O.R.	WOUNDED Off.	WOUNDED O.R.	MISSING Off.	MISSING O.R.	D. OF INJ. Off.	D. OF INJ. O.R.	INJURED Off.	INJURED O.R.
D.H.Q.	-	-	-	5						
M.T.S.	-	-	-	-						
Div.Train.	-	-	-	6	-	-	-	-	1	2
Div.Emp.Coy.	-	1	-	-						
44th Bde.RFA	-	6	12	82						
117th Bde.RFA	1	6	2	60						
74th D.A.C.	-	2	-	5						
74th M.T.M.Bn	-	1	-	2						
5th F.Co.RMRE	-	-	-	5						
8th F.Co.RARE	-	-	-	4						
439 F.Co.R.E.	-	-	-	2	-	-	-	-	-	1
1/12 D.W.Lancs	-	-	-	4						
74th Div.Sigs	1	-	2	8						
229th Inf.Bde.										
229th Bde.HQ	-	-	1	-						
229th LTMB	-	-	-	5						
16th Devons.	2	54	14	243	-	14				
12th Som.L.I.	6	43	12	335	1	42				
14th B.Highlrs	3	60	19	243	-	17				
230th Inf.Bde.										
230th Bde.HQ	-	-	5	1						
230th LTMB	-	-	-	6						
10 E.Kents	3	32	11	199	1	26	-	-	-	1
15th Suffolks	-	26	7	172	-	1	-	-	-	3
16th Sussex	1	41	15	356	3	50	-	-	-	3
231st Inf.Bde.										
231st Bde.HQ	-	1	-	-						
231st LTMB	-	-	-	6						
24th R.W.F.	7	54	14	379	1	20	-	1	-	1
24th Welsh	3	52	14	229	1	10	-	-	-	-
10th K.S.L.I.	4	68	8	301	-	1				
74th M.G.Bn.	3	25	8	142	1	1				
229th F.Amb.	-	6	-	2						
230th F.Amb.	-	-	-	30						
231st F.Amb.	-	-	-	6						
Div.M.T.Coy.	-	-	-	-						
TOTAL DIVISION	**34**	**459**	**145**	**2712**	**8**	**182**	**-**	**1**	**1**	**9**

Attd. Troops.

UNIT.	KILLED Off.	KILLED O.R.	WOUNDED Off.	WOUNDED O.R.	MISSING Off.	MISSING O.R.	D. OF INJ. Off.	D. OF INJ. O.R.	INJURED Off.	INJURED O.R.
58th D.A.C.	-	-	-	-	-	-	-	-	-	1
80 A.Bde.RFA	-	6	5	40	2	-	-	-	-	-
104 A.Bde.RFA	2	1	7	38	-	-	-	-	-	1
230th Bde.RFA	1	-	2	13	-	-	-	-	-	-
290th Bde.RFA	-	-	-	-	-	-	-	-	-	1
291st Bde.RFA	-	1	1	7	-	1	-	-	-	1

Appendix XV

The following letter has been received from Lieut-General Sir R.H.K.BUTLER. K.C.M.G. C.B. Commanding III Corps:-

74th Division.
****

It is with the greatest regret that I bid "au revoir" to the 74th Division.

During the brief period which the Division has been with the III Corps, it has not only fought with gallantry and determination, but also with that spirit of mutual co-operation and comradeship which ensures success.

I wish also to convey my personal thanks to General GIRDWOOD, the Staff, and all ranks of the 74th Division for their loyal support and for the manner in which they have always "played up". I trust that it may be my good fortune, at no distant date, to have the Division in my Command again in further victorious operations.

R.H.K.BUTLER.

III Corps H.Q.
26th September 1918.

Lieutenant-General,
Commanding III Corps.

Major-General E.S.GIRDWOOD, C.B. Commanding 74th (Yeomanry) Division has sent the following reply:-

Lieut-Gen. Sir R.BUTLER. Commanding III Corps.

Personally and on behalf of all ranks of the 74th Division I beg to thank you for your kind message received today which I know will give the utmost satisfaction to all AAA May we soon be taking part in further victorious operations under your leadership.

Major-General GIRDWOOD.

Distribution:-

Unit	Copies	Notes		
229th Inf.Bde.	60	copies for distribution down to Platoons.		
230th Inf.Bde.	60	do	do	
231st Inf.Bde.	60	do	do	
C.R.A.	50	do	down to Batteries and Sections of D.A.C.	
C.R.E.	30	do	down to Sections of Field Companies and Pioneer Bn.Platoons.	
74th M.G.Bn.	18	copies for distribution down to Sections.		
A.D.C.for G.O.C.	2 copies.	A.P.M.	1 copy.	
"G"	6 copies.	D.A.D.O.S.	1 copy.	
"Q"	6 copies.	D.A.D.V.S.	1 copy.	
74th M.T.Coy.	2 copies.	Camp Comdt.	1 copy.	
A.D.M.S.	12 copies.	S.C.F.	1 copy.	
74th Div.Sigs.	3 copies.	985 Emp.Coy.	1 copy.	
74th Div.Train.	7 copies.			

WAR DIARY
INTELLIGENCE SUMMARY

Army Form C. 2118.

A & Q Branch
Headquarters (94) Division
October 1916

Place	Date	Hour	Summary of Events and Information	Remarks and references to Appendices
NORRENT FONTES	3		Divisional A.Q. closed at NORRENT FONTES W.30.a.7.8. Sheet 36A at the end of which time command passed from 19" to 94" Division.	
W.36.a.7.8	4		Reconnaissance made for new Advd N.Q. and Rlhd selected at S.12.d.7.8. Railhead moves to CHOCQUES and supplies taken by Decauville to S.13.a.0.6	
"	5		Div H.Q. closed at W.30.a.7.8 and opened at S.12.d.7.8 at same hour.	
S.12.d.7.8			Headquarters were situated in money HALPEGARBE Annobay. No room huts had to be erected as no building available. Refilling point for supplies fixed at T.2.d.6.4. Supplies being drawn from railhead by M.T.	
"	9/10		2.29" Inf Bde relieved 31" Inf Bde	appendix I
"	8		Administrative Instructions relative to the relief.	
"			Railhead moves to BEAUVRY.	
"	11		C.A.M. MONTGOMERY, Ayrshire Yeo appointed Staff Capt 230 Inf Bde Vice Major M.M. PARRY JONES M.C. & S.O.2 appointed G.S.O.2 XIX Corps Vice Major	
"	12		W.M BECKWITH. D.S.O. A. of J. Coldstream Guards appointed G.S.O.2 vice Major	
"	13		Parry Jones. A.N.Q. closed at S.12.d.7.8 and opened at FOURNES CHATEAU.	
FOURNES CHATEAU	17		Supply refilling point fixed at V.2.a.3.6 & supplies dumped there by M.T. Supplies drawn from Beauvry Railhead at MARQUILLIES & dumped at 03 0d 9 y SANTES which was refilling point for 19"	
"	18		Adv D.H.Q closed FOURNES CHATEAU at 1430 and opened at throne huts at WATTIGNIES CHATEAU W.1.C.&.3 at same time.	

A.H. Burkhart Major
D.A.Q.M.G. (94) Division

Army Form C. 2118.

WAR DIARY or INTELLIGENCE SUMMARY.

(Erase heading not required.)

A&Q Branch
Headquarters 74'(Yeo) Division
October 1918

Place	Date	Hour	Summary of Events and Information	Remarks and references to Appendices
WATTIGNIES CHATEAU WIERS	19		Refilling point for 20' selected at P.23.d.3.3. Sheet 36 and supplies dumped there by M.T.	
"	20		Ration M.T. today moved to WATTIGNIES. Supply refilling point for 21' selected at X.5.a.5.8 and supplies dumped there by M.T.	
			D.H.Q. closed at CHATEAU WATTIGNIES WIERS at 12.00 & opened at PONT À TRESSIN M.21.a.3.3 & 37 at same hour	
PONT A TRESSIN M.21.a.33 Sheet 37	21		Refilling point for 22' selected at R.23.c.3.9. 2/Lt. G.F. WITTS General List, appointed Evacuation officer with limits rank of Captain.	
"	22		Broad Gauge Supply railhead changed to MARQUILLIES as from 23'/24' inst. Orders issued for relief of 230 Inf. Bde. by 229 Inf. Bde. on night 23/24.	
"	23		Relief postponed for night 24'/25'. Major W.M. BECKWITH D.S.O. Coldstream Guards R.A.O. assumed duties as A.S.O. 2 today	Appendix II
"	25		D.D.C. moved to Allenton Venereal Diseases Ball Cmds.	
"	26		Personnel Railhead moved to DON. Divisional Reception Camp moved to TEMPLEMARS W.14.b.5.3. Sheet 36.	
"	27		Draft order for formation of a Divisional Mounted Squadron issued.	Appendix III
"	31		Intimation received that supply railhead will now close on 2 November. Intimation received that the 2nd Mounted Squadron will now be formed & orders issued to these accordingly.	
			East of the HAUTE DEULE Canal Bullets as a rule were good and buildings first intact. Water both for men + animals, was also plentiful in this area. It was found necessary to evacuate the village of MARQUAIN & order to the neighbouring villages of HERTAIN & LAMAIN.	

Signed...
A.A. & Q.M.G. 74 (Yeo) Division

WAR DIARY
or
INTELLIGENCE SUMMARY

Army Form C. 2118.

A+Q Branch
Headquarters 74 (yeo) Division
October 1918

Place	Date	Hour	Summary of Events and Information	Remarks and references to Appendices

PONT À TRESSIN
W.21.a.3.3
	31		**Strength:-**
			The strength of the division under the various headings on 5.", 12.", 19.", 26." October was
			     Effective Strength Ration Strength Fighting Strength
			     Off. O/R Off. O/R Off. O/R
			     601 12637 537 11168 246 5128
			on 26." Oct. 609 12535 520 11241 239 5304
			
			Sick:-
			Nos. evacuated sick for week ending:-
			5." October 7 Officers 180 Other Ranks
			12." October 3 " 126 "
			19." October 9 " 241 "
			26." October 10 " 229 "
			Total for month 29 776
			
			Casualties for the month:-
			            Officers Other Ranks
			Killed 6 68
			Wounded 26 348
			Missing 1 28
			Injuries - 14
			Total for month 33 458
			
			Reinforcements:-
			Total Reinforcements received during the month
			23 Officers + 96 Other ranks
				Appendices
				IV

A/Q Branch
Headquarters 74 (yeo) Division
October 1918

War Diary Appendix I

SECRET.　　　　　　　　　　　　　　　　　　　　　　Copy No. 16

C.Q. 505/1

ADMINISTRATIVE INSTRUCTIONS RELATIVE TO
74th DIVISION ORDER No. 97.

1. The 231st Infantry Brigade will hand over to the 229th Infantry Brigade all Trench and Area Stores including, Packsaddles, Food Containers, and Petrol Tins.
   The 229th Infantry Brigade will forward to this office by the 12th inst, a list of the Stores taken over, signed by the Staff Captains of the two Brigades concerned.

2. The S.A.A. Section of the D.A.C. is located at T.2.a.1.9. All demands for S.A.A. and Fireworks will be made through Brigades and not by individual Units. The Orderlies attached to Brigades from the S.A.A. Section will invariably be used as Guides.

3. Transport Lines will not be exchanged. In future Transport Lines should be located so as to make it unnecessary to alter them on inter Brigade reliefs.

Headquarters.　　　　　　　　　　　　　　　　　　　Lieut-Colonel
　　　　　　　　　　　　　　　　　　　　　　　　　　A.A. & Q.M.G.
8th October 1918.　　　　　　　　　　　　　　　　　74th (Yeo) Division.

Copies to :-
No. 1.	G.O.C.	11.	D.A.D.V.S.
2.	"G"	12.	Div. Train.
3.	3rd Corps.	13.	D.A.D.O.S.
4.	C.R.E.	14.	D.A.P.M.
5.	Signals.	15.	19th D.A.
6.	74th M.G. Battn.	16.	War Diary.
7.	229th Inf. Bde.	17.-18	File.
8.	230th Inf. Bde.	19.	Salvage Officer.
9.	231st Inf. Bde.	20-25	Spare.
10.	A.D.M.S.		

Diary Appendix II

C.A. 547/1.

Hd.Qrs. 229th Bde.   O.R.A.   Div.Sigs.   O.Comdt.   Div.Rec.Camp.
         230th Bde.   C.R.E.   Div.Train.   985 E.Coy.   D.A.D.O.S.
         231st Bde.   A.D.M.S. Div.M.G.Bn. Div.M.T.Coy.   D.A.D.V.S.

It is necessary to repeat again that the enemy is as unscrupulous in his methods as he is bestial in his habits, forewarned is forearmed, we do not wish to be caught napping.

We are all now aware that the enemy leaves delay action fuses and mines behind him in his retreat and we are prepared to deal with this particular form of warfare, but we are up against a far more deadly and insidious form of time fuse which he has left behind, one which is far reaching in its effects and which will affect not only us but our children and our children's children if we are not on the alert and ready for it when we meet it.

The enemy has deliberately released from hospitals all patients suffering from Venereal Disease and from now onwards we may expect to find prostitutes in every village and every town who are diseased, who are probably in the pay of the enemy, and whose business it is to spread as much disease in our Army in as short a time as possible.

The ravages of Venereal Disease cannot be made too widely known at the present stage of the war especially amongst young troops who may yet be wanting in worldly experience.

We are winning this war by grit and determination but these qualities are no use without MEN, any man therefore is playing into the enemy's hands, who becomes non-effective by exposing himself to infection by intercourse with the cast-off prostitutes the enemy has left behind to ensnare him.

Disease may cause far more casualties than bullets, we must look to it that the war is not prolonged by loss of men from causes which can be prevented.

25/10/18.

Major General,
Commanding 74th (Yeomanry) Division.

SECRET.
****

Copy No. 16

C.Q. 505/1

ADMINISTRATIVE INSTRUCTIONS RELATIVE TO
74th DIVISION ORDER No. 97.

1. The 231st Infantry Brigade will hand over to the 229th Infantry Brigade all Trench and Area Stores including, Packsaddles, Food Containers, and Petrol Tins.
   The 229th Infantry Brigade will forward to this office by the 12th inst, a list of the Stores taken over, signed by the Staff Captains of the two Brigades concerned.

2. The S.A.A. Section of the D.A.C. is located at T.2.a.1.9. All demands for S.A.A. and Fireworks will be made through Brigades and not by individual Units. The Orderlies attached to Brigades from the S.A.A. Section will invariably be used as Guides.

3. Transport Lines will not be exchanged. In future Transport Lines should be located so as to make it unnecessary to alter them on inter Brigade reliefs.

Headquarters.

8th October 1918.

Lieut-Colonel
A.A. & Q.M.G.
74th (Yeo) Division.

Copies to :-
No.1.	G.O.C.	11.	D.A.D.V.S.
2.	"G"	12.	Div. Train.
3.	3rd Corps.	13.	D.A.D.O.S.
4.	C.R.E.	14.	D.A.P.M.
5.	Signals.	15.	19th D.A.
6.	74th M.G.Battn.	16.	War Diary.
7.	229th Inf.Bde.	17.-18	File.
8.	230th Inf.Bde.	19.	Salvage Officer.
9.	231st Inf.Bde.	20- 25	Spare.
10.	A.D.M.S.		

Diary  Appendix II

C.A. 547/1.

Hd.Qrs. 229th Bde.	O.R.A.	Div.Sigs.	O.Comdt.	Div.Rec.Camp.
230th Bde.	C.R.E.	Div.Train.	985 E.Coy.	D.A.D.O.S.
231st Bde.	A.D.M.S.	Div.M.G.Bn.	Div.M.T.Coy.	D.A.D.V.S.

It is necessary to repeat again that the enemy is as unscrupulous in his methods as he is bestial in his habits, forewarned is forearmed, we do not wish to be caught napping.

We are all now aware that the enemy leaves delay action fuses and mines behind him in his retreat and we are prepared to deal with this particular form of warfare, but we are up against a far more deadly and insidious form of time fuse which he has left behind, one which is far reaching in its effects and which will affect not only us but our children and our children's children if we are not on the alert and ready for it when we meet it.

The enemy has deliberately released from hospitals all patients suffering from Venereal Disease and from now onwards we may expect to find prostitutes in every village and every town who are diseased, who are probably in the pay of the enemy, and whose business it is to spread as much disease in our Army in as short a time as possible.

The ravages of Venereal Disease cannot be made too widely known at the present stage of the war especially amongst young troops who may yet be wanting in worldly experience.

We are winning this war by grit and determination but these qualities are no use without MEN, any man therefore is playing into the enemy's hands, who becomes non-effective by exposing himself to infection by intercourse with the cast-off prostitutes the enemy has left behind to ensnare him.

Disease may cause far more casualties than bullets, we must look to it that the war is not prolonged by loss of men from causes which can be prevented.

E.S.Girdwood

25/10/18.

Major General,

Commanding 74th (Yeomanry) Division.

DIARY *Appendix III*

Headquarters		A.I. 245/M.
229th Inf.Bde	A.D.M.S.	
230th Inf.Bde.	D.A.D.V.S.	
231st Inf.Bde.	O.C.251 (T)Coy.R.E.	
C.R.A.	D.A.P.M.	
O.C. 74th M.G.Bn	Area Commdt. BAISIEUX.	
O.C. Div.Train		

The attached Draft Order is forwarded for your information and immediate action.

Nominal Rolls of Officers and O/Rs selected will be forwarded so as to reach this Office by 1200 on 29th

Brigades will in addition to the numbers required to complete establishment select 1 Troop Officer and 10 ORs as a Waiting List from which casualties will be replaced. These names will be added to the Nominal Rolls rendered.

Any suggestions for adjustments in regard to the composition of the personnel should be put forward at once, but this must not delay the selection of the personnel detailed or the rendering of the Nominal Rolls punctually

H.J.Birtchnell, Major
for Lieut.-Colonel,

27/10/18.   A.A. & Q.M.G. 74th (Yeomanry)Division.

Copies to: "G"
O.C. Signals.
C.R.E.

DRAFT ORDER.

A.I.245/M

Headquarters
229th Inf.Bde.   A.D.M.S.
230th Inf.Bde.   D.A.D.V.S.
231st Inf.Bde.   O.C 251(T)Coy R.E.
C.R.A.   D.A.P.M.
O.C. 74th M.G.Bn   Area Commdt. BAISIEUX
C.C.Div.Train   C.P.E.

---

1. A Mounted Squadron will be formed forthwith to enable touch to be kept with the enemy in the event of his making a rapid retirement.

2. Capt. H.P.FREEMAN,M.C., Montgomery Yeomanry (attached 25th R.Welsh Fusiliers) is appointed to Command the Unit with local rank of Major.

3. Personnel etc. will be found by Units as laid down in attached table ("B" Teams may be drawn upon but such withdrawals must be suitably replaced.)

4. Establishment will be in accordance with attached Table.

5. Personnel and Vehicles etc. will assemble at 10 a.m. on ......

   Billets from Area Commandant BAISIEUX.
   Personnel to be fully equipped.
   Vehicles fully equipped and horsed.

6. Other Ranks to bring the unexpired portion of the days Ration- Iron Rations and 1 Day's Ration. 2 Days Rations and forage (less fuel and hay) will be issued in addition to any Rations drawn for consumption while in Billets. This issue will be taken with the Squadron in the event of an advance.

Lieut.-Colonel,
A.A. & Q.M.G. 74th (Yeomanry) Division.

27/10/18.

Copies to:- "G"
            O.Signals

74th (Yeomanry) Division Mounted Squadron.
H.Qrs & 3 Troops War Establishment.

Officers	W.O.	St.Sergts & Sergts	Artificers	Trumpeters	Drivers	Rank & File
(a) H.Q. 1 Major,Commanding 1 Capt. 2nd-in-Cmd. (b) 3 Troops. 3 Capts) Troop or) Leaders Lieuts)	H.Q. 1 SSM.	(a) H.Q. 1.S.Q.M.S. 1 Vet.Sgt (b) 3 Trps 6 Troop Sergts.	(a) H.Q. 1 Cpl.Shoeing Smith (b) 3 Troops 3 Shoeing Smiths	H.Q. 2.	3.	(a) Squadron H.Q. 2 Batmen 2 Grooms 1 Storeman 7 Signallers (includes 1 Sergt) 2. R.A.M.C. 1 Interpreter or Intelligence Police. (b) 3 Troops 87 ORs (Includes Batmen and Grooms of Troop Leaders.)
TOTAL 5 Officers	1.	8	4	2	3	102.

TRANSPORT FOR ABOVE.

Horses and Mules.

Riding Horses	Draught.	Pack Mules For L.Gs.	Vehicles.		
120 (Includes 1 Interpreter) (Excludes Batmen)	6.	8.	7 Bicycles.	3 Limbered G.S.Wagons rations & forage for 2 days (forage - oats only - rations (less fuel) and ammunition.	

MOUNTED SQUADRON.   PERSONNEL TO BE FOUND BY UNITS.

DETAIL.	229th Bde.	230th Bde.	231st Bde.	Divnl. Arty.	M.G.Bn.	Train.	A.D.M.S.	REMARKS.
5 Officers { Squadron Leader.	1							Not yet selected.
{ 2nd in Comd.		1	1					Not yet selected.
{ 3 Troop Leaders.								x To be detailed by D.A.D.V.S.
1 S.S.M.	1							
1 F.Q.M.S.	1							
1 Vet.Sgt. x								
1 Corpl.S.Smith.	1	1	1					
3 Cold Shoers.	1	1	1					
3 Drivers.	1	2	3*	1				* To include Sgt.
7 Signallers (incl 1 Sgt)	2							
1 Interpreter or 1 Intelligence Police (Mtd) %								% To be detailed by D.A.P.M.
6 Troop Sergts.	2	2	2					
2 Trumpeters. ♂	1	1						♂ Includes Batman & Groom for Sqdn.Ldr.
92 Corpls & Privates. **	29	29	31 ø					x To be detailed by A.D.M.S.
2 R.A.M.C. x							2	
Vickers M.G.Group (Mtd)	To be arranged by O.C. 74th Divnl. M.G.Bn.							
119 Riding Horses.	To be provided by Corps.							
6 Draught Horses.	2	2	2					
6 Pack Mules.	2	2	2					
7 Bicycles.	1	1	1	1	1			
3 Wagons Limbered.	1	1	1					

** The Bde finding 2nd in Cmd will provide in addition to the 2 e.batman and groom for the 2nd in Cmd. The remaining Bdes will provide 1 Storeman in addition.

No 3

War Diary
"A" & "Q" Branch
Hd Qrs 74th (Yeo) Division
From 1st to 30th JUNE 1918
VOLUME XVI

DAAG Appendix IV

74th (YEOMANRY) DIVISION.

CONSOLIDATED LIST OF CASUALTIES FOR PERIOD 1st - 31st Oct.

UNIT.	KILLED Off.	KILLED O.R.	WOUNDED Off.	WOUNDED O.R.	MISSING Off.	MISSING O.R.	D. OF INJ. Off.	D. OF INJ. O.R.	INJURED Off.	INJURED O.R.
D.H.Q.	-	4	1	1	-	-	-	-	-	-
M.V.S.	-	-	-	-	-	-	-	-	-	-
Div. Train.	-	-	-	-	-	-	-	-	-	-
Div. Emp. Coy.	-	-	-	1	-	-	-	-	-	-
H.Q.RA.	-	-	1	-	-	-	-	-	-	-
44th Bde. RFA	-	-	1	2	-	-	-	-	-	-
117th Bde. RFA	1	-	2	9	-	-	-	-	-	2
74th D.A.C.	-	-	-	1	-	-	-	-	-	1
74th M.T.M.Bs	-	2	-	5	-	-	-	-	-	-
H.Q. R.E.	-	-	-	1	-	-	-	-	-	-
5th F.Co. RMRE	-	-	-	1	-	-	-	-	-	-
5th F.Co. RARE	-	-	-	-	-	-	-	-	-	-
439 F.Co. R.E.	-	1	-	1	-	-	-	-	-	-
1/12 L.N.Lancs	1	-	-	1	-	-	-	-	-	-
74th Div. Sigs.	-	1	-	3	-	-	-	-	-	-
229th Inf. Bde.										
229th Bde. H.Q.	-	-	-	-	-	-	-	-	-	-
229th LTMB.	-	-	-	-	-	-	-	-	-	-
16th Devons.	-	2	1	21	-	-	-	-	-	-
12th Som. L.I.	-	11	6	64	-	-	-	-	-	-
14th R. Highlrs	1	11	5	47	-	-	-	-	-	-
230th Inf. Bde.										
230th Bde. HQ	-	-	-	-	-	-	-	-	-	-
230th LTMB	-	-	-	-	-	-	-	-	-	-
10 E. Kents	1	6	2	64	-	6	-	-	-	6
15th Suffolks	2	14	1	27	-	6	-	-	-	1
16th Sussex	-	4	1	29	-	-	-	-	-	-
231st Inf. Bde										
231st Bde. HQ	-	-	1	-	-	-	-	-	-	1
231st LTMB	-	-	-	-	-	-	-	-	-	-
25th R.W.F.	-	3	1	18	-	-	-	-	-	-
24th Welsh	-	2	-	14	-	2	-	-	-	2
10th K.S.L.I.	1	3	3	21	-	20	-	-	-	-
74th M.G. Bn.	-	1	-	12	-	-	-	-	-	-
229th F. Amb.	-	-	-	1	-	-	-	-	-	-
230th F. Amb.	-	7	-	4	-	-	-	-	-	-
231st F. Amb.	-	-	-	-	-	-	-	-	-	-
Div. M.T. Coy.	-	-	-	-	-	-	-	-	-	-
TOTAL DIVISION	**7**	**68**	**26**	**348**	**-**	**28**	**-**	**-**	**-**	**14**
Attd. Troops.										
87th Bde. RFA	-	1	2	4	-	-	-	-	-	-
88th Bde. RFA	-	-	-	1	-	-	-	-	2	-
179th Bde. RFA	-	-	-	1	-	-	-	-	-	1

Major D.A.A.G.
74th (Yeomanry) Division.

WAR DIARY
74th (Yeomanry) Division
"A" & "Q" BRANCH
From 1st to 31st OCTOBER 1918
VOLUME XX

W.D. 8

War Diary
"A" & "Q" Branch
14th (Yeomanry) Division
for
month of
NOVEMBER 1918.

WAR DIARY / INTELLIGENCE SUMMARY

Army Form C. 2118.

A & Q Branch
Headquarters
42 (Yeomanry) Division
November 1918

Place	Date	Hour	Summary of Events and Information	Remarks
PONT A TRESSIN M.21.a.3.3 Sheet 37	4		Personnel railhead moved to LOOS	
	5		Divl Reception Camp moved to PONT A TRESSIN. Corps Reception Camp receives and sends them forward. Divl Reception following day. Personnel from the trains & sends them forward.	
"	6		Intimation received that Lt. (T/Capt.) C Mackintosh, Royal Scots (T.F.) Staff Capt 229 "Sd" Bde has been appointed Staff Capt "A" & "Q" Branch. Supply Railhead moved to BAISIEUX M.17 Central Sheet 37 Refilling Point for whole Division at M.17.b.3.2.	
"	7		Rations drawn from BAISIEUX by Horse Transport. Intimation received that the 29 & 34 "B" & 2 Portuguese Bde & 1 Section of 1.P. Field Ambulance are to be attached to the Division. 22 "B" to the 29 "Bde, 1 34 "B" 229 Inf Bde. They will bring 1 Cook and M. Transport 230 Inf Bde, 2 F. I/Payno Facultification and 2 M. L. a.s.o. Battalion. They will form an 11 cadre to be retained by the Division from 13 onwards.	
"	8		Strength 29 "B" 900 and 100 animals 34 "B" 700 and 100 animals Section Field Ambulance 50 men and 20 animals. Intimation received that Lt A H Grant 3 "B" South Lancashire Regt att 37 Division has been appointed Staff Capt 229 Inf Bde vice Lt(T/ Capt) C Mackintosh to 25 3 Tank Brot.	
	9		M.T. dump supply of 0.28.b.97 abt sh 37 ordered at M.21.a.33 Ditto Ammo at 0.18.c.27 at 12.00 Sheet 37 M.T. Supply authoris at P.13.a.5.0 Staff Capt 229 Inf Bde Lt A H Grant assumed duties	
OISY-LE- FAUBOURG	10			
	11		Lt Col W. Y. Inq Duncan D.A.Q.M.G.	

Army Form C. 2118.

WAR DIARY
or
INTELLIGENCE SUMMARY

Army: A.S. Branch
Headquarters: 9th (Scottish) Division
Month and year: November 1918

(Erase heading not required.)

Place	Date	Hour	Summary of Events and Information	Remarks and references to Appendices
OISERY	11		Intimation received that an Armistice with Germany had been signed. D.H.Q. closed at OISERY at 12.00.	
LE ZARZ FRASNES LEZ BUISSENAL	11		D.H.Q. opened at FRASNES LEZ BOISSENAL 1234 Z7 at 12.00. The roads from TOURNAI via ROMMIES-MELLES-QUARTES & FRASNES LEZ BUISSENAL to new H.Q. were fair with room for only one way M.T. There were several indicators on the roads which caused great difficulty in getting convoys with supplies forward. They arrived at 22.00 t supplies were dumped at L27 C67.	
	12		Lt. Col. A.C. TEMPLE DSO G.S.O.1 appointed G.S.O.1 X Army & proceeded today. Major (T/Lt.Col.) C.N.F. BROAD D.S.O. assumed duty as G.S.O.1. Major W.M. BECKWITH D.S.O. Coldstream Guards (R.O.) G.S.O.2 appointed G.S.O.1 30. Devon and to Lieut. Col. Bt. Major A.F. SANDERSON Gordoners (Bucks. hands.) L9 G.S.O.2 35 Division appointed G.S.O.2 vice Major BECKWITH.	
	13		Major BECKWITH proceeded to join 30. Division	
	14		Refilling points were as follows: 929 L7 ded. Supply Co. left at 17 c23 23.01.23 51 groups at L17 c60. Supplies were drawn from BASSIEUX whilst remains supply railhead.	
	15		Intimation received that the advance to the German Frontier will commence on 15 inst. & that III Corps will be transferring to II Army at 12.00 on 16 inst.	
	16		Intimation received that Nov. 242 (Army) Bde R.F.A. would join the Division on Nov 6 inst. Major A.E. SANDERSON D.S.O. assumed duty as G.S.O.2.	

Sgd. R.W. Charles
Lt. Col. Gen. Staff 9th Div.

WAR DIARY or INTELLIGENCE SUMMARY

Army Form C. 2118.

A.T.¶ Branch
Headquarters
74 (Yeomanry) Division
November 1918

Place	Date	Hour	Summary of Events and Information	Remarks and references to Appendices
FRASNES L&Z	17		Refilling point for 830" Inf Bde Group and M.G.B" moved to K.32.b.39. Div. Arty. to K.32.b.39. 931st Inf Bde. Group to J.30.d.2.0. Pioneer L.17.d.2.3.	
BUISSENAL L23 a 2.7	18.		242 (Army) Bde R.F.A. joined the Division	
	19		S.R.P.S moved as follows 931 Group to RUMILLIES P.15.a.3.0. Div artillery to MELLES K.32.A.3.0. 242 (Army) Bde R.F.A. K.32.A.3.0. Newts53	appendix I
	22°		Intimation received that a supplementary years despatch would be called for. Particulars sent to all units formation	
	24		Intimation received that forms for Demobilization purposes are being issued to Units.	
	25		Preliminary Reconnaissance of new area made. Proposed Distribution 230 Inf Bde Group & 931st Inf Bde Grp less 931st Field Ambulance in GRAMMONT ONKERZEELE & OVERBOULAERE 231st Field Ambulance at Convent OLIGNIES & Bde HQ in GRAMMONT. 230 Inf Bde Group GAMMERAGES, BIÉVÈNE, THOLLEMBEEK & HERINNES with 24 Cas at GAMMERAGES. Rest Cps at WANNEBECQ, PAPIGNIES, IZIERES, DEUX ACREN & HOVE & VIANE. Train at OLIGNIES. D.H.Q, MGB & Pioneers in LESSINES.	
	27		Staff Capt. made reconnaissance of new areas	
	30		Distribution circulars Nos 1 & 2 issued Ins 2 books with Columns	

R.F. Autchard(?)
Lt. Col. G.S. (Gen) Division

WAR DIARY
or
INTELLIGENCE SUMMARY.
(Erase heading not required.)

Army Form C. 2118.

2nd Branch
Headquarters
4th (Cavalry) Division
November 1918

Place	Date	Hour	Summary of Events and Information	Remarks and references to Appendices
FRASNES LEZ BUISSENAL L 23 a 27	30		**Strength:-** Effective Fighting Division on 2nd November 611 officers & 12,918 other ranks. 30 November 694 officers & 13,721 other ranks. Fighting Strength - on 2nd November 227 officers & 6004 other ranks. 30 November 318 officers & 7309 other ranks. **Sick** evacuated sick during month 25 officers & 873 other ranks. **Casualties** during the month Killed 2 officers 16 other ranks Wounded 7 " 168 " Missing 1 " 2 " Injured - " 9 " Total Casualties for month 9 officers & 195 other ranks. Reinforcements received during the month 78 officers and 1911 other ranks. 200.9 4th (Cavalry) Division	

WAR DIARY NOVEMBER
Appendix I

III Corps
No. A.983/18.

H.Q. 229th Bde.	C.R.A.	Div.Sigs.	C.Comdt.
230th Bde.	C.R.E.	Div.Train	985 E.Coy.
231st Bde.	A.D.M.S.	Div. M.G.Bn.	Div. Rec.Camp.

SUPPLEMENTARY NEW YEAR'S DESPATCH, 1919.   CA325/77

1. (a) There will be a supplementary New Year's Honours Despatch. The particular period to be covered will be from midnight, 16/17th Sept. 1918, to 11 a.m. November, 1918, but, as special cases names may also be submitted of those who may have been omitted from the New Year's Gazette (period February 25th – September 16th).
   Full particulars regarding the number of recommendations which may be sent in to cover both the above will be issued to all concerned as soon as possible after November 19th.
   (b) This Supplementary New Year's Despatch, 1919, is additional to any Final War Despatch, regarding which particulars have not yet been received from the Army Council.

2. Recommendations for the Supplementary Despatch will not be submitted until after the New Year's Gazette proper has been announced. The date by which recommendations must reach the Military Secretary, General Headquarters, will be notified later.

3. (a) Headquarters of Formations will be responsible for the submission of recommendations concerning all those who were under their Command or administered by them at 11 a.m. on November 11th, 1918.
   If there is any doubt in the case of a unit on the move at that hour it will count as part of the Formation it has just left.
   (b) At the same time any reward recommended for an Officer or man who may have left a Formation in which he is considered to have earned reward, must form part of those of the officer making the recommendation.
   (c) No recommendation will be sent to the formation to which an officer or man may have been transferred. An exception may be made in the case of a recommendation for the Commander of a Formation or Unit which has been transferred complete.
   (d) Recommendations on behalf of Commanders will come out of the allotment to the unit which they command.

4. The proportion of Honours to Mentions for officers will be 2 to 5. A separate allotment for Honours and Mentions will be given for "other ranks", the proportion being 3 medals to 1 Mention.
   The number of recommendations submitted for the Distinguished Conduct Medal, will in no case be larger than those for the Meritorious Service Medal.

5. (a) Except in special circumstances, or for particular gallant services, no officer should be recommended who has received two rewards in any of the following Gazettes, or Supplements, bearing the same date:–
            4th June, 1917.
            1st Jan, 1918.
            3rd June, 1918.
   Two rewards are to be regarded as either two promotions, Brevet or substantive, or one promotion, and one decoration or two decorations.
   (b) If an Officer or man received an Honour in the Gazette bearing date 3rd June, 1918, a recommendation for an Honour in this Supplementary Despatch should be most exceptional. (See para. 59 (a) of S.S. 477)
   (c) The name of an officer or other rank who received an honour in the New Year's Gazette, 1919, for period closing September 16th, cannot be submitted for a second honour.

                                                               P.T.O.

6. Special attention is drawn to the amendments to para 64 (a) of S.S. 477 which are about to be issued, with regard to recommendations for the reward of the Meritorious Service Medal.

7. The Postal Services will be given a separate allotment, and in no circumstances should the name of a man belonging to them be submitted for reward out of the general allotment.
  Should it be desired to recommend any man, his name should be sent to this Office separately.

8. Recommendations for the grant of the Royal Red Cross (Classes 1 and 11), and of Indian decorations may be in excess of the allotment made.

9. (a) Recommendations for different Honours should not be submitted on the same schedule.
  (b) Recommendations of officers or other ranks belonging to different arms of the Service should not be submitted on the same schedule. (vide para. 7 (a) of S.S. 477)
  It is pointed out that a Yeomanry Officer belongs to the Cavalry A Yeomanry Officer must not therefore be recommended on the same form as an Officer who holds a commission in the Infantry.

10. Formations and Units will ensure that they have sufficient supplies of A.F. W. 3121 in hand so that there may be no delay in submitting the recommendation when called for.

W.J. Butchart

Major,
D.A.A.G. 74th (Yeomanry) Division.

22/11/18.

909

COPY.

WAR DIARY
"A" & "Q" Branches
74th (Yeomanry) Division
for month of
DECEMBER 1918

WAR DIARY
INTELLIGENCE SUMMARY

Army Form C. 2118.

A & Q Branch
Headquarters 74th (Yeomanry) Division
December 1918.

Place	Date	Hour	Summary of Events and Information	Remarks and references to Appendices
FRASNES LEZ BUSSENAL L23A27	7		First draft of Instructions to be sent from the Division for Demobilization ordered to proceed on 11th inst.	Appendix I
"	8		Orders issued for advanced Billeting Parties to proceed onwards on 11th.	
"			Orders received to send 19 O.R. to 5th Army Demobilization Concentration Camp at LA MADELEINE for duty.	
"	9		Orders received to prepare Historical Documents, "Demobilizers" and Pivotal Officers and men.	
"			Capt A. GALLOWAY Scottish Rifles, G.S.O.3 of the Division ordered to proceed to G.H.Q. for duty under the D.M.L. also that he would not be replaced.	
"	10		Departure of advanced Billeting parties all cancelled as Corps unable to furnish lorries. Parties ordered to proceed on 13th.	
"	12		Capt A. GALLOWAY left for G.H.Q. Administrative instructions for move to new area issued.	Appendix II

A.G. Rutherford Major
D.A. & Q.M.G. 74th (Yeo) Dn.

WAR DIARY
or
INTELLIGENCE SUMMARY.

A.T. Branch.
Headquarters 74 (Yeo) Division.
December 1918.

Army Form C. 2118.

Place	Date	Hour	Summary of Events and Information	Remarks and references to Appendices
FRASNES	13		Traffic orders for move of MT issued.	Appendix II
LES BOUSSEVAL			Personnel railroaded. Trains 8 A.T.4.	
L.23 a 2.7	14		Divisional Headquarters closed FRASNES-LEZ-BUISSENAL at 12.00 and opened at the Hotel de Ville LESSINES at 17.00	
LESSINES	15			
"	16		Australian Aust. Sqn Camp moved to OLLIGNIES	
"	17		Supply railhead moved to GHISLENGHIEN	
"	19		Supplies from this date onwards drawn by Horse transport to refilling points at LESSINES & BIEVENE. The 230 D/P/Pk group drawing from BIEVENE also 44 Bde RFA and the remainder of the Division from LESSINES S.	

Strengths:-
Effective Strength a, y Dec. 648 officers & 13650 OR
" b " " 68 " 887 "
" " " " 689 " + 13149 OR

Sick:
15 Officers and 464 OR were evacuated sick during the month.

A.S. Autchartey
D.A.Q.M.G. 74(Yeo) Div.

FORM "D"

List No. 5.

Division, etc. **231st. INFANTRY BRIGADE**   Week-ending **1st. JANRY. 1918.**

Name of Unit, etc	STRENGTH				ANIMALS			GUNS			Remarks
	(a) Effective		(b) Ration		(a) Horses	(b) Mules	(c) Camels	(a) F.A.	(b) Maxim or Vickers	(c) Lewis	
	O.	O.R.	O.	O.R.							
Hqrs, 231st. Inf. Bde.	4	26	3	33	7	-	-	-	-	-	
Signal Sec.	-	-	1	31	4	5	-	-	-	-	
24th.(Denbigh Yeo.) Bn.R.W.F.	5 25	651	23	565	11	71	-	-	-	16	Increase. 1-24 from Hosp. 1-1 from Leave Decrease. 2-7 to Course 4 to Water D
25th. (Montgomery Welsh Horse Yeo.) Bn.R.W.F.	22	676	15	600	10	68	-	-	-	16	Decrease. 13 ORs. to Hosp.
24th.(Pembroke & Glamorgan Yeo.) Bn.Welsh Rgt.	19	647	20	592	12	72	-	-	-	16	Increase. 13 ORs. from Hosp Decrease. 14 ORS. to Hosp. 1 - Died 5 - Spec Duty
10th.Bn. (Shropshire & Cheshire Yeo) K.S.LI.	26	648 84	18	621	12	73	-	-	-	16	Increase. 10 ORs. from Hosp Decrease. 1-6 to Hosp.
210th.Machine Gun Coy.	8	206	7	201	11	57	-	-	16	-	Increase. 231st.R.W.F. 2-31 Reinfs. 1 from Hosp. Decrease. 1-1 to Leave
Water Duty Personnel	-	-	1	19							
TOTAL	104	2854 98	87	2643 (19)	67	346	-	-	16	64	

58. 2662

A.P. & S.D., Alex./1608/25A/10.17/30M.(V.& G.)
1.2.18.
1400

A/ Staff Captain
231st. Infantry Brigade.

P.T.O.

FIGHTING STRENGTH.

of

231st. INFANTRY BRIGADE.

UNIT.	STRENGTH OFFS.	ORS.	REMARKS.
24th.(Denbigh Yeo) R.W.F.	17	560	**Increase.** 24 ORs.from Hosp. / 43 " Draft / 2 Offs.from Hosp. **Decrease.** 2 Offs.5 ORs.to Hosp / 1 - 14 - to Leave / 1 - to U.K. / 5 - to Trade Test.
25th.(Montgomery & Welsh Horse Yeo.) R.W.F.	14	638	1 Off.1 OR.from BHQ / 1 - 1 - from Course / 39 - from Base / 1 - from Hosp. 2 Offs.6 ORs.Leave / 1 - 10 - Hosp. / 3 - to U.K.Leave / 1 OR.to Trade Test / 5 - to Spec.Duty
24th.(Pembroke & Glamorgan Yeo.) Welsh Rgt.	15	598	1 Off.Reinf. / 49 ORs.from Hosp. 1-10 to Hosp. / 1- 1 to Leave / 1 - 5 to Spec.Duty
10th.(Shropshire & Cheshire Yeo.) K.S.L.I.	19	633	1.58 from Hosp. / 1 from Course 2-11 to Hosp. / 2- 2 to Courses / 1 to 210th.M.G.C / 4 to Leave
210th.Machine Gun Company	6	164	2 ORs.from Battns. 1-2 to Hosp. / 1-0 to U.K.Leave / 1 to Battn. / 1 to Spec.Duty.
231st.Light Trench Mortar Battery.	2	32	3 ORs.from Hosp.
TOTAL	73	2625	

25.1.18.
1400.

A/Staff Captain
231st.Infantry Brigade.

List No. 1.

FORM "D"

Division, etc. 231st. Infantry Brigade.   Week-ending 4th. Janry 1918.

Name of Unit, etc	STRENGTH				ANIMALS			GUNS			Remarks
	(a) Effective		(b) Ration		(a) Horses	(b) Mules	(c) DONKEYS	(a) F.	(b) Maxim or Vickers	(c) Lewis	
	O.	O.R.	O.	O.R.							
Hqrs, 231st. Inf. Bde.	5	27	4	30/2@	10	-	8	-	-	-	Decrease du(Orderlies,
	-	-	1	37	4	5	-	-	-	-	(Linemen etc (returned to Regts. @ Natives
24th. Bn. (Denbigh Yeo) R.W.F.	23	505	21	431/14@	12	80	69	-	-	16	Decrease. 1 Off. to A.O. 1 Off. to G.H 11 ORs. to Hos
25th. Bn. (Montgomery & Welsh Horse Y. R.W.F.	26	557	24	514	10	69	70	-	-	16	Increase. 1 Off. from Ba Decrease. 1 Off.1 Or.Co off Ration St 8 ORs. to Hosp 1 OR.to Milit. R1
24th. Bn. (Pembroke & Glamorgan Yeo.) Welsh Rgt.	19	506	17	465	12	73	72	-	-	16	Increase. 2 Offs. 12 Ors. from Hosp. Decrease. 1 Off.14 ORs. to Hosp.
10th. Bn. (Shropshire & Cheshire Y.) K.S.L.I.	24	552	21	520	12	73	69	-	-	16	Increase. 1-30 from Hosp Decrease. 1.18 to Hosp. 1 to R.F.C.
210th. Machine Gun Company	8	170	7	166	11	57	-	-	16	-	
	104	2317	95	2163/16	71	357	288	-	16	64	

A.P. & S.D. Alex./No. 1184/7.8.17/20000 (50025A/182) V.&G.   P.T.O.

5.1.18.
1200.

Captain
Staff Captain
231st. Infantry Brigade.

1.	2. STRENGTH				3. ANIMALS			4. GUNS			5.
Name of Unit, etc	(a) Effective		(b) Ration		(a)	(b)	(c)	(a)	(b)	(c)	Remarks
	O.	O.R.	O.	O.R.	Horses	Mules	Camels	F.A.	Maxim or Vickers	Lewis	

FIGHTING STRENGTH

of

231st. INFANTRY BRIGADE.   4.1.18.

UNIT.	STRENGTH Offs.	ORs.	REMARKS.	
24th.Bn.(Denbigh Yeo) R.W.F.	17	426	Increase. 1 OR.from Hosp 1 - from B.H.Q.	Decrease. 11 ORs.to Hosp. 2 Offs.4- to Courses Transport Off.&QMr. not included
25th.Bn.(Montgomery & Welsh Horse Yeo) R.W.F.	20	512	1 Off.from Base 2 ORs.from B.H.Q.	1-1 to Course 1 Special Duty 8 to Hosp.
23th.Bn.(Pembroke & Glamorgan Yeo) Welsh Regt.	13	463	2-12 from Hosp.	1- 14 to Hosp.
10th.Bn.(Shropshire & Cheshire Yeo) K.S.L.I.	18	515	1 -30 from Hosp. 4 from Bde.	1 -18 to Hosp 1 to Special Duty.
210th.Machine Gun Company.	7	166	1 - 28 Draft 2 from Hosp.	12 ORs. to Hosp. 1 - to Sec.Duty.
231st.L.T.M.B.	2	25	1 ORs.Reinf.	1 - 1 to Course.

Note:- The Transport Officers and Quarter-masters are- of each Battalion are excluded from the Fighting Strengths this week.

TOTAL.   87 - 2207

5.1.18.
1200

Captain
Staff Captain
231st. Infantry Brigade

FORM "D"

List No. ____

Division, etc. 231st. Infantry Brigade.   Week-ending 11th. Janry. 1918.

Name of Unit, etc	STRENGTH				ANIMALS			GUNS			Remarks
	(a) Effective		(b) Ration		(a) Horses	(b) Mules	(c) Camels	(a) F.A.	(b) Maxim or Vickers	(c) Lewis	
	O.	O.R.	O.	O.R.							
Hqrs, 231st. Inf. Bde.	4	26	5	27	10	-	X	-	-	-	
Signal Section	-	-	1	37	4	5	-	-	-	-	
25th. Bn. (Denbigh Yeo) R.W.F.	21	513	20 19	432/2	X 12	79	-	-	-	16	Increase. 1 Off. 43 ORs. from X Natives. (14o/s) Decrease. 2 Offs. 9 ORs. for 66y 2 ORs. to M.G. Corp
25th. Bn. (Montgomery Yeo & Welsh Horse) R.W.F.	21	651	22	611	10	69	-	-	-	16	Increase. 1 Off. 101 OR from Base. 5 ORs. from Coms Decrease. 3 Off. 10 Ors to Courses
24th. Bn. (Pembroke & Glamorgan Yeo) Welsh Rgt.	20	580	20	542	12	73	-	-	-	16	Increase. 3-91 rejoined. Decrease. 13 ORs. to Hosp
10th. Bn. (Shropshire & Cheshire Yeo) K.S.L.I.	26	577	22	542	12	73	-	-	-	16	Increase. 2 Offs. Reinf. 48 ORs. from Hosp 1 B.H.Q. Decrease. 23 ORs. to Hosp. 1 - Commission
210th. Machine Gun Company	8	165	8	162	11	57	-	-	16	-	Increase. 1 OR. from Hosp 2 - from Batt Decrease. 7 ORs. to Hosp. 1 - to Comms
TOTAL	100	2512	98	2353/2	71	356	-	-	16	64	

A.P. & S.D., Alex./1608/25A/10.17/30M.(V.&G.)
11.1.18.
1400

Captain   P.T.O.
Staff Captain
231st. Inf___

FIGHTING STRENGTH.

of

231st. INFANTRY BRIGADE.   11.1.18.

UNIT.	STRENGTH. OFFS.	ORs.	REMARKS.
24th.Bn.R.W.F.	16	457	**Increase.** 43 ORs.from Hosp. / 2 - from Course / 1 - 104 from Base / 5 from Courses **DEcrease.** 1 Off. 9 ORs.to Hosp. / 2 - to 210 M.G.C / 1 - to R.F.C. / 3 -10 to Courses / 2 to Hosp.
25th.Bn.R.W.F.	18	609	**Decrease.** 13 ORs.from Hosp. / 1 o from A.S.C. **Increase** 3 Offs. 91 ORs.from Hosp
24th.Bn.Welsh Rgt.	16	541	**Increase** 2 Offs.from Reinfs. / 48 Ors.fromHosp. / 1 - 3 from Courses / 1 OR. from Dump. / 2 ORs.from Hosp. / 1 ORs.from Battns. **Decrease.** 23 Ors.to Hosp / 1 - to Cadet Course / 2 Off.& 8 to Courses / 7 ORs.to Hosp. / 1 OR. to Commission.
10th.Bn.K.S.L.I.	19	535	
210th.M.G.Co.	8	168	
231st.L.T.M.B.	3	27	1 Off. 2 ORs.from Course 2 ORs.to Course / 2 ORs.from Hosp. 1 - to Hosp.
TOTAL	80	2331	

11.1.18.
1400

Captain
Staff Captain
231st.Infnatry Brigade.

FORM "D"

List No. 3.

Division, etc. 231st. Infantry Bde.   Week-ending 18th. Janry. 1918.

Name of Unit, etc	STRENGTH				ANIMALS			GUNS			Remarks
	(a) Effective		(b) Ration		(a) Horses	(b) Mules	(c) Camels	(a) F.A.	(b) Maxim or Vickers	(c) Lewis	
	O.	O.R.	O.	O.R.							
231st. Bde. Hqrs.	4	26	5	27	10	9@	-	-	-	-	@ Natives.
Sig. Sec.			1	37	4	5	-	-	-	-	
24th. (Denbigh Yeo.) Bn. R.W.F.	25	564	22	489/2	12	79	-	-	-	16	Increase. 3 Offs. from Hosp. 1 - Reinfs. 58 ORs. from Hosp. Decrease. 1-1 to Leave 2 to Hosp. 1 to Course
25th. (Montgomery & Welsh Horse Yeo.) R.W.F.	28	661	22	615	10	69	-	-	-	16	Increase. 16 Ors. from Hosp. Decrease 4 Ors. to Hosp. 1 - to M.G.Co.
24th. (Pembroke & Glamorgan Yeo.) Bn. Welsh Rgt.	22	606	21	566	12	72	-	-	-	16	Increase. 1-38 from Hosp. 1 - Reinf. Decrease. 1-1 to Leave 10 to Hosp. 1 to D.H.Q.
10th. (Shropshire & Cheshire Yeo.) Bn. K.S.L.I.	28	634	25	599	12	73	-	-	-	16	Increase. 2-2 Reinfs. 67 from Hosp. 1 from Cadet Course Decrease. 12 ORs. to Hosp. 1 - to L.T.M B
210th. Machine Gun Coy.	8	175	8	166	11	57	-	-	16	-	Increase. 14 ORs. Reinfs. 2 - from Hosp. 2 - from Battns Decrease. 2 ORs. to Hosp.
TOTAL	115	2666	104	2502/2	71	355	-	-	16	54	

A.P & S.D., Alex./1608/25A/10.17/30M.(V.&G.)

18.1.18

A/Staff Captain
231st. Infantry Brigade.

P.T.O.

1.	2. STRENGTH				3. ANIMALS			4. GUNS			5.
Name of Unit, etc	(a) Effective		(b) Ration		(a) Horses	(b) Mules	(c) Camels	(a) F. A.	(b) Maxim or Vickers.	(c) Lewis	Remarks
	O.	O.R.	O.	O.R.							

REMARKS ON FORM "D" dated 18.1.18

DIFFERENCES BETWEEN RATION & EFFECTIVE STRENGTHS.
Rationed but not Effective.

	Offs.	ORs.
231st. Infantry Brigade. Headquarters.		
Att. from Battns.		
R.A.M.C.		2

Effective but not Rationed

24th. (Denbigh Yeo) Bn. R.W.F.

	Offs.		ORs.
Courses	3	-	9
Leave	1	-	1
Detached:-			
D.H.Q.			4
B.H.Q.			3
231st. Bde. Signals			3
231st. Bde. A.S.C.			2
231st. Bde. Water Duty			10
Dumps.			5
Party at LNAB	1	-	30
Att. C.T.C.			4
	5	-	71

25th. Bn. (Montgomery & Welsh Horse Yeo) R.W.F.

	Offs.		ORs.
Courses	5	-	7
Detached:-			
Corps. Hqrs.			2
D.H.Q.			7
B.H.Q.			5
231st. Bde. Signals.			3
Dumps.			7
Bde. Water Duty	1	-	2
Att. C.T.C.			1
	6	-	34

24th. (Pembroke & Glamorgan Yeo.) Bn. Welsh Rgt.

	Offs.		ORs.
Courses			7
Leave	1	-	1
Detached:-			
Corps. Hqrs.			2
D.H.Q.			8
B.H.Q.			3
Dumps.			16
231st. Bde. Signals.			3
	1	-	40

10th. (Shropshire & Cheshire Yeo) Bn. K.S.L.I.

	Offs.		ORs.
Courses	2	-	9
Detached:-			
Corps. Hqrs.			3
D.H.Q.			2
B.H.Q.			2
231st. Bde. A.S.C.			3
Water Duty	1	-	1
G.H.Q.	1	-	1
Dump			2
att. C.T.C.			
	4	-	23

210th. Machine Gun Company.

	Offs.		ORs.
Courses			3
Leave			5
Detached:-			
Dump.			1
			9

18.1.18.

FORM "D"

Division, etc. **231st. INFANTRY BRIGADE**　　　Week-ending **25th. JANRY. 1918.**

List No. _____

Name of Unit, etc	STRENGTH				ANIMALS			GUNS			Remarks
	(a) Effective		(b) Ration		(a) Horses	(b) Mules	(c) Camels	(a) F.A.	(b) Maxim or Vickers	(c) Lewis	
	O.	O.R.	O.	O.R.							
Hqrs, 231st. Inf. Bde.	4	26	4	22	8	-	-	-	-	-	
Signal Section	-	-	1	37	5	5	-	-	-	-	In Decrease.
24th.(Denbigh Yeo.)Bn.R.W.F.	23	651	21	565	12	71	-	-	-	16	Increase. 43 ORs.Reinfs. 43 ORs.From Hosp. Decrease. 1 - 5 to Hosp. 1 - to U.K. Leave.
25th.(Montgomery & Welsh Horse Yeo.)Bn.R.W.F.	22	690	16	638	10	68	-	-	-	16	Increase. 1 Off.from B.H.Q. 40 ORs.from Hosp. Decrease. 2-10 to Hosp. 3- 0 to U.K.Leave
24th.(Pembroke & Glamorgan Yeo.)Bn. Welsh Rgt.	22	645	19	599	12	72	-	-	-	16	Increase. 1 Off.Reinfs. 49 ORs.from Hosp. Decrease. 1-10 to Hosp. 1- 1 to B.H.Q.
10th.(Shropshire & Cheshire Yeo.) K.S.L.I.	27	680	22	640	12	73	-	-	-	16	Increase. 1-58 from Hosp. Decrease. 2-11 to Hosp. 1 to M.G.Co.
210th.Machine Gun Company	6	174	6	164	11	57	-	-	16	-	Increase. 2 ORs.from Bns. Decrease. 1-2 to Hosp. 1-0 to U.K.Leave 1 to Bn.
231st.Light Trench Mortar Battery	-	-	-	-	-	-	-	-	-	-	attached.
TOTAL	104	2866	89	2665	70	346	-	-	16	64	

A.P. & S.D., Alex./1608/25A/10.17/30p (V.&G.)　25.1.18　1400

A/Staff Captain
231st. Infantry Brigde.

P.T.O.

1.	2. STRENGTH				3. ANIMALS			4. GUNS			5.
Name of Unit. etc	(a) Effective		(b) Ration		(a) Horses	(b) Mules	(c) Camels	(a) F. A.	(b) Maxim or Vickers.	(c) Lewis	Remarks
	O.	O.R.	O.	O.R.							

FIGHTING STRENGTH

of

231st. INFANTRY BRIGADE.   18.1.18.

UNIT.	STRENGTH		REMARKS.	
	OFFS.	O.Rs.	Increase.	Decrease.
24th.(Denbigh Yeo.)Bn. R.W.F.	19	513	3 Offs.from Hosp. 1. " joined 58 ORs.from Hosp. 1 - from Course	1 Off.1 OR.to Leave 2 - to Hosp.
25th.(Montgomery & Welsh Horse Yeo)Bn. R.W.F.	18	615	1 -3 from Courses 16 from Base.	1- 2 to Courses 4 to Hosp. 2 to M.G.Co. 1 to D.H.Q. 1 to C.T.C.
24th.Bn.(Pembroke & Glamorgan Yeo.) Welsh Rgt.	17	565	1 - 33 from Hosp. 1 - 0 Reinfs.	1 - 1 Leave Egypt. 10 to Hosp. 1 to D.H.Q.
10th.(Shropshire & Cheshire Yeo.)Bn. K.S.L.I.	22	592	1 - 2 from Courses 2 - 2 Reinfs. 67 from Hosp. 1 from Cadet Course.	2 ORs.to Courses 12 - to Hosp. 1 - to L.T.M.B.
210th.Machine Gun Company.	8	166	14 ORs.Reinfs. 2 - from Hosp. 2 - from Battns.	8 ORs.to Hosp 5 - leave Egypt. 1 - to Course 1 Off.to Suez for embark to India.
231st.L.T.M.B.	2	29	3 ORs.from Hosp.	1 OR.to Hosp.
TOTAL.	86	2483		

18.1.18.
1400

A/Staff Captain
231st.Infantry Brigade.

List No. 6.

FORM "D"

Division, etc. 231st. INFANTRY BRIGADE **Week-ending** 8th. FEBRY. 1918.

Name of Unit, etc	STRENGTH				ANIMALS			GUNS			Remarks
	(a) Effective		(b) Ration		(a) Horses	(b) Mules	(c) Camels	(a) F.A.	(b) Maxim or Vickers	(c) Lewis	
	O.	O.R.	O.	O.R.							
Hqrs, 231st. Inf. Bde.	4	26	3	33	9 4	12	-	-	-	-	
Signal Sec.	-	-	1	37		5	-	-	-	-	
24th. (Denbigh Yeo.) Bn. R.W.F.	25	724	20	608	11	71	-	-	-	16	Increase. 1 Off.Reinf. 6 ORs.Reinfs 68 ORs.from 7 ORs.from T Decrease. 2 Offs to Co 1 Off.to Hos 5 ORs.to Ho
25th. (Montgomery & Welsh Horse Yeo.) Bn.R.W.F.	22	732	17	660	10	68	-	-	-	16	Increase. 68 ORs. Reinf Decrease. 5 ORs.to Hos 1 OR.Spec.Du
24th. (Pembroke & Glamorgan Yeo.) Bn.Welsh Rgt.	23	691	21	643	12	72	-	-	-	16	Increase.
10th. (Shropshire & Cheshire Yeo.) Bn. K.S.L.I.	26	755	18	694	12	73	-	-	-	16	Increase 6 1-81 from Ho 1- 5 from Co 4 from le 7 Reinfs. Decrease. 1- 3 to Irre (F 14 to Hosp. 1- 7 to Leav
210th. Machine Gun Company	8	202	6	198	11	57	-	-	16	-	Increase. 3 ORs.from C Decrease. 4 ORs.to Hosp 1 - 2 to Cou
TOTAL	108	3130	86	2873	69	358	-	-	16	64	

A.P. & S.D., Alex./1608/25A/10.17/30M.(V.&G.)
8.2.18.

A/Staff Captain
231st. Infantry Brigade.

P.T.O.

1.	2.				3.			4.			5.
	STRENGTH				ANIMALS			GUNS			
Name of Unit. etc	(a) Effective		(b) Ration		(a) Horses	(b) Mules	(c) Camels	(a) F.A.	(b) Maxim or Vickers.	(c) Lewis	Remarks
	O.	O.R	O.	O.R.							

FIGHTING STRENGTH

of

231st. INFANTRY BRIGADE.   8.2.18.

UNIT.	STRENGTH OFFICERS — O.RS.	REMARKS.
24th.(Denbigh Yeo) Bn.R.W.F.	17 — 686	Increase: from Hosp. Reinfs. / Decrease: to Hosp.
25th.(Montgomery & Welsh Horse Yeo.) Bn.R.W.F.	13 — 660	Increase: 1 from Spec D. ; 3 from Hosp. ; 1 – 59 Reinfs. ; 1 – 5 from Leave ; 1 – 10 from Courses / Decrease: 1 – 3 to Spec.Duty ; 4 to Hosp. ; 1 to Course
24th.(Pembroke & Glamorgan Yeo.) Bn.Welsh Regt.	16 — 640	1 – 0 Reinf. ; 82 From Hosp.
10th.Bn.X.X.X.X. (Shropshire & Cheshire Yeo.) K.S.L.I.	15 — 700	Increase: 1 – 81 from Hosp. ; 1 – 5 from Courses ; 4 from Leave ; 7 Reinfs. / Decrease: 1 – 3 to Irregular ?Force. ; 1 – 7 to Leave ; 14 ORs. to Hosp.
210th. Machine Gun Company	6 — 198	3 ORs. from Courses 1 – 2 to Course ; 4 to Hosp.
231st. Light Trench Mortar Battery	2 — 31	1 – 3 from Courses —
TOTAL	69 — 2915	

8-2-18
1400

A/Staff Captain
231st. Infantry Brigade.

FIGHTING STRENGTH.

of

231st. INFANTRY BRIGADE.   1.2.18.

UNIT	NUMBERS OFFS. - ORS.	REMARKS
24th.(Denbugh Yeo.) Bn.R.W.F.	17 - 573	**Increase.** 1 - 24 from Hosp. / 1 - 21 from Leave — **Decrease.** 2 - 7 to Courses / 4 to Water Duty.
25th.(Montgomery & Welsh Horse Yeo.) Bn.R.W.F.	11 - 592	**Increase.** 1 - 0 from Leave / 2 from Course / 1 from Spec.Duty / 1 from Base — **Decrease.** 1 - 1 to Spec.Duty / 13 to Hosp. / 6 to Leave / 14 to Deir Semied / 5 to Water Duty / 2 - 8 to Courses
24th.(Pembroke & Glamorgan Yeo.) Bn Welsh Rgt.	16 - 591	**Increase.** - 13 ORs.from Hosp. — **Decrease.** 14 ORs. to Hosp. / 1 - Died / 5 - to Water Duty
10th.Bn.(Shropshire & Cheshire Yeo.) K.S.L.I.	15 - 629	**Increase.** 1 - 4 from Courses / 3 from Hosp. / 1 from Interview R.F.C. / 7 from Salvage Duty — **Decrease.** 1 - 6 from Hosp. / 1 - 1 Conducting Off. (Leave) / 1 - 5 Water Duty / 1 - 1 Leave / 1 - 5 to Courses / 1 to R.F.C.
210th. Machine Gun Company	7 - 201	2. 31. from M.G. Base / 1. 5 from leave / 1 from Hosp. 1. 0 to leave
231st. Light Trench Mortar Battery	1 - 28	1 OR from Spec.Duty 1 - 2 to Course
TOTAL	67 - 2614	

1.2.18.
1400

A/ Staff Captain
231st. INfantry Brigade.

List No. **7.**

FORM "D"

Division, etc. **231st. INFANTRY BRIGADE.** Week-ending **15th. FEBRY. 1918.**

1.	2.				3.			4.			5.
	STRENGTH				ANIMALS			GUNS			
Name of Unit. etc	(a) Effective		(b) Ration		(a) Horses	(b) Mules	(c) Donkeys Camels	(a) F.A.	(b) Maxim or Vickers.	(c) Lewis.	Remarks
	O.	O.R.	O.	O.R.							
Hqrs, 231st. Inf. Bde.	4	25	4	37	9	12	-	-	-	-	1 OR. to H⊘ 1 Off. 1 OR. 1 Le
Signal Sec.	-	-	1	38	4	5	-	-	-	-	Increase. 8- 5 Reinfs. 3- 7 from H⊘ 2- 3 from C⊘ 26 from D. Decrease. 2 Offs. to 1 1 Off. U.K. 4 ORs. to H⊘
24th.(Denbigh Yeo.)Bn.R.W.F	33	719	30	623	11	95	4	-	-	16	
25th. (Montgomery Yeo.& Welsh Horse Yeo.) Bn. R.W.F.	22	732	18	670	10	93	4	-	-	16	Increase. 1- 1 from C⊘ 1- 3 from H⊘ 14 from S: Decrease. 1- 6 to Lee 1 to Tr 1 to M. 4 to Ho
24th. (Pembroke & Glamorgan Yeo.) Bn. Welsh Rgt.	25	682	24	626	11	97	4	-	-	16	Increase. 2-10 from H 4- 0 Reinfs. Decrease- 17 ORs. to H 10 Spec.Dut
10th. (Shropshire & Cheshire Yeo. Bn. K.S.L.I.	30	756	22	705/2@	12	99	4	-	-	16	@ Natives. Increase. 4- 24 from Decrease. 22 ORs. to H 1 OR. to Sp
210th. Machine Gun Company	9	214	8	208	11	57	-	-	16	-	Increase. 13 ORs. Rein 1--1 from Ho 1-1 from Le 1 from 25 Decraese. 3 ORs. to Ho 3 - to Le
Brigade Water Personnel	-	-	1	20	-	-	-	-	-	-	
TOTAL	123	3128	108	2925	68	458 848	16	-	16	64	

A.P. & S.D., Alex./1608/25A/10.17/30m.(V.&G.)

A/Staff Captain

P.T.O.

15 2 18
1400

1.	2.				3.			4.			5.
Name of Unit, etc	STRENGTH				ANIMALS			GUNS			Remarks
	(a) Effective		(b) Ration		(a) Horses	(b) Mules	(c) Camels	(a) F.A.	(b) Maxim or Vickers	(c) Lewis	
	O.	O.R.	O.	O.R.							

FIGHTING STRENGTH
of
231st. INFANTRY BRIGADE.   15.2.18.

UNIT.	STRENGTH OFFS. - ORS.	REMARKS.	
		Increase.	Decrease.
24th.(Denbigh Yeo.) Bn.R.W.F.	27 - 617	8 - 5 Reinfs. 3 - 7 from Hosp. 2 - 3 from Courses	2 Offs.to Leave 1 Off. to U.K.Leave 4 ORs.to Hosp. 30 ORs.at ENAB not incl. 4 ORs.Spec.Duty.
25th.(Montgomery & Welsh Horse Yeo.) Bn.R.W.F.	14 - 670	14 from Spec.Duty 1 - 1 from Course 1 - 7 from Hosp.	1 - 6 to Local Leave 4 from Hosp. 1 to Trade Test 1 to M.G.Co.
24th.(Pembroke & Glamorgan Yeo.)Bn. Welsh Regt.	22 - 626	2 -10 from Hosp. 4 - 0 Reinfs.	17 to Hosp. 10 to Spec.Duty
10th.(Shropshire & Cheshire Yeo.) Bn.K.S.L.I.	19 - 696	2 - 5 to Leave 22 to Hosp. 4 to Course 1 to Spec.Duty	4-24 from Hosp. 1- 1 from Leave 1- 1 from Conducting Leave Party
210th.Machine Gun Company.	8 - 208	-13 Reinfs. 1 - 1 from Hosp. 1 - 1 from Local Leave 1 from 25/RWF.	3 to Hosp. 3 to Local Leave
231st.Light Trench Mortar Battery	2 - 33	2 from Local Leave.	
TOTAL	92 - 2850		

15.2.18.
1400

A/Staff Captain
231st.Infantry Brigade.

FORM "D"

List No. 8

Division, etc. __231st Infy Bde.__   Week-ending __22nd Feby 1918__

Name of Unit, etc	STRENGTH				ANIMALS			GUNS			Remarks
	(a) Effective		(b) Ration		(a)	(b)	(c)	(a)	(b)	(c)	
	O.	O.R.	O.	O.R.	Horses	Mules	~~Camels~~ Donkeys	F.A.	Maxim or Vickers	Lewis	
Hqrs, 231st Infy Bde.	4	25	5	36	9	12	-	-	-	-	1 Offr from Spec Duty.
Signal Sect.	-	-	1	56	22	5	-	-	-	-	Increase 18 ORs & 18 anmls 1 Cable Wagon
24th (Denbigh Yeo) Bn R.W.F	37	747	31	640	11	95	4	-	-	16	Increase 2 Offrs Rcrnts 32 ORs from Hosp Decrease 1 1 Co Lost Wk 4 Co Trade Test 2 Co Hosp
25th (Montgomery & Welsh Horse Yeo) Bn R.W.F.	26	753	22	695	10	99	4	-	-	16	Increase 4. 25 ... Decrease ...
24th Pembroke & Glamorgan Yeo) Bn Welsh Rgt	25	717	24	657	11	97	4	-	-	16	Increase 50 ORs from Ho Decrease 15 ORs to Hosp
10th (Shropshire & Cheshire Yeo.) Bn K.S.L.I	31	772	21	716/2	12	98	4	-	-	16	Increase 2. 26 from Hosp Decrease 1. 10 to Hosp
210th Machine Gun Coy.	9	217	8	209	11	57	-	-	16	-	Increase 6 ORs Rcrts Decrease 3 ORs to Hosp 2 ORs to Cmd
Brigade ... Personnel	-	-	3	20	-	-	2	-	-	-	
TOTAL	132	3231	115	3039/2	86	257	16	-	16	64	

A.P. & S.D., Alex./1608/25A/10.17/30M.(V.&G.)

22.2.18
1800

Capt
Staff Captain

P.T.O.

1.	2.				3.			4.			5.
	STRENGTH				ANIMALS			GUNS			
Name of Unit, etc	(a) Effective		(b) Ration		(a) Horses	(b) Mules	(c) Camels	(a) F.A.	(b) Maxim or Vickers.	(c) Lewis	Remarks
	O.	O.R.	O.	O.R.							

FIGHTING STRENGTH.

of
231st Infantry Brigade   22.2.18.

Unit	Strength Offs	Strength ORs	Remarks	
			Increase	Decrease
24th Bn (Denbigh Yeo) Bn. R.W.F.	29	639	2 Offs. Reinfs. 32 ORs from Hosp.	26 ORs to Hosp. 5 ORs to Leave 4 ORs to Trade Test
25th Bn (Montgomery & Welsh Horse Yeo) Bn. R.W.F.	18	695		
24th Bn (Pembroke & Glamorgan Yeo) Bn. Welsh Regt.	12	463	50 ORs from Hosp. 9 ORs from Leave 1 OR from Trade Test.	5 ORs to Hosp. 3 Offs 133 ORs to Jerusalem 2 Offs to Leave
10th Bn (Shropshire & Cheshire Yeo.) Bn. R.W.F.	18	710	1-1. from Leave 2. 26 from Hosp	1.1. to Desert Mtd. Corps 1.1. to Course 1.10. to Hosp. 1.1. to Leave
210th Machine Gun Company	8	209	6 ORs Reinfs	3 ORs to Hosp 2 ORs to Courses
231st Light Trench Mortar Battery	3	29	1.1. ORs from 24 R.W.F. att.	2 ORs to Leave 2 ORs to Hosp 1 OR to Course
TOTAL	88	2745		

22.2.18
1400

Capt
Staff Captain.
231st Infantry Brigade

List No. 9

FORM "D"

Division, etc. 231st Indy Bde.　　Week-ending 1st March 1918

Name of Unit, etc.	STRENGTH				ANIMALS			GUNS			Remarks
	(a) Effective		(b) Ration		(a)	(b)	(c)	(a)	(b)	(c)	
	O.	O.R.	O.	O.R.	Horses	Mules	~~Camels~~ Donkeys	F.A.	Maxim or Vickers	Lewis	
Hqrs 231st Bde	4	26	5	42	9	12	.	.	.	.	2 Guides on.
Signal Sect	-	-	1	38	4	5	.	.	.	.	
24th (Denbigh Yeo) Bn. R.W.F.	37	752	21	654	11	95	4	.	.	16	Increase. 2. 6 from Leave 20 from Hosp 3 from Trsd. Decrease 1. Os Hosp. 6 ToR8 Rd 2. 3 Os Convs 1. 10 from Base 1. 0 from M.G.C. Decrease. 7 OR to Hosp. 4 - to M.G.C. 2. 5 - to Convs 1. 6. to Leave
25th (Montgomery & Welsh Horse Yeo) Bn. R.W.F.	24	747	19	688	10	93	4	.	.	16	
24th Pembroke & Glamorgans Yeo) Bn. Welsh Rgt.	26	686	24	613	11	96	4	.	.	16	Increase. 1 Off Reinft 47 ORs from Hos Decrease 13 OR to Hosp
10th (Shropshire & Cheshire Yeo) Bn. K.S.L.I.	30	785	21	732	12	98	4	.	.	16	Increase 27 ORs from Ho 4 - Reinfts. Decrease 18 OR to Hosp
210 Sig Coy.	8	219	9	212	11	87	-	.	16	-	Increase 5 ORs from Ba 1. 1. - from Conv Decrease. 1. O to Remounts (S/R) 2 ORs to Hosp 1 - to Conv
Water Duty Personnel	.	.	1	21	.	.	.	.	.	.	
TOTAL	132	3215	111	3000	68	486	16	.	16	64	

A.P. & S.D., Alex./1608/25A/10.17/30M.(V.&G.)

1.3.18
1400

Victor Paht Capt
Staff Captain

P.T.O.

1.	2. STRENGTH				3. ANIMALS			4. GUNS			5.
Name of Unit, etc	(a) Effective		(b) Ration		(a) Horses	(b) Mules	(c) Camels	(a) F.A.	(b) Maxim or Vickers.	(c) Lewis	Remarks
	O.	O.R.	O.	O.R.							

Fighting Strength
of
231st Infantry Brigade — 1.3.18

Unit	Strength Offs	Strength ORs	Remarks — Increase	Remarks — Decrease
24th (Denbigh Yeo) Bn. R.W.F.	26	643	2 ORs from Hosp 6 " from Leave 3 " from Trade Test	3 ORs to Course 3 ORs to Hosp 6 ORs to R.E. Flecy 4 ORs to 210 M.G.C.
25th Bn. (Montgomery & Welsh Horse Yeo) Bn. R.W.F.	16	688	1 - 6 from Leave 1 - 10 from Base 3 from Courses 2 from Spec.D	2 - 5 to Courses 1 - 6 to Leave 1 - 1 to B.H.Q. 7 to Hosp. 4 to M.G.C. 4 to Spec. Duty 1 to L.T.M.B.
24th (Pembroke & Glamorgan Yeo) Bn. R.W.F.	21	613	1. O Reinfs 47 from Base 3. 119 from Duties at Jerusalem	16 ORs to Hosp
10th (Shropshire & Cheshire Yeo) Bn. K.S.L.I.	18	727	2. 24 from Hosp 14 Reinfs 11 from Leave 3 from Courses 1 from Spec. Duty	1 - 5 to Leave 1 - 6 to Courses 18 to Hospital
210th Machine Gun Company	8	212	1. 1 from Course 1. 5 from Battns	1. O Regimental D. 2 to Hospital 1 to Course
231st Light Trench Mortar Battery	2	28	1 OR from 25 RWF	1 - 1 to Course
TOTAL	91	2911		

1.3.18
1400

Capt.
Staff Captain
231st Infantry Brigade

FORM "D"

List No. 10

1. Division, etc. 231st Indy Bde.   3. Week-ending 8th March 1918

Name of Unit. etc	STRENGTH				ANIMALS			GUNS			Remarks
	(a) Effective		(b) Ration		(a) Horses	(b) Mules	(c) Camels	(a) F.A.	(b) Maxim or Vickers	(c) Lewis	
	O.	O.R.	O.	O.R.							
Hqrs 231st Bde. Signal Section	4	27	5 1	49 59	9 4	12 5	. .	. .	Vickers	. .	
24th (Den/Cgh Yeo) Bn. R.W.F.	38	749	32	666	11	94	4	.	.	16	Increase. 2.4 from Courses 1.12 from ENA 9 from Leave 10 from Hosp Decrease. 2. 8 to Courses 1. 1 to Leave 4 Transferred 4 to MGC 7 Casualties 5 to Hosp
25th (Montgomery & Welsh Horse Yeo) Bn. R.W.F.	24	757	21	686	10	92	4	.	.	16	Increase 1. 3 from Course 1. 1 from Divn 7 from Hosp. Decrease 4 from Cour 7 from Hos
24th (Pembroke & Glamorgan Yeo) Bn Welsh Rgt.	28	678	27	607	11	96	4	.	.	16	Increase 14 from Hos Decrease 14 OR to Hos 5 OR to M.
10th (Shropshire & Cheshire Yeo) Bn. K.S.L.I.	29	778	20	712	12	98	4	.	.	16	Increase 8 ORs from # from Decrease 33 ORs to H 1 - 3 - Casu 4 - to M 1 - Colt.
210th Machine Gun Coy.	9	228	8	220	11	87	.	.	16	.	Increase 14 ORs from 1. 1 - from Decrease 6 - 4 to H. 1 to 214
Water Personnel	-	-	1	21	-	-					
TOTAL	135	3197	115 114	3000 2999	68	485	16	.	16	64	

A.P. & S.D., Alex./1608/25A/10.17/30M.(V.& G.)

8.3.18

Capt. Staff Captain   P.T.O.

1.	2. STRENGTH				3. ANIMALS			4. GUNS			5.
Name of Unit, etc	(a) Effective		(b) Ration		(a) Horses	(b) Mules	(c) Camels	(a) F.A.	(b) Maxim or Vickers.	(c) Lewis	Remarks
	O.	O.R.	O.	O.R.							

Fighting Strength of 231st Infantry Brigade   8.3.18

Unit	Strength		Remarks	
	Off/s	ORs	Increase	Decrease
24th (Denbigh Yeo) Bn. R.W.F.	26	666	2 · 4 from Courses 1 · 12 from E.I.V.A.B. 1 · 10 from R.A.I.A.R.E.H 1 · 0 Reinfs 10 from Hosp. 7 from Leave 2 from Trade Test	1 · 1 to Leave 4 to M.G. Cy. 2 · 3 to Course 4 Casualties 5 to Hosp 4 to Trade Test
25th (Montgomery & Welsh Horse Yeo) Bn. R.W.F.	18	686	1 · 2 from Course 1 · 1 from Divnl Horse S 7 from Hosp 1 from Water Duty 2 from Trade Test	4 ORs to Course 7 to Hosp 3 to Trade Test 1 to B.H.Q.
24th (Pembroke & Glamorgan Yeo) Bn. Welsh R.	23	607	1 · 4 to Course 1 · 1 13 Corps Reinf. Camp	1 · 5 to Course 1 · 1 to Corps Reinf. Camp 14 to Hosp 1 KILLED 5 to M.G. Coy.
10th (Shropshire & Cheshire Yeo) Bn. K.S.L.I.	17	700	1 · 3 from Course 1 · 1 from Leave 23 from Hosp 1 from B.H.Q.	1 · 0 KILLED 5 Wounded 33 to Hosp 2 · 7 to Courses 6 to Leave 4 to M.G. Cy. 1 to L.T.M.B.
210th Machine Gun Company	8	220	1 · 0 from Hospital 14 from Battns	1 · 3 to Course 4 to Hosp 1 to Trade Test 1 to 231st M.G. Cy.
231st Light Trench Mortar Battery	2	33	2 ORs from Course 2 from Leave 1 from K.S.L.I.	
TOTAL	94	2912		

8.3.18   Staff Captain Capt
                                            231st Infy Bde.

FORM "D"

List No. 11

Division, etc. 231 Inf. Bde. 14 Div.   Week-ending 15th March

Name of Unit, etc	STRENGTH				ANIMALS			GUNS			Remarks
	(a) Effective		(b) Ration		(a) Horses	(b) Mules	(c) ~~Camels~~ Donkeys	(a) F.A.	(b) Vickers	(c) Lewis	
	O.	O.R.	O.	O.R.							
Hqrs 231 Bde Signal Section	4	27	54 1	46 49	13 4	12-20 9					
24th (Denbigh Yeo) Bn R.W.F.	38	731	32	655	11	94	4			16	Increase ...
25th (Montgomery & Welsh Horse Yeo) R.W.F.	24	643	19	591	10	93	4			16	Increase Joined on Posting ... Casualties 93 ... On leave 1 Off.
24th Bn (Pembroke & Glamorgan Yeo) Welch Regt	31	617	30	547	11	96	4			16	Increase Rejoined 2 Off 5 OR Reinforcements 5 Off 1 OR Decrease Off OR Killed 1 2 Wounded - 13 Hosp. 3 42 Trans Out 1 0
10th Shropshire & Cheshire Yeo Bn K.S.L.I.	29	659	21	591	12	98	4			16	Increase Reinf Off Pl Decrease Killed 1 13 Wounded 2 68 Sick 33 Missing 1 To LTMB 5 Leave to UK
210th Machine Gun Coy.	9	227	8	216	11	87			16		Increase Attached 1 OR Decrease Hosp. 2 OR
Water Duty Personnel	-	-	1	21 19			5				Relieved by DWO Increase ...
	135	2904	117	2766	72	489	21	-	16	64	

A.P. & S.D., Alex./1608/25A/10.17/30M.(V.& G.)   P.T.O.

15-3-18

1.	2.				3.			4.			5.
	STRENGTH				ANIMALS			GUNS			
Name of Unit, etc	(a) Effective		(b) Ration		(a)	(b)	(c)	(a)	(b)	(c)	Remarks
	O.	O.R.	O.	O.R.	Horses	Mules	Camels	F. A.	Maxim or Vickers.	Lewis	

Fighting Strength
231st Infantry Brigade

Unit	Strength Off	Strength O/R	Remarks - Increase	Remarks - Decrease
24th (Denbigh Yeo) Bn R.W.F.	28	654 14 68	Quartermaster and Transport Officers including 1 O/R from D.H.Q.	2 O/R Wounded. 4 — to L.T.M.B. 6 — to Leave
25th (Montgomery and Welsh Horse Yeo) Bn R.W.F.	17	591	From Base 5/11 1 O/R; Guns 1; Leave 1, 3; Base .2; T.O & QM included	Killed Off —, O/R 9; Missing Off 1; Evacuated Off 3, O/R 83; To L.T.M.B. 4; From Servant Off on Leave evacuated 2
24th Bn Pembroke & Glamorgan Yeo Bn) Welsh Reg.	28	547	Rejoined Off 2, O/R 5; Reinf. 5, 1; QM & T.O. included.	Killed Off —, O/R 2; Wounded 13; Hosp. Sick 3, 42; Trade Test 10
10th Bn (Shropshire and Cheshire Yeo) Bn K.S.L.I.	19	585 27 612	Reinf Off 4, O/R —; Fr. Courses 2, 2; — Leave 1, 1	Killed Off 1, O/R 13; To Hosp. —; Wounded 2, 68; Sick 33; Missing 1; To L.T.M.B. 8; Leave U.K. 1, —; GHQ 1, 1
210th M.G. Cy.	8	216		To Hosp. 2; Course 1
231 Light Trench Mortar Battery	3	49	From Leave Off 1, O/R 1; Attached 17	On Leave 2; To Hosp Sick 1
Total	103	2642		

15/3/18

Staff Capt 231 Inf Bde

FORM "D"

List No. 12

Division, etc. 231st Infantry Brigade Week-ending 30/3/18

Name of Unit, etc.	STRENGTH				ANIMALS			GUNS			Remarks
	(a) Effective		(b) Ration		(a) Horses	(b) Mules	(c) Camels	(a) F.A.	(b) Maxim or Vickers	(c) Lewis	
	O.	O.R.	O.	O.R.							
1st Inf Bde Headquarters & Signals	4	27	4	53	8	20					
	-	-	1	41	4	6					3 since return
R.W.F.	34	726	28	651	12	95	4			16	
R.W.F.	24	637	16	566	9	93	4			16	Increase 1 off 130R. Decrease
Pembroke Glamorgan Welsh Rgt	33	662	28	552	11	94	4			16	Increase... Decrease...
Shropshire & Cheshire KSLI	32	699	25	615	12	98	4			16	Increase... Decrease...
MG Coys	10	221	8	207	11	87	-		16	-	
Labour Only Personnel			1	14			5				
	137	3152	111	2699	61	493	21	-	64		

P.T.O.

1.	2.				3.			4.			5.
	STRENGHT				ANIMALS			GUNS			
Name of Unit, etc.	(a) Effective		(b) Ration		(a)	(b)	(c)	(a)	(b)	(c)	Remarks
	O.	O.R.	O.	O.R.	Horses	Mules	Camels	F. A.	Maxim or Vickers	Lewis	

Fighting Strength

Unit	Strength Off	O.R's	Remarks Increase	Decrease
24th (Denbigh /eo) Bn. R.W.F.	27	669	From Cas. Cr. 1 Off. - Hosp. 13 - Courses 2 3 - D.H.Q. 1 - Leave 5 6 temp. detached Off. Cadet included	To Hosp. #88 5 O.R. Jelichin 1 Courses 4 5 ZEITOUN 1 1 Cadet Course 1 R.E 2 K.T.M.B. 4
25th (Montgomery & Welsh Horse /eo) Bn R.W.F.	14	575	1-12 from Base 1 1 Leave 1 Spcl. Duty 2 ZEITOUN 1 JERUSALEM 1 Grade list	3-9 Courses 1 JERUSALEM 3 Grade list 8 Hosp. 6 Leave 1-1 Cairo 4 L.T.M.B.
24th Bn. (Pembroke & Glamorgan /eo) Welsh Reg.	26	551	41 O/R from Hosp. 1 Off. Reinf.	11 O/R to Hosp. 2 M.G.C. 14 Courses 1 Leave 2 Cadet Course 4 L.T.M.B. 1-1 Leave U.K. 1-1 ZEITOUN - INSTRUCTOR
10th Bn. (Shropshire & Cheshire /eo) K.S.L.I.	23	615	Off O/R 1 3 Reinf. 13 from Hosp. 1 8 from Leave 1 2 - Courses 1 - KANTARA	18 to Hosp. 6 - Grade list 11 - Leave 5 - Courses 11 - RAMALLAH
210th M.G.C.	8	213	Off O/R 1 from Courses 1 Attached	Off O/R 1 2 to Hosp. 1 3 Courses 1 3 Leave
231st L.T.M.B.	3	63	2 Off. from Leave 14 Pioneers joined	Off 1 Course 1 Grade list
	101	2686		

3/3/18

Staff Captain
231 Infantry Brigade

FORM "D"

List No. 12

Division, etc. 231 Infantry Brigade 2. 74th Div Week-ending 23/3/18

Name of Unit, etc	STRENGTH				ANIMALS			GUNS			Remarks
	(a) Effective		(b) Ration		(a) Horses	(b) Mules	(c) Camels Donkeys	(a) F.A.	(b) Maxim or Vickers	(c) Lewis	
	O.	O.R.	O.	O.R.							
Inf. Brigade	4	24	4	58	8	20	–				Increase 1 off from leave, 1 OR... Decrease 1 Off & 1 OR leave
M.G. Section			1	41	4	9					
1 Denbigh Bn R.W.F	36	781	30	658	11	95	4			16	Increase 18 OR from hosp, 1 OR dety. Decrease 3 OR last week showed mend
Bn (Mont- & Welch & Flt) R.W.F	23	644	18	576	9	93	4			16	Increase 15 OR taken on. Decrease 1 Off, 14 OR taken off, 1 Charger struck off 16/3/18
2 Pembroke Glamorgan R.W.F	32	634	30	546	11	94	4			16	Increase 33 OR rejoined, 1 Off. Decrease 13 OR to hosp, 1 trade list, 1 to M.G.C., 1 destroyed, 1 evacuated
1 (Shropshire Cheshire) K.S.L.I.	31	680	23	604	12	98	4			16	Increase 2 Off 3 OR Reinf., 2-36 OR from Hosp, 2-36. Decrease 1 Off 10 OR to hosp... 4 Off OR leave KANTARA...
M.G. Coy	10	222	9	211	11	87	–		16	–	Increase 1 off from M.G.C. Depot, 10 OR from Hosp, 2 attached. Decrease 8 OR to hosp
On Duty Personnel			1	13	–	5					
	136	2944	116	2697	66	496	21		16	64	

A.P. & S.D., Alex./1608/25A/10.17/30m.(V.&G.)

P.T.O.

Staff Captain

1.	2.				3.			4.			5.
	STRENGTH				ANIMALS			GUNS			
Name of Unit, etc	(a) Effective		(b) Ration		(a)	(b)	(c)	(a)	(b)	(c)	Remarks
	O.	O.R.	O.	O.R.	Horses	Mules	Camels	F. A.	Maxim or Vickers.	Lewis.	

FIGHTING STRENGTH
231st INFANTRY BRIGADE

UNIT	STRENGTH		REMARKS	
	Officers	O/R	Increase	Decrease
24th (Denbigh &c) Bn. R.W.F	29	660 / 651	from Trade test 7 O/R. On population 1 O/R. from hosp. 18 Draft 1 off. Trade 1 off. L.T.M.B. 1 off.	Trade test 3 O/R, M.G.C. 1, Hosp. 2 off 3, Cadet Course 2 off 5, Leave 1, 2 off 13 O/R
25th (Montgomery and Welsh Horse (c)) Bn. R.W.F.	16	589	1 Zeitoun, 2 Hosp., 4 Leave, 12 Reinf., 1 Trade test, 22	1 off 7 O/R L.T.M.B., 5 Trade test, Hosp sick, 6 Leave, F.P.C., 1 off 24
24th Bn (Pembroke & Glamorgan (c)) Welsh Reg.	28	546	1 off rejoined, 10 O/R from leave	1 off leave, 8 O/R
10th Bn (Shropshire & Cheshire (c)) K.S.L.I.	22	612	2 off 3 O/R Reinf, 2 6 from Course, 10 from leave, 33 from Hosp., 1 struck off list, 5 53	1 off 10 O/R to hosp., 5 Trade test, Cadet Course, 1 9 leave, 1 duty Kantara, 2 26
210th M.G. Coy.	9	213	1 off from M.G.C. Depot, 1 off from Hosp., 1 Course, 3 Leave, 2 Attached	2 O/R to Hosp., 2 Courses
231st Light Trench Mortar Battery	3	49		
TOTAL	107	2666		

22/3/18

Staff Captain
231st Infantry Brigade

Form "Z"

No. 13

~~Daily~~ / Weekly casualty report up to ~~7 p.m.~~ / noon, Saturday. Friday

231 Inf Bde Division. 14 Date 30/3/18

Unit. (Each unit to be shown separately.)	Date	Killed		Wounded		Missing		Sick Admitted	
		O.	O.R.	O.	O.R.	O.	O.R.	O.	O.R.
231st Bde Hqrs	23/3/18 to 30/3/18	-	-	-	-	-	-	-	-
24 Bn (Denbigh Yeo) R.W.F.	23/3/18 to 30/3/18	-	-	-	-	-	-	1	5
25th (Montgomery and Welsh Horse Yeo) Bn R.W.F.	do	-	-	-	-	-	-	-	6
24th Bn (Pembroke & Glamorgan Yeo) Welsh Reg	do	-	-	-	-	-	-	-	11
10th Bn (Shropshire & Cheshire Yeo) K.S.L.I.	do	-	-	-	-	-	-	-	11
210th M.G. Coy	do	-	-	-	-	-	-	-	2
231st L.T.M.B.	do	-	-	-	-	-	-	-	-
Totals								1	35

The space below, and the back of this form, will be used to report Officers' casualties; in each case, unit, battalion, name, rank, initial, nature of casualty, and date will be shown.

× Captain D.L. EDWARDS. R.W.F.
Sick Admitted 28/3/18

Staff Capt
231 Inf Bde

Form "Z"   12

No. _____

231 Infantry Brigade Daily / Weekly casualty report up to 7 p.m. Friday / noon, Saturday 23/3/18
Division. 74th   Date

Unit. (Each unit to be shown separately.)	Date	Killed		Wounded		Missing		Sick Admitted	
		O.	O.R.	O.	O.R.	O.	O.R.	O.	O.R.
Hqrs 231 I.f Bde.	15/3/18 to 22/3/18								1
24th (Denbigh Yeo) Bn R.W.F.	15/3/18 to 22/3/18							2	3
25th Bn (Montgomery & Welsh Horse Yeo) R.W.F.	15/3/18 to 22/3/18								4
24th Bn (Pembroke & Glamorgan Yeo) Welch Reg.	15/3/18 to 22/3/18								13
10th Bn (Shropshire and Cheshire Yeo) K.S.L.I.	15/3/18 to 22/3/18							1	6
210th M.G. Coy	15/3/18 to 22/3/18								8
231st L.T.M.B.	15/3/18 to 22/3/18								
Totals								3	35

The space below, and the back of this form, will be used to report Officers' casualties; in each case, unit, battalion, name, rank, initial, nature of casualty, and date will be shown.

Staff Captain
231st Infantry Brigade

24th (Denbigh Yeo) Bn R.W.F.

3rd R.W.F. Lt. J.T. ROBINSON Sick admitted to hosp 18/3/.
to 2Lt J.J. EDWARDS " — 19/3/.

10th Bn (Shropshire & Cheshire Yeo) K.S.L.I.
3/. Shropshire Yeo.
  2Lt. D.S RAPSON. Sick Admitted to hosp 18/.

Staff Capt
231st Infantry B.

Form "Z"

No. 11

Daily / ~~Weekly~~ casualty report up to 7 p.m. / ~~noon, Saturday.~~

231 Inf Bde 16th Division.   Date 15/3/18 Friday

This Column must not be written upon.

Unit. (Each unit to be shown separately.)	Date	Killed O.	Killed O.R.	Wounded O.	Wounded O.R.	Missing O.	Missing O.R.	Sick Admitted O.	Sick Admitted O.R.
Hqrs 231 Inf Bde	—	—	—	—	—	—	—	—	—
24 Bn (Denbigh Yeo) R.W.F.	8/3/18 to 15/3/18				3*				
			*Including 1 Remain at duty						
25th Bn (Montgomery & Welsh Horse Yeo) R.W.F.	8/3/18 to 15/3/18	1	9	5	54	1	1		29
24 Bn (Pembroke & Glamorgan Yeo) Welch Regt	8/3/18 to 15/3/18		1		2			3	42
10th Bn (Shropshire & Cheshire Yeo) K.S.L.I.	8/3/18 to 15/3/18	1	13	2	68		1		33
210 M.G. Coy	8/3/18 to 15/3/18								2
231 L.T.M.B.	8/3/18 to 15/3/18								1
Totals		3	24	7	125	1	2	3	107

The space below, and the back of this form, will be used to report Officers' casualties; in each case, unit, battalion, name, rank, initial, nature of casualty, and date will be shown.

Staff Capt
231 Inf Bde

Nominal Roll of Casualties - Officers

25th (Montgomery & Welch Horse Yeo) RWF

Off Killed

3rd S.W.B. 2/Lt H.L.A. KEYSOR

Wounded

Montgomery Yeo   Lt E.H. FARMER
                 Lt J.A.S. FOULKES-JONES
Welch Horse   Major J.C. REES Remaining at duty
                 Capt W.P. ROCH Since reported missing
4 Bn RWF   2/Lt S JOHN

24th Bn (Pembroke & Glamorgan Yeo) Welsh Reg

Off Killed

Pembroke Yeo. Lt (a/Capt) D.L.P. MORGAN

Sick Admitted

3rd Welsh Reg   2/Lt J.N. BAIRD   To Hosp 11/3/18
1/5 Welsh Reg   —   H.S. PRYCE   12/3/18
1/1 Pembroke Yeo. —   R.W. SERLE   13/3/18

10th Bn (Shropshire & Cheshire Yeo) Bn K.S.L.I.

Off Killed

Cheshire Yeo   Capt H. ALDERSEY

Wounded

4 Bn K.S.L.I.   2/Lt W.F. PRATT
3 Bn K.S.L.I.   2/Lt W.E. HALLOWES

Staff Capt
231 Inf Bde

Form "Z."

List No. 10

~~Daily~~ / Weekly casualty report up to ~~7 p.m.~~ ~~noon, Saturday.~~ 0900 FRID.

231st Inf Bde 74th Division.   Date 8th March 1918.

Unit. (Each unit to be shown separately).	Date	Killed. O.	Killed. O.R.	Wounded O.	Wounded O.R.	Missing. O.	Missing. O.R.	Sick Admitted O.	Sick Admitted O.R.
Hqrs. 231st Infy Bde	1.3.18 to 8.3.18	-	-	-	-	-	-	-	1
24th (Denbigh Yeo) Bn R.W.F.	1.3.18 to 8.3.18	-	2	-	5	-	-	-	5
25th (Montgomery & Welsh Horse Yeo) Bn R.W.F.	1.3.18 to 8.3.18	-	-	-	-	-	-	-	7
24th (Pembroke & Glamorgan Yeo) Bn Welsh Rgt	1.3.18 to 8.3.18	-	1	-	1	-	-	-	13
10th (Shropshire & Cheshire Yeo) Bn K.S.L.I.	1.3.18 to 8.3.18	1	0	-	3	-	-	-	33
210th Machine Gun Coy	1.3.18 to 8.3.18	-	-	-	-	-	-	-	4
231st Light Trench Mortar Battery	1.3.18 to 8.3.18	-	-	-	-	-	-	-	-
Totals.		1	3	-	9	-	-	-	63

The space below, and the back of this form, will be used to report Officers' casualties; in each case unit battalion, name, rank, initial, nature of casualty and date will be shown.

8.3.18

Capt.
Staff Captain
231st Infantry Bde

Nominal Roll

Cheshire Yeo. att 10th (Shropshire & Cheshire Yeo) Bn. K.S.L.

Major P.K. GLAZEBROOK D.S.O. KILLED 7.3.18

Form "Z."

List No. 9

~~Daily~~
Weekly casualty report up to ~~7 p.m.~~ ~~noon, Saturday~~ 0900 FRIDAY

231st Inf Bde / 74 Division.   Date 1st March 1918

Unit. (Each unit to be shown separately).	Date	Killed.		Wounded.		Missing.		Sick Admitted	
		O.	O.R.	O.	O.R.	O.	O.R.	O.	O.R.
Headquarters, 231st Inf Bde	23.2.18 to 1.3.18	-	-	-	-	-	-	-	-
24th (Denbigh Yeo) Bn. R.W.F.	23.2.18 to 1.3.18	-	-	-	-	-	-	-	8
25th (Montgomery & Welsh Horse Yeo) Bn. R.W.F.	23.2.18 to 1.3.18	-	-	-	-	-	-	-	4
24th (Pembroke & Glamorgan Yeo) Bn. Welsh R.	23.2.18 to 1.3.18	-	-	-	-	-	-	-	15
10th (Shropshire & Cheshire Yeo) Bn. K.S.L.I.	23.2.18 to 1.3.18	-	-	-	-	-	-	-	18
210th Machine Gun Company	23.2.18 to 1.3.18	-	-	-	-	-	-	-	-
231st Light Trench Mortar Battery	23.2.18 to 1.3.18	-	-	-	-	-	-	-	-
	Totals.	-	-	-	-	-	-	-	45

The space below, and the back of this form, will be used to report Officers' casualties; in each case unit battalion, name, rank, initial, nature of casualty and date will be shown.

1.3.18

Capt
Staff Captain
231st Inf Bde

Form "Z."

List No. 8

~~Daily~~ / Weekly casualty report up to ~~7 p.m.~~ / ~~noon, Saturday~~ 0900 FRIDAY

231st Infy Bde 74th Division.   Date 22nd Feby 1918

Unit. (Each unit to be shown separately):	Date.	Killed. O.	Killed. O.R.	Wounded. O.	Wounded. O.R.	Missing. O.	Missing. O.R.	Sick Admitted. O.	Sick Admitted. O.R.
Headquarters, 231st Infantry Bde	15.2.18 to 22.2.18	-	-	-	-	-	-	-	-
24th (Denbigh Yeo.) Bn. R.W.F.	15.2.18 to 22.2.18	-	-	-	-	-	-	-	2
25th (Montgomery & Welsh Horse Yeo) Bn. R.W.F.	15.2.18 to 22.2.18	-	-	-	-	-	-	-	5
24th (Pembroke & Glamorgan Yeo) Bn. Welsh R.	15.2.18 to 22.2.18	-	-	-	-	-	-	-	15
10th (Shropshire & Cheshire Yeo) Bn. K.S.L.I.	15.2.18 to 22.2.18	-	-	-	-	-	-	1	10
210th Machine Gun Company	15.2.18 to 22.2.18	-	-	-	-	-	-	-	2
231st Light Trench Mortar Battery	15.2.18 to 22.2.18	-	-	-	-	-	-	-	2
Totals.		-	-	-	-	-	-	1	37

The space below, and the back of this form, will be used to report Officers' casualties; in each case unit battalion, name, rank, initial, nature of casualty and date will be shown.

22.2.18

Staff Captain
231st Infantry Brigade

Nominal Roll of Officers - Admitted Sick

1/1 Shropshire Yeo. att 10th Bn. K.S.L.I. Lt. E.A. Downes
sick - 18.2.18

Form "Z."

List No. 7.

~~Daily~~ / Weekly casualty report up to ~~noon, Saturday~~ 0900 FRIDAY
231st. Inf. Bde. 74th. Division.   Date 15th. Febry. 1918.

Unit. (Each unit to be shown separately):	Date.	Killed.		Wounded.		Missing.		Sick Admitted.	
		O.	O.R.	O.	O.R.	O.	O.R.	O.	O.R.
Hrqs, 231st. Inf. Bde.	8.2.18 to 15.2.18	-	-	-	-	-	-	-	1
24th. (Denbigh Yeo.) Bn. R.W.F.	8.2.18 to 15.2.18	-	-	-	-	-	-	-	4
25th. (Montgomery & Welsh Horse Yeo.) Bn. R.W.F.	8.2.18 to 15.2.18	-	-	-	-	-	-	-	4
24th. (Pembroke & Glamorgan Yeo.) Bn. Welsh Rgt.	8.2.18 to 15.2.18	-	-	-	-	-	-	-	17
10th. (Shropshire & Cheshire Yeo.) Bn. K.S.L.I.	8.2.18 to 15.2.18	-	-	-	-	-	-	-	22
210th. Machine Gun Company	8.2.18 to 15.2.18	-	-	-	-	-	-	-	3
231st. Light Trench Mortar Battery	8.2.18 to 15.2.18	-	-	-	-	-	-	-	-
	Totals.	-	-	-	-	-	-	-	51

This Column must not be written upon.

The space below, and the back of this form, will be used to report Officers' casualties; in each case unit battalion, name, rank, initial, nature of casualty and date will be shown.

15.2.18.
1400

A/Staff Captain
231st. Infantry Brigade.

P.T.O.

Form "Z."

List No. 6.

~~Daily~~ Weekly casualty report up to 7 p.m. noon, Saturday. ~~0900 Friday~~

231st. Inf. Bde. 74th Division.   Date 8th. Febry. 1918.

Unit. (Each unit to be shown separately).	Date	Killed.		Wounded.		Missing.		Sick Admitted	
		O.	O.R.	O.	O.R.	O.	O.R.	O.	O.R.
Hqrs, 231st. Infantry Brigade.	1.2.18 to 8.2.18	-	-	-	-	-	-	-	-
24th. (Denbigh Yeo.) Bn. R.W.F.	1.2.18 to 8.2.18	-	-	-	-	-	-	2	3
25th. (Montgomery & Welsh Horse Yeo.) Bn. R.W.F.	1.2.18 to 8.2.18	-	-	-	-	-	-	1	5
24th. (Pembroke & Glamorgan Yeo.) Bn. Welsh Rgt.	1.2.18 to 8.2.18	-	-	-	-	-	-	-	20
10th. (Shropshire & Cheshire Yeo.) Bn. K.S.L.I.	1.2.18 to 8.2.18	-	-	-	-	-	-	-	14
210th. Machine Gun Company	1.2.18 to 8.2.18	-	-	-	-	-	-	-	4
231st. Light Trench Mortar Battery	1.2.18 to 8.2.18	-	-	-	-	-	-	-	-
Totals.		-	-	-	-	-	-	3	46

The space below, and the back of this form, will be used to report Officers' casualties; in each case unit battalion, name, rank, initial, nature of casualty and date will be shown.

8.2.18.

A/Staff Captain
231st. Infantry Brigade

P.T.O.

NOMINAL ROLL OF OFFICERS ADMITTED SICK.

South Wales Borderers att.24th.Bn.R.W.F. 2/Lt.A.A.STIFF sick 4.2.18.
Denbigh Yeo.att.24ty.Bn.R.W.F. Capt.G.S.Topham   sick 7.2.18.

Southe.Wales Borderers att.25th.Bn.R.W.F. 2/Lt. H.L.A.KEYSOR sick 2.2.18.

Form "Z."

List No. 5.

~~Daily~~
Weekly casualty report up to ~~7 p.m.~~ ~~noon, Saturday~~ 0900 FRIDAY

231st. Inf. Bde. 74th. Division. Date 1st. Febry. 1918.

Unit. (Each unit to be shown separately).	Date	Killed.		Wounded.		Missing.		Sick Admitted	
		O.	O.R.	O.	O.R.	O.	O.R.	O.	O.R.
Hqrs, 231st. Infantry Brigade.	25.1.18 to 1.2.18	-	-	-	-	-	-	-	-
24th. Bn. (Denbigh Yeo) R.W.F.	25.1.18 to 1.2.18	-	-	-	-	-	-	-	4
25th. (Montgomery & Welsh Horse Yeo.) Bn. R.W.F.	25.1.18 to 1.2.18	-	-	-	-	-	-	-	13
24th. (Pembroke & Glamorgan Yeo.) Bn. Welsh Rgt.	25.1.18 to 1.2.18	-	-	-	-	-	-	-	14
10th. (Shropshire & Cheshire Yeo.) Bn. K.S.L.I.	25.1.18 to 1.2.18	-	-	-	-	-	-	1	6
210th. Machine Gun Company.	25.1.18 to 1.2.18	-	-	-	-	-	-	-	-
231st. Light Trench Mortar Battery	25.1.18 to 1.2.18	-	-	-	-	-	-	-	-
Totals.		-	-	-	-	-	-	1	37

The space below, and the back of this form, will be used to report Officers' casualties; in each case unit battalion, name, rank, initial, nature of casualty and date will be shown.

One O.R. 24th Bn Welsh Regt died of heart failure 30.1.18.

1.2.18
1400

/ Staff Captain
231st. Inf. Bde.

NOMINAL ROLL OF OFFICERS ADMITTED SICK.

3rd.Bn.K.S.L.I.att.10th.Bn.K.S.L.I. 2/Lt.J.de C.Peel sick 29.1.18.

Form "Z."

List No. 4

~~Daily~~ / Weekly casualty report up to 7 p.m. ~~noon, Saturday~~ 0900 hrs.

231st Inf Bde 74th Division. Date 25.1.18

Unit. (Each unit to be shown separately):	Date.	Killed.		Wounded.		Missing.		Sick Admitted.	
		O.	O.R.	O.	O.R.	O.	O.R.	O.	O.R.
Hqrs, 231st Infy Bde	18.1.18 to 25.1.18	-	-	-	-	-	-	-	-
24th (Den:bigh Yeo) Bn R.W.F.	18.1.18 to 25.1.18	-	-	-	-	-	-	2	5
25th (Montgomery & Welsh Horse Yeo) Bn R.W.F.	18.1.18 to 25.1.18	-	-	-	-	-	-	1	10
24th (Pembroke & Glamorgan Yeo) Bn Welsh Re	18.1.18 to 25.1.18	-	-	-	-	-	-	1	10
10th (Shropshire & Cheshire Yeo) K.S.L.I.	18.1.18 to 25.1.18	-	-	-	-	-	-	2	11
210th Machine Gun Company	18.1.18 to 25.1.18	-	-	-	-	-	-	1	2
231st Light Trench Mortar Battery	18.1.18 to 25.1.18	-	-	-	-	-	-	-	-
Totals.		-	-	-	-	-	-	7	38

The space below, and the back of this form, will be used to report Officers' casualties; in each case unit battalion, name, rank, initial, nature of casualty and date will be shown.

25.1.18

Staff Captain
231st Infantry Brigade

Nominal Roll of Officers - admitted Sick

Denbigh. Yeo att 24th Bn. RWF Capt R J Hodges sick 19.1.
Welsh Rgt att 24th B.RWF 2/Lt. E Thomas. sick 23.1.1

R.W.F. att 25th Bn. R.W.F 2/Lt. R.S.D. Thomas sick 24.1.18
Monmouth Rgt att 24th Bn. Welsh Rgt 2/Lt T.B. Williams sick 25.1.1
Shropshire Yeo. att 10th Bn. K.S.L.I. Lieut O. Cawley sick 21.1.
Cheshire Yeo att 10th Bn. K.S.L.I. Major P.K. Glazebrook D Sick 24.1.1
9th Royal Berks seconded 210th M.g Coy Lieut H. Wade sick 19.1.1

Form "Z."

List No. 3.

~~Daily~~ Weekly casualty report up to ~~7 p.m.~~ noon, Saturday. ~~0900 Friday~~

231st. Infantry Bde. Division.   Date 19th. Jany. 1918.

Unit. (Each unit to be shown separately).	Date	Killed.		Wounded. Accidental		Missing.		Sick Admitted	
		O.	O.R.	O.	O.R.	O.	O.R.	O.	O.R.
Hqrs, 231st. Infantry Brigade.	11.1.18 to 18.1.18	-	-	-	-	-	-	-	-
24th.(Denbigh Yeo.)Bn. R.W.F.	11.1.18 to 18.1.18	-	-	-	-	-	-	-	2
25th.(Montgomery & Welsh Horse Yeo) Bn. R.W.F.	11.1.18 to 18.1.18	-	-	-	-	-	-	-	4
24th.(Pembroke & Glamorgan Yeo.) Bn. Welsh Rgt.	11.1.18 to 18.1.18	-	-	-	-	-	-	-	10
10th.(Shropshire & Cheshire Yeo.) Bn. K.S.L.I.	11.1.18 to 18.1.18	-	-	-	-	-	-	-	12
210th.Machine Gun Company	11.1.18 to 18.1.18	-	-	-	1	-	-	-	7
231st.L.T.M.B.	11.1.18 to 18.1.18	-	-	-	-	-	-	-	1
Totals.		-	-	-	1	-	-	-	36

The space below, and the back of this form, will be used to report Officers' casualties; in each case unit battalion, name, rank, initial, nature of casualty and date will be shown.

18.1.18
1400

A/Staff Captain
231st. Infantry Bde.

Form "Z."

List No. 2.

~~Daily~~ / Weekly casualty report up to 7 p.m. ~~noon, Saturday (90)~~ Friday.

231st. Inf. Bde. Division. Date 11.1.18

This Column must not be written upon.

Unit. (Each unit to be shown separately):	Date.	Killed.		Wounded.		Missing.		Sick Admitted.	
		O.	O.R.	O.	O.R.	O.	O.R.	O.	O.R.
Hqrs, 231st. Infantry Brigade.	4.1.18 to 11.1.18	-	-	-	-	-	-	-	-
24th. Bn. (Denbigh Yeo) R.W.F.	4.1.18 to 11.1.18	-	-	-	-	-	-	1	9
25th. Bn. (Montgomery & Welsh Horse Yeo) R.W.F.	4.1.18 to 11.1.18	-	-	-	-	-	-	1	2
24th. Bn. (Pembroke & Glamorgan Yeo) Welsh Rgt.	4.1.18 to 11.1.18	-	-	-	-	-	-	-	13 ~~23~~
210th. Machine Gun Company	4.1.18 to 11.1.18	-	-	-	-	-	-	-	7
231st. L.T.M.B.	4.1.18 to 11.1.18	-	-	-	-	-	-	-	1
10th. Bn. (Shropshire & Cheshire Yeo) K.S.L.I.	4.1.18 to 11.1.18	-	-	-	-	-	-	-	23
	Totals.	-	-	-	-	-	-	2	55

The space below, and the back of this form, will be used to report Officers' casualties; in each case unit battalion, name, rank, initial, nature of casualty and date will be shown.

11.1.18
1400

Captain
Staff Captain
231st. Infantry B.

P.T.O.

NOMINAL ROLL OF OFFICERS (N.S ADMITTED SICK)   11.1.18

2/Lieut. W.Barker 7th.R.W.F.at.25th.Bn.R.W.F.   3.1.18.
Lieut.C.E.Burten Monmouth Regt.att.24th.Bn.R.W.F.   8.1.18.

Form "Z."

List No. 1.

~~Daily~~ Weekly casualty report up to ~~noon, Saturday~~ 9.00 Friday.

231st. Inf. Bde. Division.   Date 4th. Janry. 1918.

Unit. (Each unit to be shown separately).	Date	Killed.		Wounded.		Missing.		Sick Admitted	
		O.	O.R.	O.	O.R.	O.	O.R.	O.	O.R.
Hqrs, 231st. Infantry Brigade.	29.12.17 to 4.1.18	-	-	-	-	-	-	-	-
24th. Bn. (Denbigh Yeo) R.W.F.	29.12.17 to 4.1.18	-	-	-	-	-	-	-	11
25th. Bn. (Montgomery & Welsh Horse Yeo) R.W.F.	29.12.17 to 4.1.18	-	-	-	-	-	-	-	8
24th. Bn. (Pembroke & Glamorgan Yeo) Welsh Regt.	29.12.17 to 4.1.18	-	-	-	-	-	-	1	14
10th. Bn. (Shropshire & Cheshire Yeo) K.S.L.I.	29.12.17 to 4.1.18	-	-	-	-	-	-	1	18
210th. M.G.Co.	29.12.17 to 4.1.18	-	-	-	-	-	-	-	12
231st. L.T.M.B.	29.12.17 to 4.1.18	-	-	-	-	-	-	-	-
Totals.		-	-	-	-	-	-	2	63

The space below, and the back of this form, will be used to report Officers' casualties; in each case unit battalion, name, rank, initial, nature of casualty and date will be shown.

5.1.18.
1200

Captain
Staff Captain
231st. Infantry Brigade

NOMINAL ROLL OF OFFICERS ADMITTED SICK.

Pembroke Yeo.att.24th.Bn.Welsh Rgt.   Lieut.L.D.C.ROSE sick   29.12.1
4th.Bn.K.S.L.I.att.10th.Bn.K.S.L.I.   2/Lieut.E.W.RODEN sick   28.12.1

Form "Z"

No. 4

Daily / ~~Weekly~~ casualty report up to 7 p.m. / ~~noon, Saturday.~~

231st Inf. Bde / 74 Division. Date 12.3.18

Unit. (Each unit to be shown separately.)	Date	Killed		Wounded		Missing		Sick Admitted	
		O.	O.R.	O.	O.R.	O.	O.R.	O.	O.R.
10th (Shropshire & Cheshire Yeo) Bn. K.S.L.I.	12.3.18	-	-	-	9*	-	-	-	-
*. 1 Accidentally Wounded									
Totals		.	.	.	9	.	.	.	.

The space below, and the back of this form, will be used to report Officers' casualties; in each case, unit, battalion, name, rank, initial, nature of casualty, and date will be shown.

13.3.18

Capt.
Staff Captain
231st Infantry Bde

Nominal Roll.   12.3.18

10th (Shropshire & Cheshire Yeo) Bn K.S.L.I.

WOUNDED - Other Ranks

230408 L/Cpl. YAPP W.   230496 Pte HALFORD T.R.
33288 Pte POWELL N. (accidentally)
34098 Pte DAVIES A.T.   6485 Pte BULLOCK J.
329014 Pte HEYES A.   231076 Pte GUEST W.
230825 Pte SELLARS R.A.   26482 Pte MASSEY E.

(9)

Form "Z."

List No. _____

Daily / **Weekly** casualty report up to 7 p.m. / noon, Saturday.

231 Bde. 74th Division. Date 12-3-18

Unit. (Each unit to be shown separately).	Date.	Killed. O.	O.R.	Wounded. O.	O.R.	Missing. O.	O.R.	Sick Admitted. O.	O.R.
10th K.S.L.I.	12-3-18				9				
230408 L/Cpl Yapp W.									
230496 Pte Halford J.R.									
33288 Pte Powell N. (Accidentally wounded)									
34098 Pte Davies A.J.									
6485 Pte Bullock J.									
32924 Pte Heyes A.									
231076 Pte Guest W.									
230825 Pte Sellars R.A.									
26482 Pte Massey C.									
Totals.		—	—		9	—	—		

The space below, and the back of this form, will be used to report Officers' casualties; in each case unit battalion, name, rank, initial, nature of casualty and date will be shown.

J. Higginson Capt & Adjt
LIEUT. COL.
10TH (SHROP. & CHESH. YEO. BATT?)
K.S.L.I.

"A" Form
MESSAGES AND SIGNALS.

Army Form C. 2121
(In pads of 100.)

No. of Message..........

Prefix......Code......m.	Words.	Charge.	This message is on a/c of:	Recd. at.........m.
Office of Origin and Service Instructions	Sent			Date..........
....	At.......m.		..........Service.	From..........
....	To			
....	By		(Signature of "Franking Officer.")	By..........

TO { DAG GHQ
14 Div
RECORD MEF

Sender's Number.	Day of Month.	In reply to Number.	AAA
* R478	15		

Ref form Z for 10/3/18

231023 Pte HOLLOWOOD E
10th KSLI reported missing
now reported killed aaa

Ref Form Z for 1/5/18

220677 Pte WILLIAMSON R
Correct number to read 230687
reported missing now
reported sick aaa

Addressed DAG GHQ repeated
14 Div and Record MEF.

From	231 Inf Bde
Place	
Time	1850

The above may be forwarded as now corrected.   (Z)

....
Censor.   Signature of Addresser or person authorised to telegraph in his name.

* This line should be erased if not required.
(7981) Wt. W492/M1647 130,000 Pads 5/17 D. D. & L. E1187

"C" Form.
MESSAGES AND SIGNALS.

Army Form C. 2123.
(In books of 100.)
No. of Message 258

Prefix	Code	Words	Received.	Sent, or sent out.	Office Stamp.
	£ s. d.		From	At .... m.	
Charges to Collect			By	To	15/8/18
Service Instructions				By	

Handed in at .... PTR Office 11.55 Received 11.50 m.

TO .... 231 Inf Bde

Sender's Number.	Day of Month.	In reply to Number.	AAA
AP78	15	A477	

230687 Pte Williamson
R

FROM 10 KSLI
TIME & PLACE 1755

"C" Form.
MESSAGES AND SIGNALS.

Army Form C. 2128.
(In books of 100.)

No. of Message 250

Prefix	Code	Words	Received.	Sent, or sent out.	Office Stamp.
	£ s. d.		From	At .... m.	
Charges to Collect			By 3H	To	
Service Instructions				By	

Handed in at **Pile** Office **14.27** m. Received **11.40** m.

TO: 231 Inf Bde

*Sender's Number.	Day of Month.	In reply to Number.	AAA
Ad 77	15		
231023 Pte		Hollowood E	
reported missing	now	killed	
230687 Pte		Williamson R	
reported missing	now	sick	

FROM TIME & PLACE: 10th RWF 1435

*This line should be erased if not required.

"A" Form
MESSAGES AND SIGNALS.

Army Form C. 2121 (In pads of 100.)

Prefix....S...Code............m.	Words.	Charge.	This message is on a/c of:	Recd. at............m.
Office of Origin and Service Instructions	Sent			Date..........
	At............m.		..............Service.	From..........
	To..........			
	By..........		(Signature of "Franking Officer.")	By..........

TO {	DAG GHQ
	7th Divn
	RECORDMEF

Sender's Number.	Day of Month.	In reply to Number.	AAA
* A471	14/3/18		

Reference Form "Z" for 11.3.18
AAA 72960 Pte ~~Pte~~ FREEGUARD
C V 25/RWF previously
reported missing now not
missing admitted to Hospital
sick AAA addressed DAG
GHQ repeated RECORDMEF and
7th Divn

From	25th Bde
Place	
Time	9100

The above may be forwarded as now corrected. (Z)

....Censor. Signature of Addressor or person authorised to telegraph in his name.
* This line should be erased if not required.
(7981) Wt. W492/M1647 130,000 Pads 5/17 D.D.&L. E1187

"C" FORM.
MESSAGES AND SIGNALS.

Army Form C. 2123.
(In books of 100.)

No. of Message ....

Prefix......Code......Words......	Received	Sent, or sent out	Office Stamp
£ s. d.	From........	At ....m.	
Charges to Collect	By........	To ....m.	
Service Instructions		By........	

Handed in at .... Office .... m. Received .... m.

TO   **231 Brigade**

*Sender's Number.	Day of Month.	In reply to Number.	AAA
R.8.	14		

Reference form Z 9th
March aaa No 355536 a/cpl
Green T wounded in action
9th Guns. aaa Not
previously reported aaa Reference
form Z March H
aaa No 72960 pte Sheeguard
C. previously reported missing
aaa Now not missing
aaa Admitted hospital sick
aaa

FROM
PLACE & TIME   **25 RWF**

* This line should be erased if not required.
(3566.) Wt. W528/M1970. 100,000 Pads. 5/17. H. W. & V., Ld. (E. 1213.)

Form "Z"

No. 3

~~Daily~~ / Weekly casualty report up to ~~7 p.m.~~ / noon, Saturday.

231st Inf. Bde. Division. Date 16th March 1918.

Unit. (Each unit to be shown separately.)	Date	Killed		Wounded		Missing		Sick Admitted	
		O.	O.R.	O.	O.R.	O.	O.R.	O.	O.R.
24th (Denbigh Yeo) Bn. R.W.F.	11.3.18	-	-	-	-	-	-	-	-
25th (Montgomery & Welsh Horse Yeo) Bn. R.W.F.	11.3.18	-	2	1	12	1	1	-	-
24th (Pembroke & Glamorgan Yeo) Bn. Welsh Regt.	11.3.18	-	-	-	-	-	-	-	-
10th (Shropshire & Cheshire Yeo) Bn. K.S.L.I.	11.3.18	-	-	-	-	-	1	-	-
210th Machine Gun Coy.	11.3.18	-	-	-	-	-	-	-	-
Totals		=	2	1	12	1	2	-	-

The space below, and the back of this form, will be used to report Officers' casualties; in each case, unit, battalion, name, rank, initial, nature of casualty, and date will be shown.

12.3.18

Capt
Staff Captain
231st Infantry Bde.

NOMINAL ROLL 11.3.18

25th (Montgomery & Welsh Horse Yeo.) Bn. Welsh Rgt.

WOUNDED - Officers -
2/Lt. S. JOHNS. 4th Bn R.W.F. (1)

MISSING -
Capt. W.P. ROCH   Welsh Horse Yeo. (1)

KILLED - Other Ranks
356011 Pte JONES D.W.: 72929 Pte. HIGGINBOTTOM J. (2)

WOUNDED
72956 Pte PARSONS C.H.: 201605 Pte ROBERTS W.: 10499 Pte BRIDGWATER
315670 Pte CAVANAGH W.: 7940 Pte KYNES T.: 355829 Pte JONES W.:
355154 C/pl LEWIS H.: 815955 Pte HOWELLS P.: 356001 Pte ROCH W.:
242756 Pte PREDDINGH: 355111 Pte WILLIAMS G.W.: 201683 Pte LORD
MISSING
72960 Pte FREEGUARD C.V. (12)

10th (Shropshire & Cheshire Yeo) Bn. K.S.L.I. (1)

MISSING - Other Ranks
220677 Pte WILLIAMSON R.

(1)

"C" FORM.
MESSAGES AND SIGNALS.

Army Form C. 2123.
(In books of 100.)
No. of Message...........

Prefix....Code....Words....	Received.	Sent, or sent out.	Office Stamp.
£ s. d.	From........	At.........m.	
Charges to Collect	By...JG...	To........	
Service Instructions		By........	

Handed in at........Ino........Office 22.35.m. Received 23.3.m.

TO   231 Brigade
     G09

*Sender's Number.	Day of Month.	In reply to Number.	AAA
7109	11	—	AAA

Form	Z	march	11th
aaa	Killed	no	356011
Pte	Jones	DW	aaa
72939	Pte	Higginbotham	J
aaa	wounded	2 Lieut	S
John	aaa	72956	Pte
Parsons CH	aaa	201605	
Pte	Roberts W	aaa	
10499	Pte	Bridgewater W	
aaa	315670	Pte	Cavanagh
W	aaa	7940	Pte
Kynes	T	aaa	355524
Pte	Jones	W	aaa
	355754	Cpl	Lewis
H	aaa	315955	Pte
Howells	P	aaa	356001
Pte	Roch	W	aaa

FROM
PLACE & TIME

* This line should be erased if not required.

"C" FORM.
MESSAGES AND SIGNALS.

Army Form C. 2123.
(In books of 100.)
No. of Message......143

*Sender's Number.	Day of Month.	In reply to Number.	AAA
242756 Pte Predding H aaa 355111 Pte Williams GW aaa 201683 Pte Lord G aaa missing Capt W P Roch aaa 12960 Pte Freeguard aaa all guns aaa			

HW/2336

FROM PLACE & TIME: 2/5 RWF 2255

"C" FORM.
MESSAGES AND SIGNALS.

Army Form C. 2123
(In books of 100.)
No. of Message 132

Office Stamp: 3wa 11/3/18

Handed in at ... Office ... m. Received 1704 m.

TO: 231 Inf Bde

FROM PLACE & TIME: 10BSLI 1730

Casualties 220677 Pte Williamson
Missing 230605 Cpl Fowerbuts[?]
This is reported up to time
of passing enemy dead buried
enemy arms and
equipment saved

MESSAGES AND SIGNALS.

Prefix....Code....m	Words. Charge.	This message is on a/c of:		Recd. at....m
Office of Origin and Service Instructions	Sent			Date....
	At........m	..........Service.		From....
	To......			
	By......	(Signature of "Franking Officer.")		By....

TO — The Dn

Sender's Number.	Day of Month.	In reply to Number.	
* A 453	14/3/18		AAA

Reference Form Z for the 10.6.18 AAA 355957 Pte WILLIAMS D W correct number should be 72959

From 231
Place
Time 1515

The above may be forwarded as now corrected. (Z)
............................Censor. Signature of Addresser or person authorised to telegraph in his name.
* This line should be erased if not required.
(7981) Wt.W492/M1647 130,000 Pads 5/17 D.D.&L. E1187

Form "Z"

No. 2

Daily / ~~Weekly~~ casualty report up to 7 p.m. noon, Saturday, 0900 FRIDAY

231st Infy Div ~~Brigade~~ Division. Date 10th March 1918

This Column must not be written upon.

Unit. (Each unit to be shown separately.)	Date	Killed		Wounded		Missing		Sick Admitted	
		O.	O.R.	O.	O.R.	O.	O.R.	O.	O.R.
24th (Denbigh Yeo) Bn. R.W.F.	10.3.18	-	-	-	-	-	-	-	-
25th (Montgomery & Welsh Horse Yeo) Bn. R.W.F.	10.3.18	-	2	-	10	-	-	-	-
24th (Pembroke & Glamorgan Yeo) Bn. Welsh R.	10.3.18	-	1	-	-	-	-	-	-
10th (Shropshire & Cheshire Yeo) Bn. K.S.L.I.	10.3.18	1	9	2	29	-	2	-	-
210th Machine Gun Coy	10.3.18	-	-	-	-	-	-	-	-
	Totals	1	12	3	39	-	2	-	-

The space below, and the back of this form, will be used to report Officers' casualties; in each case, unit, battalion, name, rank, initial, nature of casualty, and date will be shown.

12.3.18

Capt
Staff Captain
231st Infantry Bde

Nominal - Roll   10.3.18

25th (Montgomery & Welsh Horse Yeo.) Bn. R.W.F.

WOUNDED - Officer
Welsh Horse Yeo. Capt. W.P. ROCH remaining at duty.   (1)

KILLED - Other Ranks
355048 C.S.M. HUMPHREYS S: 355357 Pte. RICHARDS J.A.   (2)

WOUNDED
21096 Sgt. GARBETT C: 355937 Pte. MONKS C: 67468 Pte. GORE W.S:
355080 Pte. DAVIES F.: 355937 Pte. WILLIAMS D.W: 72972 Pte. PADDISON D.H
355831 Pte. HARRIS T.E: 355155 Sgt. JONES D.G: 355586 C/L. PARKMAN J
355719 L/Cpl. COOK W.   (10)

24th (Pembroke & Glamorgan Yeo.) Bn. Welsh R.

KILLED - Other Ranks
52896 Pte. GWYLYN D.   (1)

10th (Shropshire & Cheshire Yeo.) Bn. K.S.L.I.

KILLED - Officers
Cheshire Yeo. Capt. H. ALDERSEY   (1)

WOUNDED
2nd Bn. K.S.L.I. 2/Lt. W.F. PRATT: 3rd Bn. K.S.L.I. 2/Lt. W.E. HALLOWES   (2)

KILLED - Other Ranks
6258 a/Sgt. MASON H: 230486 a/L/Cpl. JONES W.B: 230548 Pte. BRACEGIRDLE
230911 Pte. WOODS J. 230824 Pte. HOLDER L.H: 230144 C.S.M. BRACE E.G
33514 Pte. FOXCROFT J: 230592 Pte. VENABLES T.E: 230592 Pte. GRIFFITHS G.E   (9)

WOUNDED
230086 Cpl. ROCHELLS E: 230281 a/L/Cpl. JONES E.G: 230192 Pte. THOMAS R.S
230058 Pte. JONES J.J: 34204 Pte. HUGHES M.H: 230691 Sgt. DISTIN W.B
230981 Pte. JENKINS J.S: 33274 Pte. FROST T: 17775 Pte. DAVIES E
9651 Pte. McKAY G: 230618 Sgt. KETTLE J.E: 230894 Pte. MOSS A:
200828 Pte. SCOTT F: 230848 Pte. WATSON T: 230966 Pte. LEWIS J.T
34220 Pte. BUNTING F.E: 34218 Pte. ETCHELLS D: 231012 Pte. DUGDALE S
14160 Pte. WOODS G: 230733 Pte. JONES F: 231037 Pte. RICHARDS J
231052 Sgt. WORTHINGTON W: 230070 C/Cpl. DOOGAN J: 230261 a/Cpl. DAVIES P
230214 L/Cpl. DYKE W: 26061 Pte. EDWARDS T: 34153 Pte. TOMLINSON J.A
15682 Cpl. BRERETON G: 231026 Pte. KEENAN D.C.   (29)

MISSING
230724 Pte. DUTTON F.D: 231023 Pte. HOLLOWOOD E.   (2)

"C" FORM.
MESSAGES AND SIGNALS.

Army Form C. 2123.
(In books of 100.)

No. of Message...........

Prefix......Code......Words......	Received.	Sent, or sent out.	Office Stamp.
£ s. d.	From..........	At.............m.	
Charges to Collect	By........	To............	
Service Instructions		By............	

Handed in at...........Pph..........Office. 1705 m. Received 1705 m.

TO	231 Bde

*Sender's Number.	Day of Month.	In reply to Number.	AAA
Pg 782	12	—	

Casualties nil no 52987
Pte FICE A missing
since 9/3/18

/Jr 1706

FROM PLACE & TIME	24th Welsh Regt 1700

*This line should be erased if not required.

"A" Form
MESSAGES AND SIGNALS.

Army Form C. 2121
(In pads of 100.)

No. of Message..............

Prefix.........Code.........m. | Words. | Charge. | This message is on a/c of:
Office of Origin and Service Instructions | Sent | | ....Service.
 | At.............m. | |
 | To............ | | (Signature of "Franking Officer.")
 | By............ | |

Recd. at............m.
Date..............
From..............
By..............

TO { 74 Div

| Sender's Number. | Day of Month. | In reply to Number. | AAA |
| A.59 | 12/3/18 | | |

Reference form Z for 9.3.18
AAA Please add 52957
Pte FICE A 24/Welsh
R.E. MISSING

Since reported
admitted to
Hospital

From: 231 Bde
Place
Time

The above may be forwarded as now corrected. (Z)
........................Censor. Signature of Addressor or person authorised to telegraph in his name.
* This line should be erased if not required.

(7981) Wt. W492/M1647 130,000 Pads 5/17 D. D. & L. E1187

"A" Form
MESSAGES AND SIGNALS.

Army Form C. 2121
(In pads of 100)

Prefix......Code......m.	Words.	Charge.	This message is on a/c of:	Recd. at......m.
Office of Origin and Service Instructions	Sent			Date......
	At......m.		......Service.	From......
	To......			
	By......		(Signature of "Franking Officer.")	By......

TO: 14 Divn

| Sender's Number. | Day of Month. | In reply to Number. | AAA |

A4/62 12/3/18

Reference form Z for 9.3.18
AAA for 355350 Pte ROSLOW
read PURSLOW AAA
Please amend

From Place: 231 Bob.
Time: 1830

"C" FORM.
MESSAGES AND SIGNALS.

Army Form C. 2123.
(In books of 100.)

No. of Message......

Prefix....Code....Words....	Received.	Sent, or sent out.	Office Stamp.
£ s. d.	From..........	At........m.	
Charges to Collect	By 98	To.........	
Service Instructions		By	

Handed in at............Office........m. Received........m.

TO 231 Bde

Sender's Number.	Day of Month.	In reply to Number.	AAA
1110	11		

Corrections form Z 9th aaa No 355845 Pte Jones T reported missing under No 355804 aaa Now wounded aaa No. 355571 Pte Llewellyn S Previously reported missing now wounded not missing aaa 355786 Pte Morris L Previously reported missing now wounded not missing aaa Form Z of 10th 355957 Pte Williams DW correct number should be 72959 aaa

AJn z 351
25 RWF.

FROM PLACE & TIME

* This line should be erased if not required.
(19629) W1523/M1970. 300,000 Pads. 4/17. McC. & Co., Ltd. (E1213).

"A" Form
MESSAGES AND SIGNALS.

Army Form C.2121
(In pads of 100.)

TO: DAG GHQ
74 Divn
RECORMEF

Sender's Number	Day of Month	In reply to Number	AAA
A451	12/3/18		

Reference Form Z for the 9.3.18 AAA 355845 Pte JONES T. previously reported as Missing under No. 355804 now reported WOUNDED AAA 355541 Pte LLEWELLYN S and 355786 Pte MORRIS L both previously reported missing now reported WOUNDED AAA addressed D.A.G. G.H.Q. repeated RECORMEF and 74th Divn

From: 231 Bde
Time: 1800

"A" Form
MESSAGES AND SIGNALS.

Army Form C.2121
(In pads of 100.)

TO: 74 Divn

Sender's Number: A490
Day of Month: 14/3/18
AAA

Reference form Z 9.8.18
AAA Please add 355526 Spr
GREEN T 25/RWF WOUNDED not
previously reported

From: 231 Bde

"O" Form.
MESSAGES AND SIGNALS.

Army Form C. 2123
(In books of 100.)
No. of Message 82

Prefix....Code....Words....	Received.	Sent, or sent out.	Office Stamp.
£ s. d. Charges to Collect	From............ By............	At............m.	
Service Instructions		To............ By............	

Handed in at............Office............m. Received............m.

TO

* Sender's Number.	Day of Month.	In reply to Number.	AAA
Dyke W		26061	Pte
Edwards T		34153	Pte
Tomlinson J A		15682	Cpl
Brereton G	2/Lt		W E
Pratt	2/Lt	Hallowes 231026	
Pte	Keenin RC		aaa
missing 230784	Pte	Dutton	
F D 231023	Pte	Hollowood	
E	aaa Enemy dead		
buried Nil	aaa Enemy		
arms and equipment			
salvaged Nil			
Officers KILLED 1 Wounded 2			
Other Ranks			
KILLED 9			
WOUNDED 29			
MISSING 2			

FROM 10 KSLI
PLACE & TIME

"C" FORM.
MESSAGES AND SIGNALS.

Army Form C. 2123
(In books of 100.)
No. of Message 82

Prefix......Code......Words......
Charges to Collect
Service Instructions

Received. From...... By......
Sent, or sent out. At......m. To...... By......
Office Stamp.

Handed in at...... Office...... m. Received...... m.

TO

* Sender's Number.	Day of Month.	In reply to Number.	AAA
pte	Jenkins	pte	Frost
47775	pte	Davies	2651
pte	McKay	G	230618
Sgt	Kettle	J E	pte
Moss	A	230828	pte
Scott	F	230848	pte
Watson	J	230966	pte
Lewis	J T	34220	pte
Bunting	F E	34218	pte
Etchells	D	231012	pte
Dugdale	J	14160	pte
Woods	G	230733	pte
Jones	F	231037	pte
Richards	J	231052	Sgt
Worthington	W	230070	L/Cpl
Doogan	J	230261	A/Cpl
Davies	R	230214	L/Cpl

FROM
PLACE & TIME

* This line should be erased if not required.

"C" Form.
MESSAGES AND SIGNALS.

Army Form C. 2123.
(In books of 100.)
No. of Message 82

Handed in at PTK Office 1.03 m. Received 9.24 m.

TO: 231 Inf Bde

Sender's Number.	Day of Month.	In reply to Number.	AAA
AM 6	10	10/3/18	
Casualties	for	today	are
Killed	Capt	H	Alderey
6238	a/Sgt	Mason	H J
230486	a/L/Cpl	Jones	W B
230548	Pte	Brucegirdle	230572
Pte	Griffiths	C E	230911
Pte	Woods	J	230824
Pte	Holder	L H	230144
Cpl	Roace	E G	33514
Pte	Foxcroft	J	230372
Pte	Venables	J E	aaa
Wounded	230086	Cpl	Rochell
E	230281	a/L/Cpl	Jones
L J	230190	Pte	Thomas
R S	230058	Pte	Jones
J J	34204	Pte	Hughes
R H	Sgt	Preston	W B

*This line should be erased if not required.

"A" Form
MESSAGES AND SIGNALS.

Prefix....Code....m	Words.	Charge.	This message is on a/c of:	Recd. at....m.
Office of Origin and Service Instructions	Sent			Date....
	At....m		........Service.	From....
	To....			
	By....		(Signature of "Franking Officer.")	By....

TO — 24 Welsh RC

Sender's Number.	Day of Month.	In reply to Number.	AAA
A 442	11/3/18		

Expedite Daily Casualty for yesterday 10.3.18 17AIB Very Urgent

P9.447   10/3/18   AAA
Casualty Wire for the 10.3.18
24 Welsh RC KILLED 52896
Pte GWYLYN D

From 231 Rob
Place
Time 1838

FORM "Z"

Div. 14th   March 10th 18

Regt N°	Rank	Name	Nature of Casualty
355048	C.S.M.	Humphrey S.	Killed Gun
355357	Pte	Richards J.C.	Killed Gun

In the Field
10-3-18

Major
The Welsh Horse
Cmdg 25th Yeo Bn R.W.Fus.

FORM "Z"

74th Divn.   March 10th

                            Nature of
Regtl No.   Rank   Name   Casualty
            Capt.   W P Roch   "Wounded" "Guns"
                                   Remained on duty
21096   Sgt   Sarbutt T.C.   "Wounded" "Guns"
355937   Pte   Monks C.   "Wounded" "Guns"
67468   Pte   Cox W S   "Wounded" "Guns"
355080   Pte   Davies F.   "Wounded" "Guns"
355957   Pte   Williams L W   "Wounded" "Guns"
72972   Pte   Paddison D J   "Wounded" "Guns"
355831   Pte   Harris J C   "Wounded" "Guns"
355755   Sgt   Jones D G   "Wounded" "Guns"
355586   L/Cpl   Sackman J   "Wounded" "Guns"
355719   L/Cpl   Cook W   "Wounded" "Guns"

In the Field   Major
  10-3-18   The Welsh Horse
                                    Comdg 25th YEO Bn R.W.F.

Form "Z."

List No. 1

~~Daily~~ / Weekly casualty report up to ~~7 p.m.~~ noon, Saturday.

231st Infy Bde / 74 Division.   Date 9.3.18

Unit. (Each unit to be shown separately).	Date	Killed. O.	Killed. O.R.	Wounded. O.	Wounded. O.R.	Missing. O.	Missing. O.R.	Sick Admitted O.	Sick Admitted O.R.
24 (Denbigh Yeo) Bn. R.W.F.	9.3.18	-	-	-	3	-	-	-	-
25 (Montgomery & Welsh Horse Yeo) Bn. R.W.F.	9.3.18	1	5	3	29	-	3	-	-
24 (Pembroke & Glamorgan Yeo) Bn. Welsh Rgt	9.3.18	1	1	-	12	-	-	-	-
10th Bn (Shropshire & Cheshire Yeo) K.S.L.I.	9.3.18	-	3	-	28	-	-	-	-
210th Machine Gun Company	9.3.18	-	-	-	-	-	-	-	-
Totals.		2	9	3	72	-	3	-	-

The space below, and the back of this form, will be used to report Officers' casualties; in each case unit battalion, name, rank, initial, nature of casualty and date will be shown.

10.3.18

Nominal Roll

9.3.18

24th Bn (Denbigh Yeo) R.W.F.

Wounded – Other Ranks

202613 Pte D.C. Jones; 56104 Pte S. Nardon; 315098 Sgt S. Roberts – remaining at duty (3)

25th (Montgomery & Welsh Horse Yeo) Bn R.W.F.

Officers Killed

3rd S.W.B. 2/Lt H.L.A. Keysor (1)

Wounded

Montgomery Yeo. Lt C.H. Farmer; Montgomery Yeo. Lt J.A.S. Foulkes-Jones; Welsh Horse Yeo. Major J.G. Rees DSO remaining at duty (3)

Other Ranks Killed

60034 Pte Fearn B; 57713 Pte Williams W.G; 355825 Pte Tapping W; 355036 Sgt Edwards J.H; 72978 Pte Downs A.E. (5)

Wounded

49589 Pte Thomas J; 355598 Pte MacArtur A; 49763 Pte Evans T.J; 355013 L/Cpl Lawson R.M; 315203 Pte Beckwith G; 355444 Pte Gulliver J; 355196 Pte Lloyd T; 355910 Pte Chapman J.A; 355330 Pte Ruslow J; 55895 Pte Watkins A.J; 61103 Pte Morris R.G; 355283 Pte Francis H.W; 355410 Cpl Taylor J; 355150 L/Cpl Powell G.P; 355749 Sgt Morris J; 90106 Pte Blackmore W; 62120 Pte May H; 67132 Pte Edlestone T; 59177 Pte Watson S; 72931 Pte Walters T.H; 26023 Pte Morris; 2741 Pte Bridges E (Mont. Yeo) Pte (W.H. Yeo)

Officers Killed

Pem & Kn Yeo Lieut (T/Capt) D.L.P. Morgan

Other Ranks Killed

59987 Pte Mead J.H.

Wounded

315782 Sgt Roberts A.T; 52481 Pte Williams W.T; 320750 Pte Nicholas N; 350260 Pte Morgan W; 356160 Sgt (T/R.S.M) Thomas R; 320202 Cpl Bowen W; Pte Nesbitt G; Pte Griffiths A; 320119 Sgt Evans W; 59013 Pte Tunnicliff W; Pte Phillips D.L; 8748 Pte Jones W.E.

25th Bn (Montgomery & Welsh Horse Yeo)

Wounded (cont) 355654 Pte Curtis A; 72999 Pte Morgan J.E; 54185 Pte Walker L; 355582 Cpl Bowen T.E; 355190 Pte Jones T; 356048 Pte Griffiths R.E; 74884 Pte Dearden S.

Missing

355571 Pte Llewellyn S; 355564 Pte Jones T; 355786 Pte Morris L

2.

NOMINAL ROLL - CONTINUED

10th (Shropshire & Cheshire Yeo) Bn. K.S.L.I.   OTHER RANK

KILLED

33247 Pte BISHOP W.H.: 34201 Pte BRADSHAW. W.H. 8359 Sgt. CHURCH

WOUNDED.

230203 A/Sgt. JONES G.O: 230386 L/Cpl. TREVOR F: 230428 L/Cpl. POOLE
230097 Pte BURROUGH G.M: 231033 Pte RHEADE: 230359 Pte PHILLIPS
230130 Pte EVANS J.G: 230078 Pte ROBERTS E: 230766 Sgt. WALLIS C.
230972 Pte DAVISON H: 230989 Pte DANIELS J: 230816 Pte NORTH P.E
33024 Pte HARRIS J: 230556 Sgt. LATHAM S: 230558 Sgt. BLACKBURN T.
230795 Sgt. RICHES C.W 230880 Pte GRIFFITHS A.D: 230315 Pte JOHNS H.G.
34110 Pte ETHERINGTON E: 230360 Pte WATKINS E: 34141 Pte EDKINS
230257 Pte JONES E.P: 230459 Pte REYNOLDS T.H: 230486 Pte BAILEY J.A:
230875 Pte DUGDALE A.S: 230614 Pte WOODCOCK H: 203609 Pte HOLLAND W
230279 Pte LOCKETT W:

Form "Z"

No.

Daily / Weekly casualty report up to 7 p.m. / noon, Saturday.

Division. _____ Date _____

This Column must not be written upon.	Unit. (Each unit to be shown separately.)	Date	Killed		Wounded		Missing		
			O.	O.R.	O.	O.R.	O.	O.R.	
	Totals								

The space below, and the back of this form, will be used to report Officers' casualties; in each case, unit, battalion, name, rank, initial, nature of casualty, and date will be shown.

A.P.& S.D., Alex./2519/25A/1:18/40M. (V.&G.)

WAR DIARY or INTELLIGENCE SUMMARY

Army Form C. 2118.

A.Q. Branch
Headquarters
74th (Yeo) Division
January 1919

Place	Date	Hour	Summary of Events and Information	Remarks and references to Appendices
LESSINES	7		The S.O.C. forwarded ribbons for medals awarded to 229th Infantry Brigade at Command	Appendix 7
"	14		Conference at III Corps H.Q. re Parade at Brussels.	
"	15		G.O.C. Conference at 9.31 & Ord. H.Q. re. parade at Brussels when it was intimated that the Division would be represented by a company of our company 10th Shropshire and Cheshire (Yeo) B.: K.S. L.I. 9. 12.: (W. Somerset Yeo) B.: Somerset L.I. and the 10: (R. East and West Kent Yeo) B.: The Buffs. One composite Coy. R.E. the Composite Coy. from Fd. 8. B's. One Composite Field Coy. and the Divisional Band. The troops present in Brussels will march past the H.M. of the Belgians on the 26th inst.	
"	21		Administrative Instructions issued for the parade at Brussels on the 26	
"	24		Rations & kit & troops at Brussels sent from GHISLENGHIEN by M.T.	
"	25		Divl Ammunition Column moved to REBAIX and opened III Corps Horse Collecting Camp. 200 Horses from the Division sent to REBAIX for demobilization 200 Horses sent to REBAIX for demobilization	
"	26		Troops returned from BRUSSELS. All troops were sent & brought back by M.T.	
	28		No Leave Train running.	
	29		No Leave Train running.	
	30		No Leave Train running.	
	31		Strengths. Effective Strength Dec 25th 1918 687 off/+ 13149 O.R. Jan 25, 1919 636 off/+ 11163 O.R. Sick 5 officers & 148 O.R. were evacuated. Left Division during the month. Demobilization 82 Officers & 3043 O.R. were dispatched for Demobilization during the month.	

Day A. Qr. Mr. Genl
74th (Yeo) Division

Appendix I

ADMINISTRATIVE INSTRUCTIONS RELATIVE TO
74th DIVISIONAL ORDER No. 119.   No..........

21st January, 1919.

RATIONS.

All Units will carry rations for consumption on the day of the move to and from BRUSSELS.

The Transport party proceeding by road on the 24th inst will draw rations for consumption on the 25th on arrival at BRUSSELS at a time to be arranged by the Officer i/c Party with the Supply Officer (Lieut Mitchell).

Rations for the whole party for consumption 26th, 27th and 28th insts will be drawn on 25th, 26th and 27th insts respectively.

Time for refilling to be arranged by Staff Captain 231 Inf. Bde and the Supply Officer.

Refilling Point will be in the Square by Church St. Pierre ANDERLECHT.

BILLETS.

Billeting Areas will be allotted to Units by Staff Captain 231 Infantry Brigade.

Billeting parties from Units as under will proceed by train leaving GRAMMONT at 1430 on 23rd and will report to Capt. R.F. Wilson, 24th Welsh Regt. on arrival at GARE DU MIDI who will point out the Areas allotted to Units.

	Offr.	O.R's.	
231st Bde.H.Q.		1	} To be detailed from
10 K.S.L.I.	1	8	}
10 Buffs.	1	8	} those taking part
12 S.L.I.	1	8	}
R.E.	1	2	} in the parade and to take
Fd. Ambce		3	} rations for consumption
M.G. Coy.	1	2	} on the 24th inst.

Bicycles will be taken for Officers.

231st Inf. Bde. will provide Billets for the following:-

Supply Personnel	1 Offr.	5 O.R's.	
M.T.P.		17 "	18 animals.
For G.O.C.		2 "	3 "
For A.A.& Q.M.G.		1 "	2 "
For A.D.C.		1 "	2 "

GUARDS.

A 24 hour guard of 1 N.C.O. and 3 men will be detailed by 231st Inf Bde to mount over Supply Dump commencing 23rd inst. Guard will report daily at 1600 to the Supply Officer at Refilling Point. The Guard will not be required after rations are issued on the 27th inst. The Guard to mount on the 23rd will report to Lieut Mitchell at GHISLINGHOM STATION at 1030 on that day and proceed with Ration lorries.

TRANSPORT.

Two G.S. Wagons from 74th Divisional Train are allotted to each Infantry Battalion and will report at 1200 on the 23rd inst rationed up to and including the 24th inst. These wagons will proceed with the Transport Convoy and will be used for drawing rations whilst at BRUSSELS. Two spare horses and driver will accompany the two wagons reporting to 10th K.S.L.I.

These wagons will be returned to Div. Train on their return on 28th inst.

SUPPLY EQUIPMENT & PERSONNEL.

The equipment (tarpaulins etc) in use at the Supply Dump will be loaded on to a G.S. Wagon for the return journey. Supply Personnel will return with the Composite Brigade Group in Busses.

Supply Officer will inform the Staff Captain 231 Inf. Bde the time wagons are required to report and also ascertain place and time of ombussing.

P.T.O.

F/Brown Lieut
for
                    Lieut Colonel,
        A.A.& Q.M.G. 74th (Yeomanry) Division.

1   229th Bde.   4. 10th Buffs.   7 A.D.M.S.   10 D.A.P.M.   13 File.
2   230th Bde.   5 12th S.L.Inf   8 M.G.Bn.   11 Camp Comdt.
3   231st Bde.   6. C.R.E.   9 Div.Train.   12 War Diary.

Vol II

WAR DIARY
"A" & "Q" BRANCH
74th (Yeo) DIVISION
FOR
MONTH OF
FEBRUARY 1919.

WAR DIARY
or
INTELLIGENCE SUMMARY
(Erase heading not required.)

Army Form C. 2118.

Headquarters
74 (Yeomanry) Division
"Q" Branch
February 1919

Place	Date	Hour	Summary of Events and Information	Remarks and references to Appendices
LESSINES	5		Draft of 3 officers and 150 O.R. ordered from 16 (Sussex Yeo) Bn R. Sussex Regt to join 17 R. Sussex Regt Division.	
"	6		Major Hubbard, C.N.F.B. R.A.D, D.S.O. R.A.S.C. & G.H.Q. & various Commanding Officers arrived to inspect. Draft of 10 officers and 200 O.R. ordered from 15th (Suffolk Yeo) Bn Suffolk Regt to join 2nd Suffolks.	
			3. Sundry H.Q. Arty detachments. D.A.Q.M.G. arrived officer strengthen demobilisation. Capt (now Major) R.Y. WEIR 1st Borderers arrived.	
	11		Draft of 10 officers and 300 O.R. ordered from 25 (Montgomery and Welsh Horse Yeo) Bn and the 24 (Pembroke and Glamorgan Yeo) Bn Welsh Regt to join 6 S. Wales Borderers, 30th Division DUNKIRK.	
"	11		Draft 5 officers and all available O.R. from 12 (W. Somerset Yeo) Bn Somerset L.I. and 16 (Royal 1st & R. North Devon Yeo) Bn Devon Regt to join 2/4 Oxon & Bucks L.I. 61st Division ETAPLES.	
	12		Draft of 3 officers and 100 O.R. ordered from 7/4 M.I.B. to join 2nd M. I. B. 2nd Division 2nd Army	
"	17		1/12 L.N. Lancs (Pioneers) ordered to join 32 Division 2nd Army. This unit to move as a whole but will volunteers returnables under A.O. 55 of 1919 only to go with only 9 animals.	
	20		Draft of 5 officers and 150 O.R. 16 (Sussex Yeo) Bn proceeded to join 17 R. Sussex. Draft of 3 officers and 100 O.R. 14 (Fife & Forfar Yeo) Bn Royal Highlanders ordered to join 8 B.H. 9th Division 2nd Army.	
"	"		Draft of 8 officers all available O.R. 16 (Sussex Yeo) Bn ordered to join 1/4 R. Sussex Regt 34 Division.	
"	"		Draft of 9 officers all available O.R. from 24 (Pembroke & Glamorgan Yeo) Bn which Regt kept personnel of it self to Welsh Regt of N. Payne and demonstration of higher training for the replacement availible O.R. of 1/4 L.N. Lancs 33 Division ordered	Appendix I
"	22		Intimation received that 3 officers availible per. of 1/4 L.N. Lancs.	

Daaf 4/9/11 Richard Major
Daa. 4/9/11 (74) Division

Army Form C. 2118.

WAR DIARY
or
INTELLIGENCE SUMMARY.
(Erase heading not required.)

O. & Q. Branch
Headquarters
74th (Yeomanry) Division
February 1919

Place	Date	Hour	Summary of Events and Information	Remarks and references to Appendices
LESSINES	23		Arrangements made for draft of 5 officers & 140 O.R. of 1/6 R.W. Lancs at entraining station.	
"	24		1/12 R.N. Lancs proceeded with 17 officers and 291 O.R. These figures include 5 officers & 140 O.R. of 1/6 R.W. Lancs.	
"	24		6 orders received for move of 9.30 Sy Bde Group to GRAMMONT on the 27th inst. and for 9.30 Sy Bde Appendix II Group and Sy Bde RYAB cadres taken from LESSINES R.F. on 24th & thereafter Appx to join the R.W. Surreys 33rd Division 8th Army.	
"			Draft of 8 officers and all available O.R. of 10th (R.E. Kent & W. Kent Yeo) Bn the Buffs to join the R.W. Surreys 33rd Division 8th Army.	
"	27		Draft of 5 officers and 110 O.R. 10th (Shropshire & Cheshire Yeo) Bn K.S.L.I. ordered to join 1/6 Cheshires 36 Division DUNKIRK.	
"			Bt. Lt. Col. R.B. COUSENS. D.S.O. R.A. left on one months leave prior to reporting to Staff College for Course commencing 1st April.	

Strength:—
Effective Strength of the Division on 1st February was 596 officers and 10371 other ranks
Sick " " " " " " " 22 " " 490 " "

Demobilization:—

Personnel:—
The total number evacuated sick during the month of February was 11 officers & 115 O.R.
The total number demobilized during the month of February was 88 officers and 3761 other ranks.

Animals:—
The total number demobilized during the month of February were 950 animals of all classes.

M.G. Buckland Major
D.A.Q.M.G. (Yeo) Division

SECRET. Diary I   Copy No. 9

ADMINISTRATIVE INSTRUCTIONS RELATIVE to MOVE of 1/12th. L.N. LANCS.,
to 2nd. Army.

Headquarters,
74th. (Yeomanry) Division.
20th. February, 1919.

1. The 1/12th. L.N.Lancs. Regt. complete with Equipment, Harness, Saddles, and Vehicles, but with only 7 riders and 2 draught horses, will entrain at GHISLENGHIEN, on 24th. Feby., for BOHN, to join the 52nd. Division, 2nd. Army. Only Volunteers and men retainable under Army Order XIV of Jany., 1919, are to be sent with the battalion.

2. PERSONNEL. All Officers and Other Ranks eligible for demobilization left behind by the Battalion will be attached to the 74th. M.G.Bn.. The O.C. 1/12th. L.N. Lancs. will send Nominal Rolls of :-
   (a) All other ranks left behind with M.G.Bn. to the D.A.G. 3rd. ECHELON, and a copy to the O.C. M.G.Bn..
   (b) All Officers left behind to this office and a copy to the M.G. Bn..

3. ANIMALS. All surplus animals will be transferred to the 74th.
M.G. Bn..   The O.R.A. will hand over 5 "X" riders to 1/12th.
L.N.Lancs., in exchange for a similar number of animals of any
class.   This exchange to be carried out before the 23rd. inst..
All animals will be watered immediately before entrainment.

4. TRANSPORT.
   (a) HORSE
   4 Train Wagons will accompany the unit.
   O.C., Train will hand over the vehicles, complete with
   harness, etc., to 1/12th. L.N. Lancs., on the 23rd. inst.
   at H.Q. of 1/12th. L.N. Lancs..   He will also
   arrange to provide the necessary teams with harness
   to take the wagons to the station on the 24th. inst..
   The O.C., 74th. M.G. Bn. will arrange to provide whatever teams may be necessary to take the remainder of
   the transport of the 1/12th. L.N. Lancs., to the station,
   details to be arranged direct between Os.C..
   (b) MOTOR.
   Three Motor Lorries will report H.Q. 1/12th. L.N. Lancs.
   on 24th. to take blankets, rations etc., to
   GHISLENGHIEN, hour at which they will report will be
   notified when train timings are received.

5. AMMUNITION. No ammunition except that carried on the man will be taken.

6. SUPPLIES. Three days rations and forage will be carried in addition to the unexpired portion

P.T.O.

7. **ENTRAINMENT.** Train timings will be intimated as soon as received.

All transport will be at the station, and report to the R.T.O., 3 hours before time of departure of the train.

Personnel will be at the station, and report to the R.T.O., 1 hour before the departure of the train.

8. **ENTRAINING STATE.** A complete entraining state showing numbers of:-

    (a) Officers and men separately.
    (b) Horses.
    (c) Four wheeled vehicles (non limbered)
    (d) Four wheeled limbered vehicles.
    (e) Two wheeled vehicles.
    (f) Bicycles.

will be sent down with the transport and handed to the R.T.O., 3 hours before the train is due to depart. A copy will be sent to this office.

9. **LOADING PARTY.** A loading party of 1 Officer, 4 N.C.Os., and 30 men will be detailed to report with the transport.

10. **BREAST ROPES.** Breast ropes and collars will be taken for all animals.

11. **WATER.** Water carts will be entrained FULL and all water bottles filled before entrainment.

12. ACKNOWLEDGE.

                              [signature]

                              Major.
D.A.A.G. 74th. (Yeomanry) Division, for
Lieut. Col. A.A. & Q.M.G.

COPIES NO :-

1. G.R.A.
2. G.R.E.
3. M.G. Bn.
4. O.C. Train.
5. R.T.O. GHISLENGHIEN.
6. D.A.P.M.
7. III Corps. "Q".
8. "Q".
9. Diary.
10. File.

MESSAGES AND SIGNALS.

War Diary February Appendix II

TO all

Sender's Number: A999
Day of Month: 24
AAA

Cancel this office No A999 and 4979 of 23rd inst aaa 230th Inf Bde and Field Ambulance will move to GRAMMONT on the 27th inst aaa Areas in GRAMMONT to be as handed out to Bde representatives and sent over by will GRAMMONT today aaa Units will send representatives to draw supplies at LESSINES at 1100 on 27th for consumption 28th aaa Train will supply transport for rations on 27th aaa on 28th and until further notice units will draw from LESSINES by first line transport at 1000 daily aaa Baggage wagons

MESSAGES AND SIGNALS.

Army Form C. 2121
(In pads of 100)

No. of Message............

...will be handed over to Units at Refilling Point BIEVENE at 15·00 on the 26th and will be returned to Train on the 28th aaa Chanl Lorries will report at T Roads at Church VANE at 9.00 on 27th aaa 2.20th Bde will arrange guides to meet Lorries aaa Ordered 3 Bdes CRE ADMS Train DAPM Supply & Sup Amn Columns Armament Amm Column LESSINES aaa acknowledge

From: 74 Divn

APO/Nat 12

WAR DIARY
Hd Qrs 74th (Yeo) DIVISION
FOR MONTH OF
MARCH 1919

Army Form C. 2118.

WAR DIARY
or
INTELLIGENCE SUMMARY.
(Erase heading not required.)

Instructions regarding War Diaries and Intelligence Summaries are contained in F. S. Regs., Part II. and the Staff Manual respectively. Title pages will be prepared in manuscript.

Headquarters
Y.L. (Yeomanry) Division
From 1st to 31st March 1919

Place	Date	Hour	Summary of Events and Information	Remarks and references to Appendices
LESSINES	3		Draft of 4 Officers & 193 O.R. sent from 2.5" (Montgomery & Welsh Horse) Yeo B" RMA to 16" Bncha (also Bordurs) 30" Division DUNKIRK. Draft of 5 Officers sub 82 other ranks sent from 2d (Pembroke & Glamorgan) Yeo "D" Welsh Regt to 6. S.W.B.	
"	4		5 Officers 102 O.R. sent from 16" (R.1st - R.N. Devon) Yeo "B" Devon Regt to 2/4 Oxf & Bucks L.I. 61st Division ETAPLES.	
"	5		5 Officers & 138 O.R. sent from 12" (Westmorland Yeo) B" Border R.I to 2/4 Oxf & Bucks R.I.	
"	7		2 Officers 110 O.R. sent from 10" (R.E & West Kent) Yeo B" The Buffs & 1st R.W. Surreys 53° Division 8° Army.	
"	8		5 Officers 110 O.R. 10" (Shrops & Cheshire Yeo) B" K.S.L.I, and 1/6" Cheshire Regt 30 Division DUNKIRK.	
"	10		1 Officer 4 O.R. 13" (Suffolk Yeo) Central 5" August 5 Suffolks 34 Dev	
"	16		5 Officers from 13" (Suffolk Yeo) Suffolk Regt sent to C.B. Commanding the Division left 8 Major General P.S. GIRDWOOD. C.B.	
"	16		take command of 26 Infantry Bde = G. Rowlands Division	
"	20		1 Off + 13 O.R. 16" Sussex Yeo B" R. Sussex Regt proceeded to 1/4 Sussex 35 Bu 2° Army	

H.O.R. Rowland B.G.

Commdg 7 GL Yeo Divn.

WAR DIARY

INTELLIGENCE SUMMARY

Army Form C. 2118.

Headquarters
74 (Yeomanry) Division
1st - 31st March 1919

Place	Date	Hour	Summary of Events and Information	Remarks and references to Appendices
LESSINES	20		5 Offs + 100 Yr. 14 (Fife + Forfar Yeo) Bn Royal Highlanders sent to 8" R.H.	
"			2 Army 9 Divn.	
"			17 Yr R.E. sent to 9 Division 2° Army	
"	21		439 Field Coy moved from SCHENDELBEKE to GRAMMONT	
"			45 Yr. sent from 75 M.G. B. to 8 M.G.B. 2 Division 2° Army	
"			5 Officers sent from 16 (Sussex Yeo) Bn. & 53 Bn R. Sussex 32 Division	
"			1 Off. 37 Yr. 8/7 R.A. sent to 2 Bn R.A. 2 Army.	
"			34 Offrs sent from Brig H'qrs to 9 Gr. B. 2 Division Army	
"	22		15 Offrs + 76 Yr. sent to 4 Suffolks 34 Division 2 Army	
"	23		168 Bn Suffolks sent to 267 Coy A.C. St ANDRE.	
"			90 Yr. sent from Inf. Train into GRAMMONT	
"	29		242 (Army) Bde R.F.A. complete drawn	
"	29		6 Yr. 10 (L.R.E. + Westkent Yeo) Bn The Buffs sent to 1 R.W. Surreys 33 Bde 2nd Army	
"	31		4 Yr. 16 (Sussex Yeo) Bn R. Sussex sent to 1/4 R. Sussex 34 Division	
"			13 Yr. 14 (Fife + Forfar Yeo) Bn. R.H. sent to 8" R.H. 9 Division	
"			Brig. Gen. THACKERAY. DSO MC Commanding 229 Inf. Bde proceeded to take command of 6 K.O.S.B. 9 Division	
			Demobilization Personnel :- 46 Officers & 1101 Yr demobilized during the month	
			Animals :- 99 Animals sold, 1103 evacuated (also demobilized) during the month 2101 Animals	

FS Rutherfordby
Bde. 74 (Yeo) Divn.

Army Form C. 2118.

WAR DIARY
INTELLIGENCE SUMMARY.
(Erase heading not required.)

Headquarters
74 (Yeomanry) Division
From 1st to 31st March 1918

Place	Date	Hour	Summary of Events and Information	Remarks and references to Appendices
LESSINES	31		Strength:- Effective Strength on 8th March 414 Officers 5172 OR. " " 29th March 291 Officers 3325 OR. " " 31st March 149 Officers 37 OR. Sick Total Sick evacuated during the month 4 Officers 37 OR. JG Sutherland MG Lt G 74th (Yeo) Divn.	

AQQ
Nil 13

War Diary
Hd Qrs 74th (Yeo) Division
for month of
APRIL 1919

Army Form C. 2118.

WAR DIARY
INTELLIGENCE SUMMARY

Headquarters 74th (Yeomanry) Division
1st to 30th April 1919

(Erase heading not required.)

Place	Date	Hour	Summary of Events and Information	Remarks and references to Appendices
LESSINES	1		Lt. Col. G.B. Cairns D.S.O. of 74 Garrison reported to Staff College Camberley and to struct off Marching in of this Division.	
"	11		35 Yr. Rail Employment Coy sent to 936 Air Employment Coy.	
"	15		1 Off. 7 Yr. & 13 (Suffolk Yeo.) B. Suffolk Regt. sent to 12th O.B.W. Coy.	
"	16		25 Yr. from 74 M.G.B. sent to 2 Bn. M.G.B. 2nd Army.	
"			53 Yr. 74 M.G.B. sent to 5 M.G.B. 2nd Army.	
"			5 Yr. from 16 (Sussex Yeo.) B. R. Sussex Regt. sent to R. Sussex 2nd Army.	
"			1 Yr. from 10 (T.E.N.W.Kent Yeo.) B. The Buffs & 1 R.W. Surreys 2nd Army	
"	17		13 Yr. from 12 (W.Somerset Yeo.) B. Somerset L.I. + 60 Yr. from 16 (R.1st R.W. Surr Yeo.)	
"			B. Dev. Devon sent to 2/4 Ox & Bucks L.I. ETAPLES	
"			30 Yr. from the 24 (Pembroke & Glamorgan Yeo) B. R. Welch Regt. and 11 Yr. from the	
"			25 (Montgomery and Welsh Horse Yeo) B. R.W.F. sent to the 6. South Wales	
"			Borderers BOULOGNE.	
"			24 Yr. from the 10 (Shrops & Cheshire Yeo) B. K.S.L.I. sent to the 1/6 Cheshire	
"			ETAPLES.	
"			1 Officer and 2 & 7 Yr. from the 2nd R.A. to R.A. 2nd Army. Lieut... report to	
"	16		Major A.E. SANDERSON D.S.O. Oxf. & Bucks L.I. 2nd I.S.O.L. Hun Divn. Brigade Guard	
"	22			
"	23		... for duty as ...	
"	25	1415	Capt. A.J.M. TUCK M.C. Staff. Mn. Major 229 by Col. commanding Bde. Major 231st Bde.	
"			Capt. R.E. ADAMS M.C. E.Surr. Regt. to England ... Regt.	
"			vice Capt. (Act. Major) D.R. WILLIAMSON RAVE (S.R.) DADS proceeded Great HA 2nd Bde ... April	
"	30		Demobilised. Animals 291, Horses 372, Mules total 863. Personnel Officers 26 April 153 Effec. 290 4 Yr.	
"			Strength week ending 5 April 252 Off. 3295 Yr. Week ending 26 April SW 3 Eur. Rank and file	
"			48 (contin)... Staff Sir Sur SN...AY	
"			Lt (A/Lt Col) Asst Ga. Blin	

WO 90 74 A
9/5/14

WAR DIARY
Hd Qrs 74th (Yeo) Dn
Period
1st to 31st MAY 19

WAR DIARY
INTELLIGENCE SUMMARY.
(Erase heading not required.)

Army Form C. 2118.

Instructions regarding War Diaries and Intelligence Summaries are contained in F.S. Regs., Part II. and the Staff Manual respectively. Title pages will be prepared in manuscript.

Headquarters 74" (Y/o) Division 1st to 31st May 1919.

Place	Date	Hour	Summary of Events and Information	Remarks and references to Appendices
LESSINES.	8"		Brig Gen C.E. HEATHCOTE. D.S.O. C.M.G. A.D.C. Commanding the Division proceeded to take over the command of XIX Corps Packet. Lt. Col. C.F. ROSSE PRICE R.F.A. Commanding 74th Divisional Ammunition Column assumed command of the Division.	
	16"		Capt. D.C. GILROY (S.R.) G.S.O. 3rd Division G. & Staff Capt. 930. Inf Bde. proceeded to report to Navy & Army Canteen Board for duty.	
			Capt. P.P. KENNON-SLANEY R.N. Divn Steward assumed duties as acting Staff Capt 930 Inf Bde.	
	22.		Capt C JONES R.A.S.C. assumed command of the Divl Train vice Major (A/Lt Col) Macnaghten Willwood R.A.S.C. proceeding home for duty in RUSSIA.	Appendix I
	27.		List of Units which are to proceed home & those to be broken up in this country issued.	Appendix II
	31st		Full appendix to as amended by orders issued on 31st inst. for move of vehicles & Franco Strength 230 &30 Field Ambulance & Bear	Appendix III
			Strengths:- Effective Strength on 31st May, 108 Officers 1670 O/R " " " 3 May, 154 " 2603 "	

H.Q. 74th (Yeo) Divn
G.O.C. 74th (Yeo) Divn.

WAR DIARY JUNE 1919
Appendix "J" I   A.3.B.2/41

1. According to the information at present available the units of the Division which will go home, and those which will be broken up in this country, and NOT go home as Cadres are given in Paras. 2 and 3.

2. The following will go home on Cadre A, with equipment:-

UNIT	AUTHORITY
(a) All Infantry Battalions.	5th. Area Q.D.1654 dd 12/5/19
(b) 448th Coy. R.A.S.C.	-do-
450th. -do-	-do-
(c) 439th Field Coy R.E.	5th. Area Q.D.1681 dd 11/5/19
(d) 117th. Bde R.F.A.	
A.B.366 and D. Batteries R.F.A.	5th. Area Q.D.1609 dd 10/5/19
H.Q.242nd (Army) Bde R.F.A.	
A.B.&C Batteries	-do-
X14 Medium T.M.Battery	5th. Area Q.D.1634 dd 11/5/19
Y14 -do-	-do-

3. The following units will be broken up in this Country and will NOT go home as cadres :-

UNIT	AUTHORITY
(a) H.Q. 74th (Yeo) Divn.	5th. Area Q.D.1609 dd 10/5/19
" 229. Inf. Bde.	-do-
" 230. "	-do-
" 231. "	-do-
H.Q. Divl. R.A.	-do-
229th. Light T.M.Battery	5th. Area Q.D.1634 dd 11/5/19
230 "	-do-
231 "	-do-
H.Q. Divnl. R.E.	
(b) 44th. Bde R.F.A. 340, 382, 425 and D Batteries	5th. Area Q.D.1609 dd 10/5/19
242 (Army) Bde R.F.A.	
D.Batty.and Bde.R.F.A.C.	-do-
74th. D.A.C.	-do-
(c) 5th R.M.R.E. Field Coy.	5th. Area Q.D.1681 dd 12/5/19
5th. R.A.R.E. "	-do-
74th. Div Sig Coy R.E.	5th Area Signals K.P.60/2/7 dd 26/5/19
(d) 74th. Battn M.G.C.	5th. Area Q.D.1654 dd 12/5/19
(e) 447th.Coy R.A.S.C.	" Q.D. 1806 dd 20/5/19
449th. Coy "	-do-
(f) 229th. Field Amb.	5th. Area Q.D.1654 dd 12/5/19
230 "	-do-
231 "	-do-
(g) 39th Mob. Vet. Section	5th. Area Q.D.1654 dd 12/5/19
(h) 955th Div. Emp. Coy	Already broken up and dispersed.

4. Corps have been asked to state whether H.Q. Divisional R.E. and H.Q. 242nd. (Army) Bde R.F.A. will be broken up in this Country or proceed home as Cadres.

27/5/19

Sgd. H.J. Butchart. Major.
D.A.A.G. 74th (Yeo) Division

WAR DIARY MAY 1919

Copies of telegrams.

Appendix II

To :-
    C.R.E. 74 Division.

A 150   31/5

74th Divisional H.Q. R.E. breaks up with 74th Divisional Head quarters to which it is now affiliated aaa (Authority 3rd Corps D. 345 dated 31st May 1919.)

From :-
    74th Division.

To :-
    C.R.A. 74 Division.

A 151   31/5

Head quarters 242 Army Brigade R.F.A. will go home as cadre aaa (Authority 3rd Corps D. 345 dated 31st May 1919.)

From :-
    74th Division.

WAR Diary MAY

74th DIVISIONAL ORDER NO. 120.

COPY NO. 11

Appendix III

30th MAY 1919.

1. The vehicles and Unit Ordnance stores and equipment of the 229th and 230th Field Ambulances, with the exception of the articles mentioned in para 2 of G.R.O. 6466 will be sent to the Ordnance Demobilisation Depot BEAUMARIS CALAIS on 2nd June 1919 by train in charge of an officer of each of the units concerned.

2. Os.C. will report to the R.T.O. or his representative at GRAMMONT Station not later than 0845 by which hour all vehicles and stores must be parked in the Station Square ready for immediate entrainment. They will at the same time hand to the R.T.O. or his representative a statement showing the strength of the unit entraining under the following headings :-

    i. Numbers of officers and men separately.
    ii. Numbers of 4 wheeled vehicles (Non-limbered).
    iii. Numbers of 4 wheeled limbered vehicles.
    iv. Numbers of 2 wheeled vehicles.

3. Loading will commence at GRAMMONT Station at 0900. The train will be ready to move off at 1200.

4. Stores will be loaded in the vehicles before entraining.

5. A Conducting party of 1 officer and 6 O.R. from each of the units concerned will accompany the vehicles and equipment and guard same on route.

6. All equipment will be clearly labelled with the name of the unit.

7. The O.C., 5th R.A.R.E. Field Coy will make all necessary arrangements with the Civilian Railway Authorities at GRAMMONT Station as to loading facilities and will be responsible that the ramp is erected and ready for use by 0800 on 2nd June. He will be present during entrainment.

8. 3 days rations will be taken in addition to the unexpired portion.

9. S.M.O. will intimate departure by wire to this office.

10. ACKNOWLEDGE by wire.

H.J. Butcher
Major,
D.A.A.G., 74th (Yeomanry) Division.

Copies to:-
    1 - 3   S.M.O.
    4   5th R.A.R.E. Field Coy.
    5   O.C., Div'l Train.
    6   D.A.D.O.S.
    7   R.T.O., HAL.
    8   O.C., 229 Brigade Group.
    9   O.C., 230th " "
    10   C.R.E.
    11   Diary.
    12 - 13.   File.

Issued at 1040
on 31st May 1919.

AO a9q 74 R
Vol 15

WAR DIARY
H.Q. 74th (Yeo) Divn
JUNE 1919

WAR DIARY
or
INTELLIGENCE SUMMARY.

(Erase heading not required.)

Army Form C. 2118.

Headquarters
1/4 (Glamorgan) Division
June 1919

Place	Date	Hour	Summary of Events and Information	Remarks and references to Appendices
LESSINES	2.		Train for vehicles of 229th and 230th Field Ambulances did not arrive until 21.00 today was therefore postponed until 3rd inst.	
"	3.		Party carried 1/HQ + A.B.& D Batteries R.F.A. (Army) B+c R.F.A. proceeded.	
"			Vehicles and stores of 229 and 230 Field Ambulance left for CALAIS	
"	4.		The surplus on reduction & Equipment Guards of 4th Bde R.F.A proceeded	Appendix I
"			Officers detailed for duty in this country, & handing in of stores were also seen x Equipment Guards	Appendix II
"	9.		of units breaking the cadres proceeded to England 439 Field Cy R.E. 117 Bde R.F.A.	Appendices III IV + V
"			The cadres of the following units proceeded to England B/242 (Army) Bde R.F.A	
"	16.		and remainder of Cadres of H.A. & R.S. Battery of H.A.R.E. Battery of 216th, 16 (R.1st and R.M Devon Yeo) B. Devon Regt.	
"			ammunition column authority of G.O. Annual Right Cry. 10 (R.E.+W.Kent Yeo) B. The Buffs	Appendices VI + VII
"			12 (Westminster Yeo) B. Suffolk Regt. 26 (Montgomery and Welsh Horse Yeo) B. R.W.F.	
"			16 (Sussex Yeo) B. R. Sussex Regt. 26 (K.E.H.) which was broken up this county & amendment	
"	19.		10 (Shropshire and Cheshire Yeo) B. K.S.L.I. was sent to stores handing in of stores on breaking up	
"	19.		The 45/51 surplus of 5 R.M. RE Field Cy R.E and 5 RARE Field Cy R.E proceeded	
"	"		The Cadres of the following Units proceeded to England 14 (Fife & Forfar Yeo) B. Royal	
"			Highlanders 15 (Suffolk Yeo) B. Suffolk Regt. 24 (Pembroke & Glamorgan Yo)	
"			B. Welch Regt.	
"	20.		Orders issued entrainment to ANTWERP of following Equipment Guards - vehicles &	Appendix VIII
"			surplus of 3 Div Bdes 439 Field Cy & U/ Bde R.F.A (Amt Train Pro. 121.)	
"	22.		The 45/51 of the following Units proceeded for disposal D Battery of Bde R.F.A of 242 (Army)	
"			Bde R.F.A. 74 Div Ammunition Column authority of G.O.	
"	23.		Equipment Guards & Vehicles 16 (R.1st & R.N. Devon Yeo) B, 16 (W Somerset Yeo) B, 14 (Fife & Forfar Yeo)	
"			Royal Highlanders proceeded to ANTWERP	
"	24.		A/Lt.A.F. JOHNSTONE Scottish Rifles Camp Cmdt D.H.Q. proceeded for demobilization by	
"			T.P. GRIFFIN Suffolk Regt. assumed duties of Camp Cmdt.	

AG BCKStewart
Brig.Genl
G.S. 1/4 (Glam) Division

WAR DIARY
INTELLIGENCE SUMMARY.

Army Form C. 2118.

Headquarters 74th (Yeomanry) Division
1st to 30th June 1919

Place	Date	Hour	Summary of Events and Information	Remarks and references to Appendices
LESSINES	24.		Equipment, Guards, Vehicles etc of following units left GRAMMONT for ANTWERP 10th (R.E. + W.Kent Yeo) Bn. The Buffs. 1/6 (Norson Yeo) Bn. Suffolk Regt and 1/5 (Suffolk Yeo) Bn. The Suffolk Regt.	
"	25.		Equipment, Guards, Vehicles etc of following units left GRAMMONT for ANTWERP 2/3rd (Montgomery & Welch Yeo) Bn. R.W.F. 2/4th (Pembroke & Glamorgan Yeo) Bn. K.S.L.I. Yeo) Bn. Yh. Welch Regt and 10th (Shropshire and Cheshire Yeo) Bn. K.S.L.I.	
"	"	1300	Orders received that at Corps H.Q. Hd. for train with Vehicles to proceed Calais on 26th.	Appendix IX
"	"	1745	Orders received for move of Vehicles of D.H.Q., H.Q.R.A., H.Q.R.E., 447 & 448 Coys R.A.S.C., Div. Train, J.A.G. 229, 230 & 231 Inf. Bdes. 3rd RMRE Fld G R.E. and 5th RMRE Fld Cy. R.E. to CALAIS. (Div. Order No. 122)	Appendix X
"	26.	1430	Orders issued for move of Equipment, Guards, Vehicles Stores etc of D.H.Q., A.B., R.C. Batteries of 242 (Army) Bde. R.F.A and 448 and 450th Coys R.A.S.C. Div. Train to ANTWERP (Div Order No. 123) 242 (Army) Bde R.F.A " 74th Div Signal Coy. Telegram received from G.H.Q. intimating that all Trains to ANTWERP cancelled until further orders. Move of Train and Vehicles of units mentioned in Div order No 122 delayed.	
"	27.		Orders issued for move of Equipment, Guards, Vehicles from GRAMMONT to CALAIS J.D. Railway and Ammn Column of 242 (Army) Bde R.F.A. "74th Div Signal Coy. (Div Order No. 124)	Appendix XI
"	28.		Standing in of Reserve Stores to I.O.S ATP completed by all units of Divn being broken up the necessary Allocation Statement about dates on which each item of Stores is to be disposed. Vehicles etc mentioned in Div Order No 122 left GRAMMONT for CALAIS. H.Q. J 229, Inf Bde + 231st Inf Bde did same.	Appendix XII

[signature]
Major-General
74th Div (Yeomanry) Division

WAR DIARY
INTELLIGENCE SUMMARY

Headquarters 74/9 Division
1/6 — 30 June 1919

Army Form C. 2118.

Place	Date	Hour	Summary of Events and Information	Remarks and references to Appendices
LESSINES	30		Amendment to Rout Order No. 123 issued giving destination of "G" Train.	Appendix XIII
"			Amendment to Dist Order No 124 issued altering date of loading to 3 July & directing that all Equipment, Stores worked upon with their Vehicles, also ready Vehicles of 231st Field Ambulance to be sent by same train.	Appendix XIV
			Strength:— for week ending 31st May 1919 Battn Strength of Division was 99 off. 1662 %. for week ending 30 June 1919 " " " 39 off. 404 %.	Appendix XV
"			The attached statement A.Z.B. 2/44/7 of 6 Jun shews the number employed as Coane Porters & as 45% absentees on the reduction of units & Equipment Guards.	

A.J. Burkhart Major
DAQMG 74 (Germany) Division

WAR DIARY JUNE
Appendices I, III, IV & V

Q.D.1947.

3rd. Corps.

1. With reference to your Q.79/19, it is regretted that it is impossible to open an I.O.S. at GRAMMONT.

2. In order to avoid moving all the vehicles of the 74th.Division from GRAMMONT to ATH the service pattern vehicles, guns and howitzers, gun parts and small arms of all natures belonging to the 74th.Division, may be kept at GRAMMONT and despatched to Base direct from that station. Para 5. of my Q.D.1943 of the 29th.May should be amended accordingly as far as 74th.Division is concerned.

3. Stores and equipment of all units belonging to the 74th. Division will be handed in to the I.O.S. ATH.

4. Lorries for transport of such equipment can be obtained if necessary from O.C., ATH & TOURNAI Sub-area.

(Sgd) M.S.LUSH, Capt,
for Lieut.Colonel, G.S.
Staff Officer for Demob.

Fifth Area,

2nd.June 1919.

-2-

A.Z.B.2/41/4

Headquarters,
   229th.Brigade.   C.R.A.   S.C.F.   O.C., M.G.Bn.
   230th.Brigade.   C.R.E.   O.C., Signals.   Camp Comdt.
   231st.Brigade.   S.M.O.   O.C., Div. Train.

1. For information reference this office A.Z.B.2/41 of 27th. May 1919.

2. With reference to para 4. of A.Z.B.2/41 of 27th.May the following corrections will be made in that letter :-

   Para 2 (d) Add

      H.Q., 242nd.(Army) Bde. R.F.A.   Authority 3rd. Corps D.345
                                                        dated 31st.May 1919.

   Para 3 (a) Add

      H.Q., Divisional R.E.   Authority 3rd. Corps D,345
                                        dated 31st.May 1919.

   Para 4. Delete the whole of this para.

3. Officers Commanding Formations and Units which are to be broken up in this Country will render a return by units, so as to reach this office by the 7th.inst. stating

      (a) Number of vehicles of each class for which train accommodation is required to convey them to the Base.

      (b) Number of Lorries required to take the Units' Stores to ATH.

(2)

4. The following Units will be broken up very shortly :-

B.A.C. of 242nd. (Army) Bde. R.F.A.

5th.R.M.R.E. Field Company.

5th.R.A.R.E. Field Company.

(Authority 5th. Area Q.D. 1939 dated 28th.May 1919)

5. The certificates referred to in G.R.O.6466 will in all cases be rendered by Os.C. Units in Triplicate to this office through the usual channels.

6. <u>Records and Documents.</u>

(a) Records and Company books of R.A.S.C., H.T. Units will be ~~sent to Record Section Head quarters of British Troops in France and Flanders~~ dealt with as laid down in D. of T. Circular No.275, dated 23/4/19, (5th.Area No.T.203/6 of 25/4/19).

(b) Admission and Discharge books of R.A.M.S. units will be sent to Record Section Headquarters British Troops in France and Flanders, for transmission to the Medical Research Committee.

Other statistical records and reports of R.A.M.C. units will be disposed of as laid down in War Office letter 24/Gen/6978 (A.M.B.) dated 13th.March 1919, forwarded under No.5 Area letter A.D.M.S. No. 6/8/A.3 of 10/5/19.

(c) All records and documents other than those dealt with in (a) and (b) above will be disposed of in accordance with G.R.O. 1597, those to be preserved being sent to the Officer in charge Home Records concerned for safe custody.

(Authority 5th.Area Q.D.1943 dated 29th.May 1919).

7. Personnel other than R.E.Signals, R.A.O.C., R.A.V.C. and R.A.S.C. (H.T., M.T. and Supply) will be disposed of as follows :-

(a) All regular officers, with the exception of Staff Officers, will follow the procedure laid down in Fifth Army A/1/2570 of March 2nd.

Regular Staff Officers will proceed home with orders to report to the War Office on arrival in ENGLAND.

(b) Orders as regards regular soldiers will be issued later. In the case of units breaking up immediately they should be left with parties forming guards over vehicles.

(c) All retainable officers (including staff officers other than regulars) and men will be reported by wire to this office with a view to reposting to cognate units still in the Area.

(d) Releasable personnel, with the exception of parties retained as guards on vehicles, etc., will be sent for dispersal through the usual demobilisation channels under allotments to be issued by this office.

/8.

(2)

8.   The foregoing instructions refer only to those units which are to be broken up in this country, i.e. Those shown in para 3. of this office A.Z.B.2/41 of 27th May 1919 as amended by this letter.

9.   Acknowledge.

H.J.C.Butchart

4.3.19.

Major,
D.A.A.G., 74th.(Yeomanry) Division.

WAR DIARY JUNE
Appendix VII

A.Z.B.2/41/4.

Headquarters,
229th Brigade.   C.R.A.   S.O.F.   O.C., M.G.Bn.
230th Brigade.   C.R.E.   O.C., Signals.   Camp Comdt.
231st Brigade.   S.M.O.   O.C., Div. Train.

Reference this office No. A.Z.B.2/41/4 of the 4/6/19 and the instructions for the breaking up of units, cancel para 7 of above mentioned letter and substitute the following :—

7. On the breaking up of units the following procedure will be followed as regards the disposal of personnel other than R.A.O.C., R.A.V.C., and R.A.S.C. (H.T., M.T. & Supply).

A. Other Ranks.

1. Cavalry, Royal Artillery, Royal Engineers (except Signal Service) Infantry, Machine Gun Corps, R.A.M.C. Releasable other ranks will be demobilised as circumstances permit unless they are required for cross posting to other Cadres by Areas.
In the event of there being any retainable other ranks for whom posting orders have not been received, nominal rolls will be forwarded direct by units to Headquarters, British Troops in France and Flanders, (Record Section) by whom posting orders will then be issued.

2. Signal Service.
Personnel will be disposed of by the C.S.O., 5th Area.

B. Officers

1. Cavalry, Infantry, R.E. (except Signal Service).
Releasable officers will be demobilised as circumstances permit unless they are required for cross posting to other Cadres by Areas. Nominal rolls of Retainable and Volunteer Officers for whom no posting orders have been received, will be forwarded by units to Headquarters, British Troops in France and Flanders.

2. Royal Artillery.
Officers will be dealt with in accordance with the provisions of G.R.O. 6849.

3. Signals, and R.A.M.C.
Officers will be disposed of under orders of C.S.O. 5th Area and A.D.M.S. respectively.

4. Machine Gun Corps.
All officers other than volunteers will be demobilised as circumstances permit unless required for cross posting to other Cadres by Areas.
Nominal rolls of any volunteer officers for whom no posting orders have been issued will be forwarded by units direct to Headquarters, British Troops in France and Flanders.

5. Regular officers will be disposed of in accordance with 5th Area A/A/2570 of March 2nd.
Staff Officers will apply for instructions to 5th Area "A" before proceeding to England.
(Authority 5th Area Q.D.2024 of 4th June 1919).

H.J. Butchart
Major,
D.A.A.G., 74th.(Yeomanry) Division.

9.6.19.

WAR DIARY JUNE
Appendix IV

A.Z.B.2/41/04.

Headquarters,
    229th. Brigade.   C.R.A.   O.C., Div Train.
    230th. Brigade.   S.M.O.   O.C., M.G.Bn.
    231st. Brigade.   O.C., SIgnals.   Camp Comdt.
    O.C., 439th.Fd.Coy.R.E.   O.C., 5th.R.A.R.E.
        O.C., 5th. R.M.R.E.

1. Rference this office No.A.Z.B.2/41/4 of 4/6/19. add the following paragraph after para 3.

3A.
    1. <u>Personal Equipment.</u>
        Personnel will retain their personal equipment, including arms where in possession (except as stated below), accoutrements and blankets, also groundsheets, steel helmets and box respirators, if in possession.
        Arms will be treated as unit equipment in the case of units where a percentage only of the personnel is armed.

    II. <u>Unit Stores and Equipment of Ordnance Supply.</u>
        Pending detailed instructions as to the disposal of various categories of stores, the whole of the unit equipment of the units to be broken up will be handed in to the nearest Intermediate Collecting Station, undr arrangements to be made by G.Os.C. Corps Packets or O.C. Sub-Areas with D.A.D.O.S., with the exception of service pattern vehicles of all natures, which will be returned to Ordnance Base Depot Directfrom the Railhead, under arrangements to be made by the formations administering the units concerned, Such vehicles etc. will be consigned to the Ordnance Base Depot laid down for the particular stores in question, as follows :-

    Guns, Gun Carriages, Limbers etc.   to CALAIS DOCKS.
    Vehicles. .. .. ..   to BEAUMARAIS.
    Small Arms .. .. ..   to VALDELIEVRE.
    Gun Parts .. .. ..   to BEAUMARAIS, CALAIS.

    The stores returned to I.C.S. will be retained in these stations until disposal instructions are issued.

    III. Units which are to be broken up and in which a percentage only of the personnel is armed will render a return stating by Units (in the case of R.A. by Batteries and in the case of the Train by Companies) the number and description of small arms in possession. Also number of Rifle Cases in possession. This return will reach this office by 1700 hours on the 16th.inst.

2.   ACKNOWLEDGE.

                (sgd) H.J.BUTCHART, Major,
                D.A.A.G., 74th.(Yeomanry) Division.

12th. June 1919.

WAR DIARY JUNE
Appendix V

A.Z.B.2/41/4.

Headquarters,
 229th.Brigade. C.R.A.   O.C.,Signals. O.C.,439 Fd.Coy.,R.E.
 230th.Brigade. S.M.O.   O.C.,Div.Train. O.C.,5th.R.A.R.E.
 231st.Brigade. Camp Comdt. O.C.,M.G.Bn. O.C.,5th.R.M.R.E.

    Reference this office A.Z.B.2/41/4 dated 12th.inst.

   Para 1. (3A. II) lines 9 onwards. The sentence " Such vehicles etc. - CALAIS " should be amended as follows :-

  " Such vehicles etc. will not be handed over to local Ordnance Officers, but will be despatched with representatives of the Unit (i.e. 1 Officer and 2 O.R. per unit) direct to CALAIS where the guns etc will be handed in to Ordnance Base Depots as follows :-

  Guns, Gun carriages, Limbers etc. to CALAIS DOCKS.
  Vehicles   to BEAUMARAIS.
  Small Arms   to VALDELIEVRE
  Gun Parts   to BEAUMARAIS CALAIS.

   The officer representing the unit after handing in the stores to the Ordnance Base Depots will return to the H.Q. of the formation administering his unit with the receipt for the guns etc. handed in. The remainder of the party will travel in possession of all their demobilisation documents, and after handing in the guns etc will proceed for demobilisation through the L. of C. Demobilisation COncentration Camp, CALAIS."

   Instructions for handing over vehicles, guns. etc. and dispersal of O.R. of Equipment Guards at Calais will be carefully carried out,

   Two days rations will be taken by parties proceeding to CALAIS this way.

            (Sgd) C.F.RUGGE-PRICE, Lieut.Col.
         Commanding 74th.(Yeomanry) Division.

14.6.19.

WAR DIARY JUNE
Appendix II

74th Division.   D.M.1/73.

1. Fifth Area Q.D.1961 of 29th May and extracts from Schedule showing strength of personnel for "Equipment Guards" of units, is forwarded herewith for information and guidance reference this office D.M.1/61 of 27th May.

2. Ref. para 1. The Fifth Area forecasts of train movements issued from this office will probably hold good, the same number of trains being required to move the equipment and vehicles as under the previous system.

3. Ref. para 2. In the case of H.Q. Units which will still be required to administer the Equipment Guards, and all units so small that in their case the 75% reduction does not apply, the "Cadre" and the "Equipment Guard" will still be one and the same thing.

4. On receipt of an allotment from this office giving numbers to proceed to CONCERT ONE, ST.ANDRE, LILLE, to connect with demobilization trains to BOULOGNE from there, Divisions and Corps Troops will select Cadres to complete this allotment as far as possible.

   A priority wire will be sent to this office giving the following information :-
        Name of the Cadres selected.
        Date of despatch to CONCERT 1.
        No. of all ranks being despatched.

5. Should it not be possible to complete allotment with "Cadre" men, it should be completed with personnel rendered available for disposal by the 75% reduction of units which are being broken up in this country.

6. The instructions laid down in para. 2 of Q.D.1961 reference despatch of Cadre parties from BOULOGNE, descriptive rolls, Colour Parties, etc., will be carefully carried out.

7. Divisions and Corps Troops units will wire this office as soon as all units are reduced to Equipment Guard strength as laid down in attached schedule.

8. Fifth Area No.Q.D.1805 referred to in para 4 of Q.D.1961 was circulated under this office No.D.M.1/52 of 22/5/19.

                                            (Sgd) E.GIBSON, Captain, R.A.
3rd.Corps "Dem".   for Major, A.Q.M.G.
2nd.June 1919.   III Corps Packet.

-2-

                                                              A.Z.D.17.

Headquarters,
    229th.Brigade.   O.R.A.   S.C.F.   O.C., M.G.Battn.
    230th.Brigade.   O.R.E.   O.C., Signals.   Camp Commdt.
    231st.Brigade.   S.M.O.   O.C., Div.Train.

1. For information and necessary action in continuation of this office No. A.Z.D.2/33 of 28th May 1919.
2. O.C. Formations and units will wire this office as soon as the units under their command are reduced to Equipment Guard strength as laid down in attached schedule.
3. Particular attention is directed to the last sentence of para 2. of 5th.Area Q.D.1961, viz:- that Colours and Standard Bearers are NOT retained with Equipment Guard.
4. Para 8. of 3rd. Corps D.M.1/73 of 2nd.June does not apply.

5. These instructions apply only to units which are going home as Cadres
6. Acknowledge.
                                                    H.Burchart
4.6.19.   Major,
                                            D.A.... , 74th.(Yeomanry) Division.

Q.D.1901.

With reference to my telegram Q.D.1894 dated 20th May, the following procedure regarding the despatch of Cadres to the U.K. will be carried out in future, and will be held to supersede the instructions at present in force :-

1. The personnel shown in the attached schedule will be known as the Equipment Guard of the unit.

This personnel will remain in this country in charge of the equipment of the unit until such time as orders are issued for the despatch of the equipment to the U.K., and will not be employed on any duties not connected with the unit.

One quartermaster or Q.M.S. should be included in the Equipment Guard. *Men who enlisted in 1914 will not be included in Equipment Guard.*

2. The remainder of the releasable personnel at present on the Cadre Establishment of the Unit will be known as the "Cadre" of the Unit, and will be despatched by the ordinary demobilisation trains to the Embarkation Camp at BOULOGNE as a party.

These Cadres will be sent in parties from the Embarkation Camp at BOULOGNE to destinations in the U.K. in accordance with lists which will be furnished to the Embarkation Camp Commandant.

The O.C. Cadre will have in his possession the Descriptive Roll of the unit, which will include the names of Officers, W.O's, N.C.O's, and clerks left behind with the Equipment Guard.

In addition to these Descriptive Rolls all personnel of Cadres will have the usual Demobilisation documents in their possession, made out as if proceeding for individual dispersal to Areas in the U.K.

The Colours of a unit and the officer or officers composing the Colour Party will be sent with the Cadre of the unit.

3. Corps Packets and O.C., LILLE Sub-area will wire this office as soon as units are reduced to the Equipment Guard specified above.

4. The instructions contained in letter, Fifth Area Q.D. 1805 of May 20th, regarding the breaking up of units in this country continue to hold good.

(Sgd) M.S.LUSH, Capt. S.O.
for Lieut.Colonel, G.S.
Staff Officer for Demob.

Fifth Area.
29th May 1919.

EXTRACT FROM SCHEDULE SHOWING STRENGTH OF PERSONNEL FOR "EQUIPMENT GUARDS" OF UNITS.

UNIT.	OFFICERS.	OTHER RANKS.
H.Q., Division.	2	5
R.H. and R.F.A.		
H.Q., Divisional Artillery.	1	4
" R.F.A., Brigade.	1	4
Army R.H. or R.F.A. Bde., Ammunition Column.	2	27
Batty, R.F.A., 18 pdrs.	1	15
Batty, R.F.A., 4.5" Howrs.	1	15
Divisional Ammunition Column.	2	60
Divisional Ammunition Column (British and Indian)	2	60
Medium Trench Mortor Batty.		1
ROYAL ENGINEERS.		
H.Q., Div., R.E.	1	5
Field Coy.	1	13
R.E. SIGNALS.		
Divisional Signal Company.	2	20
INFANTRY.		
H.Q., Inf. Bde.	1	5
Inf. Bn.	2	12
Light Trench Mortar Batty.		1
MACHINE GUN CORPS.		
Machine Gun Bn.	2	32
A.S.C.		
Divisional Train.	2	15
R.A.M.C.		
Field Ambulance	1	11 R.A.M.C.
	1 Sergt.	5 R.A.S.C.
MILITARY POLICE.		
Traffic Control Unit, Dismounted Branch.	1	5
Traffic Control Unit, Mounted Branch.	1	5

WAR DIARY JUNE
Appendices VI & VII

A.Z.B.2/41/2.

Headquarters,
    229th. Infantry Brigade.   C.R.A.
    230th. Infantry Brigade.   O.C., 74th. Divisional Train.
    231st. Infantry Brigade.

---

1.   Ordnance Stores and Equipments of units being broken up in this country will be handed in to I.C.S., ATH, on the dates mentioned in the attached schedule.

2.   All vehicles will be stripped with the exception of poles, supporting bars and swingletrees.

3.   A.Fs. G.1033 will be completed in duplicate and handed to the officer i/c I.C.S. who will sign one copy which will be retained by the unit as a receipt.

4.   Lorries will report Station Square, GRAMMONT, at 0800 hours each day. Os.C. Units will be responsible that guides collect the lorries there.

5.   O.C., Divisional Train will use the Supply Lorries to convey the Train Stores and Equipment on Tuesday the 24th. inst.

6.   Os. C. Units are responsible that sufficient men to off load at ATH accompany each lorry, as the O i/c I.C.S. cannot supply off-loading parties.

7.   Stores will be loaded and despatched as quickly as possible; lorries proceeding independently as soon as loaded.

                                        Major,
19.6.19.   D.A.A.G., 74th. (Yeomanry) Division.

Copy to :-
    Officer i/c I.C.S., ATH.

Sections 14 to 19 incl

74th.(Yeo) Division.
Headquarters.
June 19th.1919.

SCHEDULE issued with A.Z.B.2/41/2 of the 19th.June 1919.

		Total Lorries.
Saturday 21st.June.	229th., 230th. and 231st. Infantry Brigade H.Q. and L.T.M.Batteries (2 Lorries to each Brigade)	6
Monday 23rd.June.	74th.D.A.C. 3	15
Tuesday 24th.June.	74th.D.A.C. (8 Lorries) H.Q., 447 and 449 Coys Div'l Train (6 Lorries supplied by Train from Supply Lorries)	14
Wednesday 25th.June *Train 5 Lorries 0700 for 44 Bde*	74th.D.A.C. (10 Lorries) 340th.Batty, 44th.Bde.R.F.A. (5 Lorries)	15
Thursday 26th.June *Train 5 Lorries 0700 for 44 Bde.*	382nd.Batty, 425th.Batty and D.Batty. 44th.Bde R.F.A. (5 Lorries per Batty) *5 Lorries from Train*	15
Friday 27th.June *Train 1 Lorry for 44 Bde. 4 Lorries D Bty 242 Bde all at 0700*	H.Q.,44th.Bde R.F.A. (1 Lorry) D.Batty (4 Lorries), and B.A.C. (8 Lorries) 242nd.(Army) Bde. R.F.A. *from 5 Lorries*	13

Monday 30 June 1919
74 Div Signal Coy.   12

WAR DIARY JUNE
Appendix VII

A.Z.B.2/41/2.

Headquarters,
   229th. Infantry Brigade.   C.R.A.
   230th. Infantry Brigade.   O.C., 74th. Divisional Train.
   231st. Infantry Brigade.

---

1. Ordnance Stores and Equipments of units being broken up in this country will be handed in to I.C.S., ATH, on the dates mentioned in the attached schedule.

2. All vehicles will be stripped with the exception of poles, supporting bars and swingletrees.

3. A.Fs. G.1033 will be completed in duplicate and handed to the officer i/c I.C.S. who will sign one copy which will be retained by the unit as a receipt.

4. Lorries will report Station Square, GRAMMONT, at 0800 hours each day. Os.C. Units will be responsible that guides collect the lorries there.

5. O.C., Divisional Train will use the Supply Lorries to convey the Train Stores and Equipment on Tuesday the 24th.inst.

6. Os. C. Units are responsible that sufficient men to off load at ATH accompany each lorry, as the O i/c I.C.S. cannot supply off-loading parties.

7. Stores will be loaded and despatched as quickly as possible; lorries proceeding independently as soon as loaded.

                                                            Major,
19.6.19.   D.A.A.G., 74th.(Yeomanry) Division.

Copy to :-
      Officer i/c I.C.S., ATH.

Officer i/c
   I.C.S., ATH.

    Please note new schedule attached for Divisional Signal Company, who are handing in their Stores on Monday, 30th. June.

                                                          Major,
21.6.19.   D.A.A.G., 74th.(Yeomanry) Division.

    Copy to :- O.C., 74th. Div Signals.

SCHEDULE issued with addendum to A.Z.B.2/41/2 on the
21st. June 1919.

		Lorries.
Monday 30th. June	74th. Divisional Signal Company.	12.

WAR DIARY JUNE /25

74th. DIVISIONAL ORDER NO. 121.

Appendix VIII — 20th. June 1919.

1. **ENTRAINMENT.**

    The Equipment Guards mentioned, with vehicles, Ordnance stores and equipment will entrain at GRAMMONT in accordance with the attached Schedule 'A'.
    Units will entrain in the order mentioned.
    Loading will commence at 0900 each day.

2. **LOADING PARTIES.**

    A party of 75 Prisoners of War will report to a representative of the Brigade concerned, at GRAMMONT Station, at 0845 on the dates mentioned in the Schedule.
    Os.C. Equipment Guards are responsible, under the direction of the Entrainment Officer, that Officers and N.C.Os. are detailed to supervise the work of the P.O.W.
    Entrainment Officers will ensure that Capt. CLEGHORN is provided with any working parties he may require for roping, scotching, etc.

3. **ENTRAINING STATES.**

    Os.C. will report to the R.T.O. or his representative at GRAMMONT Station at 0845 on the day on which their unit is to entrain.
    They will at the same time hand to the R.T.O. or his representative a statement showing the strength of the Equipment Guard entraining, under the following headings :-

    I. Number of Officers and Men separately.
    II. Number of 4-wheeled vehicles (non-limbered).
    III. Number of 4-wheeled limbered vehicles.
    IV. Number of 2-wheeled vehicles.

4. **ENTRAINMENT OFFICERS.**

    The following will act as Entrainment Officers :-

DATE.	OFFICERS.
23rd. June 1919	Staff Captain, 229th. Infantry Brigade.
24th. June 1919	" " 230th. " "
25th. June 1919	Brigade Major 231st. Infantry Brigade.
27th. June 1919	Officer to be detailed by C.R.A.
28th. June 1919	-do-

    These Officers will be in charge of the Entrainment and assist the R.T.O. or his representative and Captain CLEGHORN.
    They will wire 'PRIORITY' to this Headquarters the completion of the entrainment, and departure of the trains, stating names and Serial Numbers of Equipment Guards which have proceeded on each

    Lieut. (A/Captain) A.M. CLEGHORN, R.A.R.E., will make all necessary arrangements with the Civil Railway Authorities at GRAMMONT Station as to loading facilities, and will be responsible that the ramp is erected and ready for use by 0800 on the 23rd. inst.
    It is probable that the R.T.O. will be unable to provide an Officer to supervise the entrainment, in which case Capt. CLEGHORN will be responsible that all vehicles are properly roped and scotched.
    Equipment Guards must have drag-ropes ready for securing vehicles in case the Railway Authorities do not provide same.

74th DIVISIONAL ORDER NO.121. (CONTD.)

5. STORES.
Stores will be loaded in vehicles before entrainment. Os.C. units will ensure that the total weights of wagons so loaded does not exceed 2 tons.

6. RATIONS.
The unexpired portion of the day's rations plus one day's rations will be taken.
The journey takes less than 12 hours.

7. AMMUNITION.
No ammunition, grenades or explosives of any sort will be taken to the Port of Embarkation or England.

8. ORDERS ALREADY ISSUED.
Attention is directed to the various orders issued under the following numbers and dates :-

    A.Z.D.2 of 19th.March.   A.Z.D.17. of 6th.June.
    A.Z.D.2 of 20th.March.   A.Z.D.4. of 14th.June.
    A.Z.D.4.of 7th.April.   A.Z.D. of 19th.June.

9½. ACKNOWLEDGE.

Major,
D.A.A.G., 74th.(Yeomanry) Division.

Issued at 15.00

Copies to :-

    1 - 4   229th.Infantry Brigade.
    5 - 8   230th.Infantry Brigade.
    9 - 12   231st.Infantry Brigade.
    12- 14   C.R.A.
    15   R.M.R.E.
    16- 17   P.A.R.E.
    18   Divisional Train.
    19   D.A.D.O.S., ATH.
    20- 21   III Corps.
    22- 23   R.T.O., HAL.
    24   Signals.
    25   Diary.
    26- 30   File.

SCHEDULE.

Date.	From.	Serial Nos.	UNITS.	approx. dep. time.
23/6	GRAMMONT.	ZE.437 ZE.438 ZE.439	14/ Royal Hdrs. 12/ Som.L.I. 16/ Devons.	2000
24/6	GRAMMONT.	ZE.440 ZE.441 ZE.442	10/ East Kent.R. 15/ Suffolks. 16/ Sussex.	2000
25/6	GRAMMONT.	ZE.443 ZE.444 ZE.445	25/ R.W.F. 24/ Welsh. 10/ Shrops.L.I.	2000
27/6	GRAMMONT	ZE.446 E.447 E.448	439 Fld.Coy. R.E. A/117 Bde.R.F.A. B/117 Bde.R.F.A.	2000
28/6	GRAMMONT	E.449 E.450 E.451 E.452	C/117 Bde R.F.A. D/117 Bde R.F.A. 117 Bde R.F.A. H.Q. 117 Bde R.F.A. Sig.Subsn.	2000

WAR DIARY JUNE

74th. DIVISIONAL ORDER NO.122.

Appendix IX   26th. June 1919.

1. **ENTRAINMENT.**

    The vehicles of the units mentioned in the attached schedule 'A' will be sent to the Vehicles Park, BEAUMARAIS, CALAIS, on the 26th. June 1919 by train in charge of an officer and two other ranks of each of the units concerned.

    The vehicles of D.H.Q. and H.Q.R.E. will proceed under the charge of the Officer i/c 447th.Coy, R.A.S.C. He will be responsible for obtaining the necessary receipts for the vehicles and handing these over to this office on his return.

    Vehicles will be entrained at GRAMMONT Station.

    Entrainment will commence at 0900 hours on the 26th. instant.

2. **ENTRAINMENT OFFICER.**

    Staff Captain 229th. Infantry Brigade will act as Divisional Entrainment Officer.

    He will be in charge of the entrainment and assist the R.T.O. or his representative and Captain CLEGHORN.

    He will wire "PRIORITY" to this Headquarters the completion of the entrainment, and departure of the train, stating names of Units whose vehicles have proceeded.

    Lieut. (A/Captain) CLEGHORN, R.A.R.E., will make all necessary arrangements with the Civil Railway Authorities at GRAMMONT Station as to the loading facilities.

    It is probable that the R.T.O. will be unable to provide an officer to supervise the entrainment, in which case Capt. CLEGHORN will be responsible that all vehicles are properly roped and scotched.

    Units must have drag ropes ready for securing vehicles in case the Railway Authorities do not provide same.

3. **LOADING PARTY.**

    A party of 100 Prisoners of War will report to the Entrainment Officer at GRAMMONT Station at 0900 hours on the 26th. inst.

    The Divisional Entrainment Officer will allocate the P.O.W. to units and determine the order in which units' vehicles will entrain.

    He will detail 25 P.O.W. for the use of 117th. Bde R.F.A. and hand them over to a representative of that Brigade.

    Officers i/c vehicles are responsible, under the direction of the Entrainment Officer, that Officers and N.C.O's are detailed to supervise the work of the P.O.W.

    The Entrainment Officer will ensure that Capt. CLEGHORN is provided with any working parties he may require for roping, scotching, etc.

4. **ENTRAINING STATES.**

    Os.C. will report to the R.T.O. or his representative at GRAMMONT Station at 0845 on the 26th. inst.

    They will at the same time hand to the R.T.O. or his representative a statement showing the strength of the units entraining, under the following headings :-

/ I.

74th. DIVISIONAL ORDER NO.122 (Contd).

  I. Number of Officers and men separately.
  II. Number of 4-Wheeled Vehicles (non-limbered)
  III. Number of 4-Wheeled limbered vehicles.
  IV. Number of 2-Wheeled vehicles.

5. ORDERS ALREADY ISSUED.
  Attention is directed to this Office A.Z.B.2/41/4 of 16.6.19.
  All Units, if they have already handed in their stores, will render in duplicate to this Office as soon as the Officer i/c vehicles returns the Certificate required by G.R.O.6466.

6. ACKNOWLEDGE.

            Major,
      D.A.A.G., 74th.(Yeomanry) Division.

Issued at 1745.

  Copies to :-

    1 - 2 229th. Infantry Brigade.
    3 - 4 230th. Infantry Brigade.
    5 - 6 231st. Infantry Brigade.
    7 - 8 R.M.R.E.
    9 - 10 R.A.R.E.
    11 - 12 Divisional Train.
    13 - 14 III Corps.
    15 - 16 R.T.O., HAL.
    17 Signals.
    18 Diary. 23 - 24 C.R.A.
X 19 - 22 File.
X 21 Camp Commdt

SCHEDULE "A" ISSUED WITH DIVISIONAL ORDER NO.122.

UNIT.	NO. of AXLES.
Divisional H.Q. (including 2 G.S. Train Wagons and 1 Limbered G.S. Train Wagon.)	11
H.Q. R.E.	1
447th. Coy R.A.S.C. (Div Train.)	42
449th. Coy R.A.S.C. (-do-)	11
229th. Infantry Brigade H.Q.	12
230th. Infantry Brigade H.Q.	12
231st. Infantry Brigade H.Q.	12
5th.R.M.R.E.	28
5th.R.A.R.E.	28
	157

Diary 18

ADDENDUM TO DIVISIONAL ORDER NO.122.

7. The personnel, other than the O.C. and 2 men proceeding with vehicles, should be sent for dispersal by train leaving GHISLENGHIEN at 1245 hours on the 28th.inst.

8. Units will on receipt of this Order wire this office numbers proceeding for dispersal on the 28th.inst.

9. Pro-forma to be used in rendering Certificate mentioned in para 5 is given below

10. Acknowledge.

H.J. Cartchart
Major,
D.A.A.G., 74th.(Yeomanry) Division.

25th.June 1919.

Certified in accordance with G.R.O. 6466 that all Ordnance Stores have been returned to the R.A.O.C. and that no equipment has been retained by the unit under my command.

WAR DIARY JUNE
Appendices X + XIII
16

74th. DIVISIONAL ORDER NO.123.

26th. June 1919.

1. **ENTRAINMENT.**

   The Equipment Guards mentioned, with vehicles, Ordnance Stores and equipment will entrain at GRAMMONT in accordance with the attached Schedule "A".

   Units will entrain in the order mentioned.
   Loading will commence at 0900 hours each day.

2. **LOADING PARTIES.**

   A party of 200 Prisoners of War will report to a representative of the unit concerned, at GRAMMONT Station, at 0845 on the dates mentioned in the Schedule.

   Os.C. Equipment Guards are responsible, under the direction of the Entrainment Officer, that Officers and N.C.Os are detailed to supervise the work of the P.O.W.

   The Entrainment Officer will ensure that Capt. CLEGHORN is provided with any working parties he may require for roping, scotching etc.

3. **ENTRAINING STATES.**

   Os.C. will report to the R.T.O. or his representative at GRAMMONT Station at 0845 on the day on which their unit is to entrain.

   They will at the same time hand to the R.T.O. or his representative a statement showing the Strength of the Equipment Guard entraining, under the following headings :-

   I. Number of Officers and Men separately.
   II. Number of 4-Wheeled vehicles (non-limbered)
   III. Number of 4-Wheeled limbered vehicles.
   IV. Number of 2-Wheeled vehicles.

4. **ENTRAINMENT OFFICER.**

   The CR.A. will detail an Officer to act as ENTRAINMENT Officer each day. Names of officers detailed to be intimated to this office. This Officer will be in charge of the entrainment and assist the R.T.O. or his representative and Captain CLEGHORN.

   He will wire 'PRIORITY' to this Headquarters the completion of the entrainment, and departure of the trains, stating names and Serial Numbers of Equipment Guards which have proceeded on each.

   Lieut. (A/Captain) A.M.CLEGHORN, R.A.R.E., will make all necessary arrangements with the Civil Railway Authorities at GRAMMONT Station as to loading facilities.

   It is probable that the R.T.O. will be unable to provide an Officer to supervise the entrainment, in which case Captain CLEGHORN will be responsible that all vehicles are properly roped and scotched.

   Equipment Guards must have drag ropes ready for securing vehicles in case the Railway Authorities do not provide same.

5. **STORES.**

   Stores will be loaded in vehicles before entrainment. Os.C. units will ensure that the total weight of wagons so loaded does not exceed 2 tons.

74th.DIVISIONAL ORDER NO.123 (Contd.)

6. RATIONS.
The unexpired portion of the day's rations plus one day's rations will be taken.
The journey takes less than 12 hours.

7. AMMUNITION.
No ammunition, grenades or explosives of any sort will be taken to the Port of Embarkation or ENGLAND.

8. ORDERS ALREADY ISSUED.
Attention is directed to the various orders issued under the following numbers and dates :-

    A.Z.D.2. of 19th.March   A.Z.D.17 of 6th.June.
    A.Z.D.2. of 20th.March   A.Z.D.4. of 14th.June.
    A.Z.D.4. of 7th.April   A. Z.D. of 19th.June.

9. ACKNOWLEDGE.

Major,
D.A.A.G., 74th.(Yeomanry) Division.

Issued at 1430.

Copies to :-

    1 - 5   C.R.A.
    6 - 8   Divisional Train.
    9   Capt.CLEGHORN, R.A.R.E.
    10   D.A.D.O.S., ATH.
    11 -12   III Corps.
    13 -14   R.T.O., HAL.
    15   Signals.
    16.   Diary.
    17 -21   File.

SCHEDULE ISSUED WITH DIVISIONAL ORDER NO.123.

DATE.	FROM.	SERIAL NOS.	UNITS.	NO. OF AXLES.	APPROX. DEP. TIME.
29th. June 1919.	GRAMMONT.	E.453	H.Q. 242nd. A.F.A.Bde.	10	2300
		E.456	A/242nd. A.F.A.Bde.	42	
		E.457	B/242nd. A.F.A.Bde.	42	
		E.458	C/242nd. A.F.A.Bde.	42	
1st. July 1919.	GRAMMONT.		448th. Coy R.A.S.C. (Div. Train)	11	2300
			450th. Coy R.A.S.C. (Div Train)	11	

WARDIARY JUNE
Appendix XIII

AMENDMENT TO DIVISIONAL ORDER NO. 123.

SCHEDULE

1. Delete "20th. June" and "1st. July". Dates of entrainment will be notified later.

2. Amend entries re. 448 and 450 Coys. R.A.S.C. to read as follows:-

DATE	FROM	SERIAL NOS.	UNIT	NO. of AXLES	NO. of Personnel	DESTINATION
-	GRAMMONT	E.459	448 Coy.R.A.S.C.	11	5	GLENCORSE
-	"	E.460	450 " "	11	5	DREGHORN

3. ACKNOWLEDGE.

H.J.Butchart

30th. June.1919
Issued at 1100.

Major
D.A.A.G. 74th.(Yeo) Division

WAR DIARY JUNE
74 (Yeo) Div
Appendix XII

Equipment and Stores handed in to I.C.S., ATH.

Divisional Headquarters	19th. June 1919.
229th. Infantry Brigade H.Q.	21st. June 1919.
230th. Infantry Brigade H.Q.	21st. June 1919.
231st. Infantry Brigade H.Q.	21st. June 1919.
229th. Light Trench Mortar Bty.	21st. June 1919.
230th. Light Trench Mortar Bty.	21st. June 1919.
231st. Light Trench Mortar Bty.	21st. June 1919.
Headquarters R.A.	19th. June 1919.
Headquarters R.E.	19th. June 1919.
H.Q. 44th. Bde R.F.A.	27th. June 1919.
340/ 44th. Bde R.F.A.	25th. June 1919.
382/ 44th. Bde R.F.A.	26th. June 1919.
425/ 44th. Bde R.F.A.	26th. June 1919.
D / 44th. Bde R.F.A.	26th. June 1919.
D/ 242nd. (Army) Bde R.F.A.	27th. June 1919.
B.A.C./242nd. (Army) Bde R.F.A.	27th. June 1919.
74th. D. A. C.	24th. & 25th. June 1919.
5th. Field Coy, R.M.R.E.	18th. & 19th. June 1919.
5th. Field Coy, R.A.R.E.	19th. June 1919.
74th. Divisional Signal Coy.	25th. June 1919.
74th. Bn. M. G. C.	20th. & 23rd. June 1919.
447th. Coy R.A.S.C. (Div Train)	24th. June 1919.
449th. Coy R.A.S.C. (Div Train)	24th. June 1919.
231st. Field Ambulance	16th. June 1919.

WAR DIARY JUNE
14

74th DIVISIONAL ORDER NO. 124.

Appendices XI & XIV

27th JUNE 1919.

1. ENTRAINMENT.

The vehicles of the units mentioned in the attached schedule 'A' will be sent to the Vehicles Park, BEAUMARAI, CALAIS, on the 4th July 1919 by train, in charge of an officer and two other ranks of each of the units concerned.

Vehicles will be entrained at GRAMMONT Station.

Entrainment will commence at 0900 hours on the 4th July 1919.

2. ENTRAINMENT OFFICER.

Staff Captain 230th Infantry Brigade will act as Divisional Entrainment Officer.

He will be in charge of the entrainment and assist the R.T.O. or his representative and Captain CLEGHORN.

He will wire 'PRIORITY' to this Headquarters the completion of the entrainment, and departure of the train, stating names of Units whose vehicles have proceeded.

Lieut. (A/Captain) CLEGHORN, R.A.R.E., will make all necessary arrangements with the Civil Railway Authorities at GRAMMONT Station as to the loading facilities.

Should the R.T.O. be unable to provide an Officer to supervise the entrainment, Captain CLEGHORN will be responsible that all vehicles are properly roped and scotched.

Units must have drag ropes ready for securing vehicles in case the Railway Authorities do not provide same.

3. LOADING PARTY.

A party of 100 Prisoners of War will report to the Entrainment Officer at GRAMMONT Station at 0900 hours on the 4th July 1919.

The Divisional Entrainment Officer will allocate the P.O.W. to units and determine the order in which units' vehicles will entrain.

Officers i/c Vehicles are responsible, under the direction of the Entrainment Officer, that Officers and N.C.O.s are detailed to supervise the work of the P.O.W.

The Entrainment Officer will ensure that Capt. CLEGHORN is provided with any working parties he may require for roping, scotching, etc.

4. ENTRAINING STATES.

Os C. will report to the R.T.O. or his representative at GRAMMONT Station at 0845 on the 4th July 1919.

They will at the same time hand to the R.T.O. or his representative a statement showing the strength of the units entraining, under the following headings :-

    I. Number of Officers and men separately.
    II. Number of 4-wheeled vehicles (non-limbered)
    III. Number of 4-wheeled limbered vehicles.
    IV. Number of 2-wheeled vehicles.

74th DIVISIONAL ORDER NO. 124 (Cont'd)
----

5. ORDERS ALREADY ISSUED.
   Attention is directed to this Office A.Z.B. 2/41/4 of 16/6/19.
   All Units will render in duplicate to this office as soon as the Officer i/c Vehicles returns the certificate required by G.R.O. 6466 on the proforma given below.

6. The personnel, other than the O.C. and 2 men proceeding with vehicles, who will be disposed of as directed by this office A.Z.B. 2/41/4 of 16/6/19, should be sent for dispersal by train leaving GUISLENGUIEN at 1245 hours on the 6th July 1919.
   Sufficient Signal personnel will be retained by O.C. Signals to work the Divisional Signal Office.

7. Units will on receipt of this order wire this office numbers proceeding for dispersal on the 6th July 1919.

8. ACKNOWLEDGE.

Issued at   Major,
                                        74th (Yeo) Division.

PROFORMA referred to in para. 5 of foregoing order :-

Certified in accordance with G.R.O. 6466 that all Ordnance Stores have been returned to the R.A.O.C. and that no equipment has been retained by the unit under my command.

Copies to :-

        1 - 6   C.R.A.
        5 - 6   Signals.
        7 - 8   230 Infantry Brigade.
          9   Capt. CLEGHORN, 5th R.A.R.D.
         10   Divl. Train.
        11 -12   / 3 Corps.
         13   R.T.O. HAL.
         14   Diary.
        15 -20   File.

SCHEDULE "A" ISSUED WITH DIVISIONAL ORDER NO.124

UNIT	NO. of AXLES
"D" Battery 242 (Army) Bde.R.F.A.	42
Bde.A.C.242 (Army) Bde.R.F.A.	75
74th. Div.Signal Coy.	49
TOTAL AXLES.	166

WAR DIARY JUNE

AMENDMENT TO DIVISIONAL ORDER NO. 124.

Appendix XIV

Para.1. ENTRAINMENT.

Line 3. After "sent" and before "to", insert "Guns" "Gun Carriages, Limbers etc., to CALAIS DOCK and Vehicles"
Lines 4 and 5. Delete from "of an officer" to "units concerned" inclusive, and substitute "of their restective Equipment Guards".
Lines 7 and 8. Delete "4th. July 1919", and substitute "3rd. July 1919".
Line 8. After "1919" add "but the train will not depart until 4th.July,1919.
Add new sub para. as follows:-

"The vehicles of the 231 Field Ambulance will be entrained "last, as it is possible that sufficient rolling stock may "not be available to permit of the vehicles of this unit "proceeding."

Para. 3. LOADING PARTY.

Line 4. Delete "4th. July.1919" and substitute "3rd.July.1919".

Para. 4. ENTRAINING STATES.

Line 3. Delete "4th.July.1919" and substitute "3rd.July.1919"

Para. 5.

Cancel the whole of this paragraph, and substitute the following:-
"5.Personnel
"The whole of the Equipment Guards of units concerned "will proceed with their Vehicles. Each of the Os.C. is "responsible that the whole party under his command is in "possession of all their demobilisation documents. After "handing in their Vehicles all Equipment Guards will "proceed for demobilisation through the L.ofC.Demobilisation "Concentration Camp, CALAIS."
"Os. Commanding will not return to this H.Q.They will "after handing in their Vehicles etc., forward the certificate "referred to in G.R.O.6466 on the PROFORMA given below "in duplicate to the O.i/c Ordnance, I.C.S. ATH, and send "a third copy to this office."
"Sufficient Signal personnel will be retained by the "O.C.Signals to work the Divisional Signal Office."
"Sufficient personnel of the 231st. Field Ambulance "will be retained by the S.M.O. to ensure adequate medical "service for the remaining troops of the Division."

Paras. 6 and 7.

Cancel the whole of each of these paragraphs.

SCHEDULE "A"
Add:-

UNIT	NO. of AXLES.
231st.Field Ambulance	25

Amend total to read as follows:-

TOTAL AXLES 191

ACKNOWLEDGE.

30th. June.1919
Issued at.....
D.A.A.G. 74th. (YEO) Division. Major.
Copies to all recipients of Divnl. Order No. 124

www.ingramcontent.com/pod-product-compliance
Lightning Source LLC
Chambersburg PA
CBHW080844010526
44114CB00017B/2370